*Ben Jonson's Parodic Strategy*

# Ben Jonson's Parodic Strategy

## LITERARY IMPERIALISM IN THE COMEDIES

## Robert N. Watson

HARVARD UNIVERSITY PRESS
CAMBRIDGE, MASSACHUSETTS
LONDON, ENGLAND   1987

Publication of this book has been aided by a grant from the
Hyder Edward Rollins Fund.

This book is printed on acid-free paper, and its binding materials
have been chosen for strength and durability.

*Library of Congress Cataloging in Publication Data*

Watson, Robert N.
  Ben Jonson's parodic strategy.

  Bibliography: p.
  Includes index.
  1. Jonson, Ben, 1573?–1637—Comedies. 2. Parody.
I. Title.
PR2638.W38     1987        822'.3        87-60
ISBN 0-674-06601-4 (alk. paper)

*To David and Cynthia, and Jon and Eileen*

# Acknowledgments

Among the many people to whom I owe deep thanks for their help and their kindness, I wish particularly to acknowledge Emily Bartels, Heather Dubrow, G. B. Evans, Karen Greif, Walter Kaiser, Gillian M. Kendall, David R. Riggs, Claire Scovell, and Barbara Bellow Watson, all of whom advised me on the manuscript with extraordinary care, generosity, and insight. I am also very grateful to the American Council of Learned Societies, and the Marion and Jasper Whiting Foundation, for the funding that allowed me to complete my research.

# Contents

Let them the deare expence of oyle upbraid
Suckt by thy watchfull Lampe, that hath betray'd
To theft the blood of martyr'd Authors, spilt
Into thy inke, whilst thou growest pale with guilt.
Repine not at the Tapers thriftie waste,
That sleekes thy terser Poems, nor is haste
Prayse, but excuse; and if thou overcome
A knottie writer, bring the bootie home;
Nor think it theft, if the rich spoyles so torne
From conquered Authors, be as Trophies worne.

    —Thomas Carew, "To Ben. Johnson," 33-42

# *A Note on Texts*

My quotations and citations of those plays available in the Yale Ben Jonson series, ed. Alvin B. Kernan and Richard B. Young, are based on that edition. These include *Every Man In His Humor,* ed. G. B. Jackson (1969); *Volpone,* ed. Alvin B. Kernan (1962); *Epicoene,* ed. Edward Partridge (1971); *The Alchemist,* ed. Alvin B. Kernan (1974); and *Bartholomew Fair,* ed. Eugene M. Waith (1963). References to Jonson's other plays are based on *The Complete Plays of Ben Jonson,* ed. G. A. Wilkes (Oxford: Oxford University Press, 1981–1982), a modern-spelling adaptation of volumes III–VI of the classic edition of Jonson's complete works edited by C. H. Herford, Percy Simpson, and Evelyn Simpson (11 vols.; Oxford: Oxford University Press, 1925–1952). References to Jonson's prose works are based on Herford, Simpson, and Simpson. References to the poems are based on *Ben Jonson: Poems,* ed. Ian Donaldson (Oxford: Oxford University Press, 1975).

# INTRODUCTION

Ben Jonson's comedies are acts of theatrical imperialism. Through an ingenious system of parody, Jonson fights for artistic *Lebensraum*. Instead of simply placing on the stage caricatured versions of hackneyed plots and motifs, as an ordinary parodist would, Jonson's strategy is to place those plots and motifs in the minds of his foolish characters. He then shows those characters trying to live out their melodramatic fantasies within the more realistic environment of Jacobean city comedy, an environment as hostile to naive fantasies as Jonson was to the works of his naive fellow-playwrights. By allowing a Jonsonian satirist to exploit and defeat all these pretenders and pretensions, Jonson symbolically asserts his dominance over his rivals and their more conventional literary modes. Dryden's famous praise of Jonson's adaptations—"He invades Authours like a Monarch, and what would be theft in other Poets, is onely victory in him"—aptly describes this strategy.[1] Jonson's thefts are not furtive: they are tactics in a proud campaign for sovereignty in the drama. He systematically subsumes the more conventional plays of his competitors, forcing them to work for his exaltation, like the Asian kings who lift Tamburlaine into greater glory by their very subjugation. Those rival plays become colonies within Jonson's empire, their native languages and value systems redefined as merely quaint by incorporation into the imperial scheme.

Like many imperialists, Jonson understands himself as more a missionary than a general, aspiring to purify and modernize what he perceives as the barbaric practices of Renaissance dramatists and the base appetites of their audiences. His method is kindred to that of Cervantes, who used parody ingeniously to reshape fiction during the same period, subsuming romance to create space for the novel.[2] While there are elements of mock-heroic in Jonson's technique, he uses self-dramatizing characters (as does Cervantes) primarily to belittle unhealthy literary forms, rather than using the forms (as does mock-heroic) to belittle the characters. He establishes his own generic space by creating truly Quixotic characters, characters who behave as if they supposed themselves central figures in a conventional plot suited to their humors. There are many good examples: Wasp, the Knowells, and the Penniboys anticipate a prodigal son story; Drugger hopes for a citizen-comedy; Celia and Bonario await a sentimental melodrama; Kitely, Corvino, and Fitzdotterel fear a cuckolding fabliau; Deliro essays a Petrarchan courtship; Dapper believes in a fairy tale; Overdo constructs a disguised-magistrate plot; Volpone mimics a legacy-hunting fable; Kastril trains for a roaring-boy interlude; Pug attempts a morality play; Truewit stages an anti-masque; Subtle and Meercraft foresee a coney-catching tale; Brainworm and Mosca undertake a classical New Comedy; and so on. As if in a Pirandello play, each character fights with the others for the privilege of staging the story in which he envisions himself as the hero.

Those who complacently await the fulfillment of their fantasies are surprised by satire. They fall into the hands of a playwright-figure who (as Jonson's surrogate) encourages the conventional and egoistical expectations to collide with each other, creating his own mordant and triumphant plot out of the wreckage. The audience's conventional expectations of plot, meanwhile, have been similarly aroused and overruled by Jonson himself.[3] The eagerness of spectators to see their expectations fulfilled was evidently a burden on Jacobean playwrights. The Prologue to Middleton and Dekker's *The Roaring Girl* complains that each spectator "comes / And brings a play in's head with him; up he sums / What he would of a roaring girl have writ; / If that he finds not here, he mews at it" (ll. 3–6).[4] Jonson turns this disease into commodity. The dynamics of reader response allow him to ambush not only a variety of hackneyed traditions, but also the intellectual complacency that sustained those traditions. His victory is truly a *coup de théâtre,* a subversive seizure of territory within the dramatic genre. Metadrama, which serves to blur the distinction between art and life in so many Renaissance plays, serves in Jonsonian comedy to insist on that distinction. The failed plays-within-the-plays warn us against our unhealthy tendency to surrender our grip on reality and our intellectual alertness, a tendency we share with Jonson's ingenuous characters and the ingenuous playwrights by whom those characters apparently suppose they have been created.[5] If we allow ourselves to be lured into mistaking the characters' melodramatic self-conceptions for Jonson's signals of his own generic intentions, we leave ourselves vulnerable to a humiliating reminder that, like the characters on stage, we have been perceiving only residual images of our previous experiences at the theater rather than the more immediate reality confronting us in Jonson's play.

In *The New Organon* Francis Bacon calls one crucial set of obstacles to scientific progress the "Idols of the Theater." The theater was his metaphor for the human tendency to subjugate what we see to what we have read, to perceive according to received authoritative schemes (such as those of Aristotle) instead of applying our own rational judgment to the information provided by our own senses. Jonson explicitly praises Bacon's warning in his critical *Discoveries*,[6] and in his comedies he literalizes the metaphor in order to warn against an obstacle to progress in the drama: the gulls in these plays are usually idolators of the theater. Gestalt and genre, as Paul Hernadi has suggested, are profoundly linked,[7] and the correlation allows Jonson to parody his dramatic rivals in the course of satirizing common human follies. He juxtaposes the human tendency to cling to established schemes for interpreting the world, with the tendency of playwrights to cling to conventional motifs of plot and character in their drama. What to us are conventions of a genre, to these characters are delusions, usually of grandeur. Like the disillusioned Caesar in *Poetaster,* Jonson sharply and persistently asks his characters "not what you play? But, what you are?" (4.6.25).[8] In revealing the foolishly theatrical way people conceive of themselves, Jonson challenges the ingenuous way many of his rivals and their admirers conceive of theater. Only if we cast away the stale melodramatic expectations we have brought to the theater, and approve instead Jonson's new approach, can we identify ourselves with the triumphant wits instead of with the fools who have paid dearly for an unrealistic and unrewarding fantasy. The subliminal plays-within-the-play are the things wherein Jonson catches our literary consciences.

Jonson's plays both are, and are about, his new type of comedy. They are what they advocate—satires on human folly, in all its gullibility and all its susceptibility to self-aggrandizing delusions. Instead of writing two separate sorts of works, one a satiric drama about London society and the other a piece of satiric criticism about the London stage, Jonson combines social satire and parodic satire synergistically.[9] He portrays the collapse of grandiose fantasy in a way that allows the theory and the practice to legitimize each other. In fact, what are generally considered his weaker plays are the ones where the two projects are most distinguishable—where the story lacks any essential critical thrust, and where the critical argument takes place almost entirely apart from the story, in the form of a prologue or a chorus.

The action of the stronger plays represents, in the form of a sequential plot, the gesture of superiority Jonson achieves by writing such a plot. The plays reenact the process Jonson may have gone through in creating them, considering in turn a series of standard story lines and then decentering or betraying them on behalf of his own sort of urbane and realistic drama. His surrogates often triumph largely because Jonson puts them at center-stage rather than on the periphery, and ends the play when they happen to be ahead. It is primarily a question of framing, to borrow a cinematic term. Icarus himself can seem a minor character when Brueghel chooses to diminish his story to a pair of bare legs in the corner of the canvas. Decentering a conventional motif, in Jonson as in Brueghel, is the artist's way of asserting his control and his independence. Jonson is, in Harold Bloom's terms, a strong poet, because his echoes of his literary rivals function less as servile imitations than as strategic reductions, making the works of those rivals appear as mere incomplete parts of his own complete work. Indeed, one of Jonson's contemporaries praised him in remarkably Bloomian terms, composing a Latin epigram in which the gods charge Jonson with plagiarizing the works of Plautus, but then conclude that Plautus had actually stolen his ideas from Jonson.[10]

The confusing multiplicity that critics have often condemned in Jonson's plotting thus becomes an artful *bricolage:* this is parody by pastiche. Yuri Tynyanov asserts that "any literary succession is first of all a struggle, a destruction of old values and a reconstruction of old elements."[11] Jonson wages that struggle for succession in a highly sophisticated way. While all generic innovations involve reshuffling elements from established genres, Jonson's innovation in comedy occurs at what Alastair Fowler calls a tertiary stage, where the generic conventions are exploited as symbols in their own right.[12] The wealth of allusions to earlier forms (Old and New Comedy, Estates Moralities, and so on) that Jonson's critics have dutifully listed are less a deferential gesture toward earlier writers than an ironic and didactic subsuming of those writers. What have been enumerated as Jonson's literary sources are in many cases only the sources from which his characters have apparently derived their doomed heroic poses and social tactics. Jonson "refunctions" (to borrow a term from Russian Formalism) these bits of literary convention. The characters who expect and embody the conventions are like lonely instruments quoting famous old melodies out of context within a piece of parodic modern music.

To understand these allusions is to recognize that Jonson's attacks on his rivals are considerably more extensive and subversive than has commonly been acknowledged: beyond the famous *poetomachia* and the explicit parodies in *Bartholomew Fair* and *The Devil Is an Ass* are countless moments when the appetites and affectations of Jonson's comic characters take on a derivative literary coloring. Alvin Kernan has observed that great satire tends to exploit characters who "create grand inflated images of themselves and pompously attempt to reconstruct the world";[13] Jonson exploits characters whose grandiose self-images oblige them to reconstruct the Globe. The idea of the *theatrum mundi,* which pervades medieval and Renaissance literature (and takes a provocative form in the name and motto of the Globe theater), hovers in Jonson's comedies somewhere between a strategy of allusion and an existential principle: in satirizing other playwrights, Jonson is also satirizing life's tendency to imitate art, the self-dramatizing instinct by which people seek to make sense of their lives.[14]

That instinct, as Stephen Greenblatt has shown, wielded remarkable power over Elizabethan minds.[15] Jonson's world as well as his plays must have been full of people striking half-conscious poses as unrequited lovers, court intriguers, family revengers, underpromoted malcontents, and underappreciated poetic geniuses. The tactics by which Jonson's roguish heroes exploit the less self-aware self-fashioners bear a clear and suggestive resemblance to the "crucial Renaissance mode of behavior" Greenblatt calls "*improvisation, by which I mean the ability both to capitalize on the unforeseen and to transform given materials into one's own scenario.*"[16] The fact that this mode is (according to Greenblatt and Steven Mullaney)[17] most starkly operative as a tool of Renaissance colonization may lend new depth to my characterization of Jonson's reformist campaign as literary imperialism. Jonson's parodic strategy may not be simply a literary innovation: it may also be viewed as an adaptation of the oblique mode of aggression practiced by his culture as a whole on its ingenuous opponents.

But though dramatic improvisation can be profitable in these plays, it is a dangerous game to begin, because there is always the risk of settling complacently into a single self-aggrandizing role and becoming the dupe of a more elaborate cheater, the subject of a more resourceful imperialist, the zany of a more adept improvisator. Indeed, Jonson's relentless attacks on the self-dramatizing instinct may reflect a lifelong struggle against his own impulses to replace reality with literary poses. Anne Barton observes that Jonson's service in the Low Countries "obviously fuelled his innate romanticism—in particular the need to validate the classical literature he loved by making it part of his own, deeply felt experience. The man who told Drummond about how he had dared one of the enemy to single combat, killed him in the sight of both the armies, and taken 'opima spolia' from him, clearly did what he did at the time because he was acting out things he had read."[18] Perhaps Jonson needed the literary models to validate his experience, rather than vice versa. Several of his poems document his frustrated hopes to replace the unromantic realities of his body with his poetic inventions. He writes in the *Discoveries,* "*I have* considered, our whole life is like a *Play:* wherein every man, forgetfull of himselfe, is in travaile with expression of another. Nay, wee so insist in imitating others, as wee cannot (when it is necessary) returne to our selves: like Children, that imitate the vices of *Stammerers* so long, till at last they become such; and make the habit to another nature, as it is never forgotten" (VIII, 597, ll. 1093–99). Characters who understand this susceptibility (as do Clement, Macilente, Face, Dauphine, and Mosca) can both mock and manipulate those who do not; the playwright who recognizes the naive conventionality of his competitors can achieve a similar and simultaneous conquest. Within the plays, to adapt a Socratic precept, the unexamined role is not worth playing; Jonson thereby implies that plays lacking his sophisticated self-consciousness about the conventions of the genre were not worth writing.

So Jonson's multiple plots become devices for carrying on the War of the Theaters by other and subtler means, and some Renaissance equivalents of Walter Mitty are his secret agents in that war, eventually immolating themselves behind enemy lines and taking much of the enemy arsenal with them.[19] Jonson's triumphs as a playwright depend on his dislike of theater: his willingness to shatter his dramatic heritage into incoherent bits is what permits him to build a superior dramatic mode. The peculiar shape of Jonsonian comedy can be explained as the result of what might be termed generic engineering. The parodic strategy gives these plays many of the complexities and capabilities that Mikhail Bakhtin attributes only to the novel. Clearly the imperialistic function of the comedies resembles that of Bakhtin's typical novel, which "fights for its own hegemony in literature . . . The novel parodies other genres (precisely in their role as genres); it exposes the conventionality of their forms and their language; it squeezes out some genres and incorporates others into its own peculiar structure, reformulating and re-accentuating them."[20] Beneath the surface action of the plays is the ruthless and resourceful struggle of a new kind of drama—satiric city-comedy—for a place in the Renaissance constellation of genres.[21] The purpose of this book is to chronicle that struggle: to show where Jonson's standard comic critique of personal vanity and social pretensions edges toward a critique of formulaic literature, and to show how that critique gives the comedies their distinctive structure and their intellectual purpose.

Some readers may feel that I have exaggerated the prominence of parody in these plays, and that Jonson is merely satirizing naive people and their vanities where I detect him satirizing naive literature and the self-dramatizing impulses of those who enjoy it. A certain amount of subjectivity is involved in deciding whether a character behaves in a certain way because Jonson is simply following a literary source, or rather because Jonson wants us to perceive that the character is following that source. It is similarly difficult sometimes to distinguish between a character named after his odd conduct, and a character whose odd behavior results from his own efforts to fulfill the role he thinks his name implies. Characters who confidently attempt to improve their social status by marriage or industry may seem to one reader to be mimicking a common role from Elizabethan popular literature, but seem to another simply to be undertaking a common project in Elizabethan life which that literature reflected. But the preoccupation with names, manners, and social status was generally understood by the Elizabethans themselves in explicitly theatrical terms.[22] Moreover, Jonson points so frequently and suggestively to the specifically literary sources of his characters' delusions that it is time to consider an essentially new way of understanding the workings of the comedies, a critical approach with implications also for their staging and editing.

It is worth remembering, furthermore, that a Jacobean audience would have been well prepared to recognize Jonson's parodic barbs. The world of London's playwrights and theatergoers was a cozy one, and inside jokes about rival companies and their plays were the rule rather than the exception. The famous War of the Theaters that occupied London's stages in the first years of the seventeenth century was a well-publicized eruption of a battle royal that went on continually—sometimes playful, sometimes vicious—among virtually all the major Jacobean playwrights. Even Shakespeare, though he put himself further above the battle than most, could not resist parodying Marlowe's popular *Tamburlaine* in *2 Henry IV* (2.4.163–167), devastating crude melodrama in the mechanicals' performance in *Midsummer Night's Dream* (5.1.108–362), and complaining in *Hamlet* (2.2.338–362) about the popularity of the rival Children's Companies, with their incongruous, stylized performances of grand tragedies and sex farces. Jonson elevated this battle beyond the simple burlesque and the isolated potshot, by making the parody, and his triumph over the parodied rival, integral to the plots of his comedies. Each of Jonson's comedies enacts a contest between his sort of drama and the works of other playwrights; each time he emerges victorious, which is not surprising, since he is in a position to make up the rules, arbitrate the disputes, and declare the finish of what pretends to be a fair fight among dramatic modes.

Nor was Jonson the only playwright of his time to employ this more involved kind of parody. Beaumont and Fletcher, in *The Knight of the Burning Pestle,* and Marston, in *The Malcontent* and

*Antonio and Mellida,* display a similarly ironic self-consciousness about dramatic conventions and make similarly sophisticated use of them.[23] Chapman, Webster, and (of course) Shakespeare made occasional gestures to show that they were sardonically alert to the traditions in which they worked. There are clear traces of the parodic strategy in Thomas Heywood's *The Wise-Woman of Hogsdon* and *A Challenge for Beauty.* It is trite to suppose that much Elizabethan and Jacobean drama was merely trite, and naive to attribute an essential naiveté to the audiences of the period. In his comedies, however, Jonson contentiously and tendentiously defines his rivals and their admirers in those reductive terms, as straw men for his critical argument. He deliberately overstates the stability, and therefore the stagnancy, of "conventional" literary forms. Whereas, against the burden of the classical past, Jonson employs an appropriative piety, playing the role of curator, his characteristic move against encroachment from contemporary competitors is this misrepresentation, which diminishes their works into something he can triumphantly subsume. By the same token, he isolates any spectators who disapprove of his plays by associating them with characters and choral commentators who childishly desire nothing more than a retelling of these same old stories. For the purposes of my argument, I speak of popular literature and its audiences as Jonson chose to depict them, rather than as the varied and self-conscious entities they may often have been.

Jonson could portray himself as sole proprietor of a new and superior dramatic mode only by reducing or ignoring the various works that impinged on his claim. It is also true, however, that he deployed the parodic strategy far more systematically and effectively than any of his rivals, and that the variations in his technique constitute an elaborate commentary on the strengths and weaknesses of that strategy. The chapters that follow sketch a subtle evolution of both attitude and method which corresponds to the arc perceived by Anne Barton, in which Jonson progresses from an openly combative attitude toward popular theater, to a brilliant assimilation of that tradition, and finally to a nostalgic immersion in it.[24] In *Every Man In His Humor* and *Every Man Out of His Humor,* Jonson simply herded his rivals onto the stage to be humiliated; this gave the plays as much entertainment value, but as little integrity of plot, as a massive street brawl. In literary terms these early plays are more like anthologies than like stories.

They are satires, but they express some reservations about the suitability of the bitter satiric spirit to the comic stage, which Jonson understood as a place of pleasure and positive social morality.

The great middle comedies, from *Volpone* to *The Devil Is an Ass,* succeed in subordinating both the rivalrous and the satiric impulses to unitary plots. Jonson invents settings and stories that perfectly coordinate the humiliation of his literary rivals with the humiliation of his self-dramatizing characters. Lovewit's house and Bartholomew Fair serve as metaphors both for the actual stages of London and for the metaphorical great stage of the world. They are places to which people naturally bring their fantasies and their money, and are finally compelled to surrender them both to Jonson's superior wit. But just as Jonson's on-stage surrogates such as Volpone and Face seem constitutionally unable to stop creating complications and simply enjoy their profits, so Jonson himself seems unable to switch off the parodic mechanism that generated his triumphs and relax on his satiric laurels. Instead, he turns that mechanism against his own dramatic pattern. These plays reveal Jonson's increasing doubts about the adequacy of satiric wit as an end in itself, reflected in an increasing willingness to parody the motifs of his own kind of city-comedy. He turns his punitive dramatic weaponry against punitive figures, and his plays become steadily more forgiving, both toward human nature and toward popular drama.

This progression leads predictably to the sentimentality that has provoked so many critics to dismiss the late plays as "dotages." In *The Staple of News, The New Inn,* and *The Magnetic Lady,* the vigorous synthesis of the middle comedies begins to fade, and the arguments about the right course for drama often become isolated in choral figures, rather than generated by the plots themselves. Even in criticizing and finally surrendering his own parodic stance, however, Jonson always makes some use of his parodic strategy, always acknowledges when he is deviating from it, and always calls our attention to the struggle between popular melodrama and sophisticated satire, a struggle that occupied his mind and London's stages throughout his career. *The New Inn* may look like a flag of surrender, but it is also a gesture of peace, brilliant in its elaborate retraction of Jonsonian parody, and powerfully poignant in its implications about the man Jonson had become.

*   *   *

This approach to Jonson opens many avenues that are beyond the scope of my book. Barely half of Jonson's comedies receive any substantial treatment here. These were chosen as the most significant instances—that is, the plays that gain the most new coherence in the light of the parodic strategy, that best exemplify the normal functions of that strategy, and that most clearly outline its evolution. (The fact that these are also, for the most part, Jonson's most admired works may indicate how essential the parodic strategy was to his dramatic energy.) The same issues I raise concerning the comedies appear prominently throughout Jonson's oeuvre. Clearly the paradoxes involved in the mutual imitation of life and art are essential to the masques. In fact, Jonson's increasing willingness to let life imitate art successfully in the last plays may result, at least in part, from the fact that, between *The Devil Is an Ass* (1616) and *The Staple of News* (1626), Jonson spent most of his time writing masques which were designed precisely to encourage the noble players to internalize the virtues and undertake or reenact the tasks the script assigned to them. Jonson's poems are also relevant, because they frequently satirize his own impulses, and the impulses of his subjects, to imagine themselves in unrealistic or anachronistic literary poses—as a great lover or a greatly beloved, as a classical god or hero, even as a Muse. Although Jonson's complex imitation theory is less directly relevant to the parodic strategy than it might at first appear,[25] his literary criticism persistently wrestles with the ambivalence of literary precedents and the dangers of imitating someone else's voice.

The theoretical implications of Jonson's parodic strategy may also deserve further study. His technique anticipates several of the central insights of contemporary critical theory, because (whether intentionally or not) it suggests that literary meanings are essentially arbitrary and self-referential. Jonson becomes, in effect, a reader-response theorist by choosing a strategy that can function only in a realm of dialogue between author and audience.[26] In a more limited way Jonson becomes a deconstructionist, by reminding us repeatedly that the supposed absolutes of meaning and morality depend on context, and that heroes and fools are distinguished less by innate qualities of the persons represented than by the degree to which their representations are either privileged or decentered in the text. "Heroic" behavior may do you no good at all, as Bonario and Surly and Overdo discover, if the context is hostile or dismissive toward your particular genre of heroism.

Jonson is highly ambivalent about this acknowledgment, however. While he implies that meaning and morality are essentially arbitrary, he also implies that he has some intellectual and ethical right to be the arbiter, and that some innate superiority, not authorial tyranny, gives his surrogates their triumph. Like Gonzalo in *The Tempest,* he envisions no sovereignty, yet he would be king on't; the latter end of his commonwealth forgets the beginning (2.1.158–159). His intertextuality usually has more to do with competition than with deconstruction, since it produces a hierarchy of texts (with his as the best and truest) out of what pretends to be a neutral pastiche. In this sense Jonsonian comedy lacks the openness of Bakhtin's ideal novel: the renowned heteroglot pleasures of Jonsonian comedy—the fascination of its rich alternative languages and the leveling force of its vital scatology—yield to the univocal authority of an implied and often represented author.[27]

A similar contradiction lurks in the purported "realism" of Jonsonian comedy and in the way Jonson purports to reward characters whose view of the world is "realistic." Certainly the plays are anti-romantic, and packed with material objects and historical place-names, but is it valid to talk about "realism" in a world that belongs to whichever character can write the most powerful script for it? Truth in Jonsonian comedy appears radically subjective and unstable, merely a competition among interpretations, among the self-serving plots the characters try to enforce, among the various genres the characters envision, each with its own gestalt. The author's version is privileged, but it has too much in common with the refuted fantasies of the decentered characters to carry the force of pure fact: the process by which it becomes privileged is too visible for comfort.

These complications may have been inadvertent side effects of the parodic strategy, but the evolution of Jonson's comic pattern suggests an increasing sensitivity to them. Denying the victory to Jonsonian wits such as Mosca and Merecraft, and Jonsonian censors such as Surly and Wasp, not only diminishes the transparently self-aggrandizing aspects of the earlier plays: by mortifying characters who assume that a Jonsonian plot will prove more viable within the play-world than the romantic plots of the other characters, Jonson acknowledges that the victories of his surrogates in earlier plays were arbitrarily imposed, not necessary enactments of what would "really" happen. By allowing the puppet show to dominate the ending of *Bartholomew Fair,* and a morality-play fiend to catalyze the ending of *The Devil Is an Ass,* Jonson implicitly retreats from his determination to impose reality on drama. In the senescence of Jonson's comic empire the literary motifs he had enslaved are allowed to reassert their indigenous cultures as no less valid than that of their conqueror. Finally, in *The New Inn* and *The Sad Shepherd,* Jonson formally surrenders to the thoroughly romantic and literary fantasies he had spent so many years subjugating to his version of reality.

This tension between the indeterminate and the authoritative in Jonson's comedies has suggestive analogues in his biography, which reveals a constant struggle between (on the one hand) his violent, individualistic, even anarchic propensities, and (on the other) his dedication to high culture, hierarchy, and authority. He was an ambitious man who climbed from a working-class background to eminence at court, a violent man who killed both in war and in a duel, an assertive innovator in literature, an individualistic spirit by temperament as well as practice. How can those things be reconciled with the aristocratic connections he cultivated and eulogized in his poems and masques, or with the arch classicism of his critical positions? By the same token, how can the essentially respectful imitation theory presented in Jonson's *Discoveries* be reconciled with the rivalrous mockery practiced in his comedies?[28]

Jonson's innovations in comedy reflect his engagement with these contradictions. In the parodic mode of satiric city-comedy Jonson found a literary form that spoke to his inner conflicts. He created a literary universe in which his repressive tendencies as a social and literary commentator could happily coexist with his boisterous appetites and competitive impulses as a comic playwright. By making the humiliation of the misbehaving gulls inseparable from a humiliation of naive rival playwrights, Jonson melded the inherent conservatism of satire with the inherent subversiveness of parody.[29] By attacking his contemporaries and the illnesses of his society in this way, he could ally himself with classical authors and align himself with traditional values, even while subverting the usual boundaries between works and between genres.

Jonson's effort to alchemize England's base dramatic heritage into literary treasure clearly parallels his battle to transcend his social inheritance, to transform his middle-class background, through his poetic powers, into something worthy of the royal court. His refusal to be a bricklayer (or even a "Johnson")[30] corresponds significantly to his refusal to be an ordinary playwright. From this perspective, the many facets of Jonson are all of a piece. His biography, which shows him constantly revising his own past; his criticism, which repeatedly advocates imitating the ancients in such a way as to express one's individual vision; his poems, which in their revisionistic classicism so often reflect the ambivalence of that imitation theory;[31] his masques, which are constantly in tension between the descriptive and the prescriptive; all these things fit with the parodic strategy of the comedies, in which Jonson again remakes a limiting inheritance into something sovereign and triumphant, something essentially self-generated and sui generis.

My hope is that the instances and topics I have chosen to explore in depth will be sufficient not only to illuminate the individual plays, but also to encourage further thinking about both the tactics and the philosophy of Jonson's entire artistic project. His parodic strategy is close to the essence of that project, as I understand it. Jonson offers to reform literature by replacing romantic indulgences with an alertness to contemporary circumstances that will allow art to resume its ideal function, as a reformer of society. That reformed society, cured of its unhealthy melodramatic fantasies, will then support authors such as Jonson who, in the great classical tradition, give it the satiric medicine it needs to retain its moral and intellectual health. As Jonson writes at the end of the Epilogue to *Every Man Out of His Humor,* the audience that learns to accept this new form of drama "may, in time, make lean Macilente as fat as Sir John Falstaff."

For Jonson this hope must have ended in bitterness. Fat he may have become, and perhaps not quite so poor as has commonly been supposed, but when he fell from royal and popular favor late in life, he surely found he had fallen far short of his dreams; and whereas Falstaff has always been loved for his faults, Jonson has always been disliked for his virtues.[32] Jonson's great kinsman in this regard is the Milton of *Paradise Lost,* and the kinship runs deep. Like Jonson, Milton tries to control and convert his audience by transmuting and incorporating a variety of subgenres, though of course in a less dismissive manner.[33] This tactic again generates some interesting correspondences to the imperial ideology of Renaissance England. In *Paradise Lost* Satan is an imperialist who tries to seduce, divide, and conquer both the old world of heaven and the new world of earth by improvising on the conventional literary motifs to which his audiences are susceptible: formulas of epic heroism, tragic revenge, and Petrarchan seduction. He seems to win some momentary power and glory within both the heavenly and earthly theaters, but Milton and his God literally hiss that play out of their poem. The analogy between the way Elizabethan England and its agents exploited Native American tribes[34] and the way Jonson and his surrogates exploit their gulls can be extended to include this third term: the way Milton and his God transume Satan's proud display of classical heroism into the Christian superstructure of *Paradise Lost*. It is certainly suggestive, furthermore, that at a time when England was supposedly becoming increasingly aware of authority as an arbitrary human construct, Jonson and Milton devoted themselves to experimenting with the way different genres legitimize different characters, the way an arbitrary authorial choice empowers one type of character while defining others—who would be sovereign in a different context, in their own native literary realms—as mere pretenders or subjects, in either sense of those words.

Clearly a high degree of literary self-referentiality does not necessarily signal a strictly literary project. Jonson marshaled his ingenious campaign on behalf of satiric city-comedy, Milton on behalf of Christian epic, but in a sense the new genres were really stalking-horses, behind which the authors could approach and destroy a set of stagnant cultural values. Imperious reformers, whether of literary modes or of social mores, are rarely loved.[35] Few writers inspire as much thought and respect with as little affection as Jonson and Milton. Their elaborate association of authority with authorship may not have helped matters. The triumphs of Jonson's satirists have been widely criticized as being too cruel, too easy, too unemotional; much the same criticism has traditionally been leveled at Milton's God, by critics from Addison and Shelley to Empson and Waldock. Too close an alliance with the author can make even the fairest sort of victor seem a bit of a bully. Conversely, an author who makes his primary surrogate so ideal and so completely triumphant may seem to be engaged in a transparently self-aggrandizing gesture, a valorized and ventriloquized act of self-flattery.

Furthermore, both authors had to combat the inertia of an audience devoted to the comforts of recognizing conventional patterns. The "affective stylistics" by which *Paradise Lost* provokes and then mortifies an unhealthy reflex in the mind of the reader[36] closely resembles the tactic at the heart of Jonson's parodic strategy. Jonson creates his wonderfully self-dramatizing gulls as Milton creates his magnificent battles in heaven: ostensibly, for the sake of declaring them irrelevant, a disappearing banquet of our favorite literary dishes. The third day of the battle discards the conventional martial heroism of the fallen and unfallen angels by displacing the Homeric epic of wrath into a brief—very brief—divine epic. These events, or rather non-events, must be simply disappointments to those who fail to see the heuristic purpose and—at least at first blush—unpleasant betrayals even to those who do see it.

Like Milton a few decades later, Jonson had to call up the possessive demons of the literary past in order to exorcise them, but woe to the exorcist who leaves the job unfinished. There is always a chance that the audience's naive attachment to familiar and colorful characters will not yield to the more subtle and abstract values the authors intend to exalt. The instinctive appeal of traditional heroes and traditional literary flourishes is what made possible Jonson's and Milton's subversions of the complacencies, moral and generic, embodied by Renaissance literature; but it is also what made those subversions so difficult and dangerous. The satirist and the moralist always risk appearing essentially negative, as critics rather than creators. From his early "Ode on the Morning of Christ's Nativity" through the early books of *Paradise Lost,* Milton openly wonders how he can reconcile his readers—and himself—to the silencing and exile of the vivid figures of classical literature, when all that the infant Christ and the infant Christian culture could offer at those moments in compensation was the mere anticipation of a more solemn music, a more refined mythology, a more humble form of heroism. By the same token, how can Jonson expect his audience to endorse the silencing of all their favorite theatrical figures merely for the sake of exalting a disillusioning wit? What, finally, is the appeal of a play that proceeds by rejecting all the plots the audience has learned to appreciate, leaving only a critical attitude to fill the narrative void? [As the ending of *Every Man Out of His Humor* suggests, Jonson's victories over his literary rivals are always in danger of becoming Pyrrhic victories.]

This may help explain why critics have been able to debate so long and hard about whether Jonson is really on the side of morality or of mischief, as about whether Milton slips out late at night to the party of Satan. It has been observed that, though Jonson clearly despises his gulls and hypocrites, they are nonetheless often his most vivid characters,[37] as Satan is commonly said to be the most vivid inhabitant of *Paradise Lost,* despite all Milton's efforts to ironize that type of vividness. Is what Milton finds himself obliged to do to Satan so different, in this sense, from what Jonson decides he must do to Petrarchan lovers like Deliro and finally (when he feels he must prove his willingness to "punish vice"; *Volpone,* Epistle, 109–110) even to cynical playwright-figures like Volpone and Mosca? Works such as *Volpone* and *Paradise Lost* are so unsettling, seem so multiple in their motives, because their structures are utterly haunted with the ghosts of the authors' past selves, and of the characters those past selves might have let live and thrive. The old epic and comic characters are still in there, defending, one might say, their own premises.[38]

It has become routine to acknowledge the anxiety of influence, the burden of the past; but the struggle of these two immensely strong poets to assert their distinctive artistic identities and moral perspectives is a daunting reminder of how desperate a task it can become, particularly for authors so deeply knowledgeable about the traditions they are trying at once to enter and escape. It must have been agonizing labor for Jonson to push all that tradition off the stage so that he would have room for his own plays, as it was for Milton to climb to the top of a mountainous literary heritage and translate, not only its countless languages, but its entire ethos, into his own voice. That Jonson and Milton found such similar ways of asserting themselves suggests that there cannot have been many ways; that they knowingly sacrificed popularity in the process suggests that there were no ways without costs.

In deploying his parodic strategy, Jonson is not merely playing tricks on his gullible characters and inside jokes on his fellow-dramatists, any more than Milton is using his peculiar mode of mock-epic in *Paradise Lost* merely to score points against his diabolical characters or his fellow-poets. Less obviously but no less essentially than Milton, Jonson was a revolutionary working in a paradoxically conservative medium, courting the audience he needed for his new form of art and the allies he needed for his guerilla campaign against the idolatries of England's theatricalized culture.

# CHAPTER ONE

# Every Man In His Humor

## THE PURGING OF
## MONSTROUS CONVENTIONS

*Every Man In His Humor* (1598), which Jonson placed first in his collected works, can be taken as a model for reading the rest of the comedies.[1] Its Prologue urges the audience to approve a realistic and ethical type of comedy, as opposed to the bombastic productions that had so often occupied the public stages. Behind this outwardly simple and sensible request lies Jonson's strategy for creating a new kind of drama, a system of integrated parodies built on a combination of Latin comedy and the "humors" comedy initiated by George Chapman's *An Humorous Day's Mirth* about a year earlier. The action of *Every Man In His Humor* represents the victory of this new dramatic mode over standard Elizabethan fare. Each of the lesser characters presumes that the play will take a conventional form that focuses on his personal aspirations and problems; more sophisticated plotters then engineer the collision of those incompatible expectations. As the wits supersede the fools in controlling the plot of *Every Man In His Humor,* satiric comedy supersedes the prodigal son fables, cuckolding farces, and romantic tragedies that were so common on the stages of London. The Prologue implies that Jonson's realism is intended merely to make his plays more effective as vehicles of social reform, but he has literary reform in mind as well. Jonson establishes this highly modernistic sort of transaction with his characters, in which they vainly compete with him for control of the play, in order to establish a dialogic transaction with his spectators by which he can modernize their hackneyed notions of what drama should be.

The reputation of *Every Man In His Humor* is mixed. It has proved durable on the stage as a piece of light comedy, and equally durable in the academy as a landmark in the brief history of "humors" theory, but it has almost always been faulted as artistically fragmentary, as lacking any core other than its loosely applied humors psychology.[2] The plot is notoriously difficult to follow or remember, a fact which critics attribute to Jonson's willingness to jury-rig his story in order to facilitate the collisions of humorous types. Perhaps, however, Jonson recognized in the scattershot plotting of *An Humorous Day's Mirth* an opportunity for systematic parody that Chapman had failed to exploit. Although *Every Man In His Humor* may be a "comedy of non-interaction," as G. B. Jackson has called it,[3] it enlists that non-interaction in the cause of reshaping the audience's understanding of the comic genre. Our ability to follow or remember stories depends above all on generic conventionalities; we read and retain in much the same way oral-tradition poets are said to have composed, proceeding less by irreducible morphemes than by signals directing us toward one of a few set patterns of language, action, or character. In *Every Man In His Humor* Jonson deliberately jumbles the associative patterns we are prepared to apply to his play. Justice Clement's explicit reproof of each character for having been so easily fooled carries within it Jonson's implicit reproof of his audience for having confidently awaited the fulfillment of those same conventional plots—infidelity in the Kitely family, a vengeful duel involving Downright and Bobadill, a rescue of the prodigal Edward Knowell by his father.[4] Even Edward's courtship of Bridget, though completed by marriage near the end of the play, is finally far less central than the audience would likely have expected: the courtship and the marriage alike occur offstage, are narrated only in the most passing way, and are peripheral to the focus of Clement's resolutions.[5] Every man may be in his own humor, but he is not finally in his own play. Only those who are in harmony with Jonson's satiric spirit are allowed to fulfill their intentions at center stage.

The Prologue emphasizes Jonson's unwillingness to

> serve th'ill customs of the age
> Or purchase your delight at such a rate
> As, for it, he himself must justly hate:
> To make a child, now swaddled, to proceed

Man, and then shoot up, in one beard and weed,
Past threescore years; or, with three rusty swords,
And help of some few foot-and-half-foot words,
Fight over York and Lancaster's long jars,
And in the tiring-house bring wounds to scars.
He rather prays you will be pleased to see
One such, today, as other plays should be:
Where neither Chorus wafts you o'er the seas;
Nor creaking throne comes down, the boys to please;
Nor nimble squib is seen, to make afeared
The gentlewomen; nor rolled bullet heard
To say, it thunders; nor tempestuous drum
Rumbles to tell you when the storm doth come;
But deeds and language such as men do use,
And persons such as Comedy would choose
When she would show an image of the times,
And sport with human follies, not with crimes—
Except we make 'em such by loving still
Our popular errors, when we know they'are ill.
I mean such errors as you'll all confess
By laughing at them—they deserve no less;
Which when you heartily do, there's hope left, then,
You that have so graced monsters may like men.

By laughing at characters who try to pose as conventional heroes, Jonson's audience will prove that it can distinguish between truly human characteristics and the conventional signatures of dramatic types. By merrily siding with the clever manipulators against those who live out the "popular errors" of bombastic drama, the audience will necessarily be siding with Jonson in his struggle against other playwrights—particularly, the allusions here suggest, against Shakespeare. The ending of the Prologue bolsters its offer of a new kind of drama with a threat to humiliate any spectator who declines the offer; Jonson uses both the carrot and the stick. He pleads for a more sophisticated audience by implying that those who fail to understand the play's critical argument will, by their unthinking devotion to familiar dramatic modes, necessarily be casting themselves as the play's gulls. Not to laugh is thus to identify oneself inadvertently with the characters at whom the other spectators are laughing.

The call for a more realistic theater, furthermore, necessarily implies a call for a more realistic approach to life itself. What is hollow bombast on the stage is surely even hollower and more bombastic on the street. In the theater, audiences have admired the monsters playwrights have made, and in society, people have admired the monstrosities other people have made of their own humanity; Jonson wants to inculcate simultaneously a taste for more naturalistic drama and a taste for more spontaneous virtue. True literature and true manhood, the Prologue suggests, go hand in hand. The follies become crimes (and therefore no longer a fit subject for comedy—Jonson has it both ways) only when we fondly accept them against our better knowledge, whether in our lives or in our theaters. We have everything to gain, and nothing to lose except some crude displays and cheap showmanship, by accepting Jonson's innovation as the ideal form of comedy and accepting the authentic wit of Jonson's gallants as the ideal form of social conduct. As Justice Clement says after burning Matthew's largely plagiarized verse, the attack on falsely based literary poses should in no way be taken as a disparagement of the achievement of authentic poets (5.5.35–42). The fact that literature has sometimes exercised an unhealthy influence over life does not preclude the possibility of a socially beneficial literature. Jonson offers satiric city-comedy—itself a form of multiple plagiarism—as an art that can chasten rather than indulge human follies, including the folly of self-dramatization.

The play proper begins by apparently announcing itself as a prodigal son story, and only an unusually wary spectator would suspect that the generic signals offered by Old Knowell might conflict with the generic intentions of Jonson. Knowell conceives of himself as the prodigal's wise father, a relationship frequently portrayed in Elizabethan literature.[6] The brief interjections by Brainworm in these opening lines are easy to overlook, and perhaps the playwright intended them to be so. Jonson invites Knowell and the audience to contribute to each other's false expectations, by allowing the old man to stand at center stage, with all eyes on him, and deliver a standard sort of soliloquy about his paternal fears and aspirations: "How happy, yet, should I esteem myself, / Could I (by any practice) wean the boy / From one vain course of study he affects" (1.1.6–8). The fact that this affectation is scholarship and poetry should of course alert us to the possibility

that Jonson considers his fears unreasonable, although the play
makes it clear that even poetry can be an evil in the hands of a
foolish plagiarist like Matthew. The irony is that the old man's
condemnation of poetry is spoken in verse and is itself a poetic
plagiarism of sorts: Knowell seems to be unconsciously adapting
a passage from *The Spanish Tragedy*,[7] which would have been the
literary rage back when

> Myself was once a student; and, indeed,
> Fed with the self-same humor he is now,
> Dreaming on naught but idle poetry.               (1.1.15–17)

Most critics have concluded that Knowell cannot be classified with
the "humorous" characters,[8] but he shares with the other gulls a
delusive attachment to an aggrandizing and dramatically conventional idea of himself. The self-same idle poetical humor that causes
him unconsciously to muddle his own words with those of Kyd's
Hieronimo is also responsible for his muddling his own identity
with a standard theatrical role.

When Old Knowell learns in the second scene that his son Edward is heading off to see a free-spirited companion, he delivers
another soliloquy that (partly because it *is* a soliloquy) seems to
identify him as the play's overseeing consciousness and his concerns as the play's concerns:

> I am resolved I will not stop his journey,
> Nor practice any violent mean to stay
> The unbridled course of youth in him; for that,
> Restrained, grows more impatient; and in kind
> Like to the eager but the generous greyhound,
> Who, ne'er so little from his game withheld,
> Turns head, and leaps up at his holder's throat.
>                                        (1.2.115–121)

There is nothing at all wrong with this as wisdom, except that it
has almost nothing to do with the reality of young Edward's
character and activities: the sententious speaker is established so
that his pose may be revealed and deflated by his dramatic context.
The words seem to be his own, but they are again an adaptation
of a well-known play, in this case Terence's *Adelphi*.[9] Henry Hol-
land Carter has suggested that Knowell reflects a standard type
illustrated by Charmides in Plautus' *Trinummus*, who must finally

forgive the son who had wasted the family's entire fortune.[10] But while it would doubtless please Knowell to see himself as this "thoroughly moral, long-suffering, and forgiving" father, the action of *Every Man In His Humor* offers very little correspondence. The parallel noted by Carter exists on Jonson's unconventional stage only to the extent that it is imposed by Knowell's conventionally melodramatic imagination.

Several critics have commented that Wellbred's letter, while sufficient to annoy Old Knowell, is hardly sufficient to provoke his gaudy fears about his son's misconduct; in the Quarto version, the letter is even less suggestive of the dissipated behavior traditional for the prodigal. Barton, for example, remarks that even the more scandalous version "still fails to motivate the elder Kno'well's anxiety in the tangible way that sons . . . do, in Roman comedy." Her diagnosis is that the old man "suffers, quite simply, from a milder form of Ferneze's broodiness [in *The Case Is Altered*] over a chick he cannot bear to release from parental surveillance."[11] I believe the heavily allusive flavor of this "broodiness" suggests that Jonson is making a literary point in addition to any psychoanalytic one. Knowell seems determined to cast himself as the prodigal's protective father, whether or not the mundane reality surrounding him will support such a pose. He proclaims his idiotic nephew Stephen "a prodigal" also, sounding very much like Polonius as he gathers *sententiae* into a spell against the waywardness of youth (1.1.62–85).[12] We may feel an urge to complain, as the play proceeds, that Jonson is not fulfilling the conventional prodigal son pattern, but any such complaint identifies us with the overly conventional thinking that allows Knowell to be gulled by a more alert satirical wit. By sounding and then renouncing echoes of our past theatrical experiences, Jonson enmeshes us in a process of literary reeducation. This is "affective stylistics" in a dramatic mode, a heuristic strategy that temporarily misleads the audience down a familiar path—a path that proves to be a dead end.

When Old Knowell next appears in soliloquy, still obsessed by the intercepted letter and still moralizing conventionally on the decline of the world and the misbehavior of the younger generation, we are compelled to reevaluate our conventionally respectful response to his earlier speeches of this kind, because we have now seen enough of Edward and enough of the plot to suspect that Knowell is overrating his role as moral guardian.[13] What before sounded duly concerned may now sound a little obsessive, foolish, and hackneyed:

> I cannot lose the thought, yet, of this letter
> Sent to my son; nor leave t'admire the change
> Of manners and the breeding of our youth
> Within the kingdom, since myself was one.     (2.5.1–4)

These seemingly heartfelt words are yet again perceptibly a literary pose. Knowell's entire long speech is actually a pastiche of passages from the classics, wandering from Juvenal's *Thirteenth Satire* to Quintillian's *Institutes of Eloquence,* then on to Juvenal's *Fourteenth Satire,* with local stops in Ovid's *Fasti* and Horace's *Epistles.* These patchwork paraphrases have been described by the play's editors as evidence of Jonson's predatory classicism.[14] My argument offers an alternative way of viewing them, as Jonson's effort to reveal Knowell's subconscious literary posing by filling his speeches with subconscious literary allusions. By having Knowell inform us that he was once a scholar himself, Jonson invites us to attribute the allusiveness to the character rather than the author (though Jonson may also be engaged in a symbolic battle here against his own tendency to play the rigidly patriarchal literary classicist rather than the spontaneous and ingenious prodigal son). If the typical Jonsonian gull is indeed a character whose words and ideas are secondhand, and whose sense of his own importance is greatly exaggerated,[15] then Old Knowell fits the category perfectly. His aging wit remains stuck in a residue of the poetic humor he thought he had abandoned in his youth.

Stephen, the country gull, demonstrates in a starker form the foolishness of pursuing an exalted role. He has an omnivorous appetite for the poses, costumes, and lines that the city and its courtly literature offer to sell him. He first appears asking Old Knowell for a book about hawking, determined to invest in the sport because "skill in the hawking- and hunting-languages nowadays" is *de rigueur,* and "a gentleman mun show himself like a gentleman"(1.1.31–50). Stephen consistently attempts to conform to one attribute or another of this role, and is consistently humiliated by the discrepancy between the role and the actual qualities he brings to it. He is always imagining that the right clothes will make him a handsome man, or the right weapon a fearsome fighter; such suppositions reflect an unhealthily theatricalized notion of the self and, in fact, gentlemanliness was commonly discussed in specifically theatrical terms by Elizabethan commentators.[16] Jonson rarely provides his poseurs with the rapt spectators they expect. When Stephen tells Brainworm, "I think my leg would show in a silk hose," Brainworm answers, "You have an excellent good leg, Master Stephen, but I cannot stay to praise it longer now, and I am very sorry for 't" (1.3.39–44). Brainworm's wry lament that he lacks world enough or time to praise Stephen properly is funny because it neatly reveals Stephen's absurd assumption that the play has no other business than elegizing the shape of his leg and the cut of his garment, as if it were an ordinary Renaissance love lyric or dialogue on courtiership. His misprision of the genre he inhabits, as much as his vanity, is what exposes him to mockery, though of course the misprision and the vanity reinforce each other.

When he meets Stephen again, Brainworm (now disguised as a soldier) sells him a rapier at an exorbitant price by exploiting his desire to strike magnificent gentlemanly poses:

> *Brainworm*   Generous sir, I refer it to your own judgment; you are a gentleman, give me what you please.
> *Stephen*   True, I am a gentleman, I know that, friend: but what though? I pray you say, what would you ask?
> *Brainworm*   I assure you, the blade may become the side or thigh of the best prince in Europe.
> *Edward*   Aye, with a velvet scabbard, I think.
> *Stephen*   Nay, and 't be mine, it shall have a velvet scabbard, cos, that's flat.                         (2.4.64–72)

Stephen revealingly misunderstands Edward's sarcastic remark, which implies that the sword will prove adequate only for posing and not for use, as an endorsement rather than a warning. Outward display always takes precedence for him over inward reality.

The decorations by which Stephen tries to signal his own nobility are verbal as well as physical. The fact that he swears by St. Peter in his love-posy merely "to make up the meter" (2.4.40) evinces his willingness to augment his behavior with meaningless flourishes in an effort to fill out conventional literary forms. The grand oaths he admires in Bobadill turn up, often in ridiculously inappropriate contexts, in his own mouth (3.5.121; 4.2.27, 75). As Old Knowell points out, Stephen's formulaic attempts at honorable quarreling are patiently forborne by Wellbred's inoffensive messenger, and therefore exposed as merely a scene Stephen was determined to rehearse, whether or not it had any justification in reality:

> You see the honest man demeans himself
> Modestly towards you, giving no reply
> To your unseasoned, quarreling, rude fashion;
> And still you huff it, with a kind of carriage
> As void of wit as of humanity. (1.2.28–32)

Stephen's huffy carriage, in other words, is neither authentically human nor theatrically effective—or, if it is effective, it works as low comedy rather than as the heroic story Stephen envisions. Even when he realizes that someone might be mocking his vain poses, that realization only more clearly exposes his egoism. As Edward chuckles at Wellbred's letter, Stephen exclaims, " 'Slid, I hope he laughs not at me; and he do—" (1.3.47). Not only is this vague threat promptly revealed as hollow bluster (1.3.64–77), but his supposition that Edward was concerned with him at all renders him ridiculous. From the audience's perspective Stephen is humiliated as much by the strategy of decentering Jonson uses against many of his gulls—by the fact that the world thinks less about him than he imagines—as he would be by Edward's laughter at any of his less subtle follies.

Edward, like Brainworm, knows how to exploit Stephen's type of folly once he sees it. He draws Stephen along for display to Wellbred by promising to enmesh his greatness in no "plot against the state," and by addressing him as

> A gentleman of your sort, parts, carriage, and estima-
> tion . . . that (hitherto) his every step hath left the stamp
> of a great foot behind him, as every word the savor of
> a strong spirit! And he! This man! So graced, gilded, or
> (to use a more fit metaphor) so tin-foiled by nature, as
> not ten housewives' pewter (again' a good time) shows
> more bright to the world than he! And he . . . this man!
> To conceal such real ornaments as these, and shadow
> their glory, as a millaner's wife does her wrought stom-
> acher with a smoky lawn or a black cypress? Oh,
> cos! . . . Come, wrong not the quality of your desert

with looking downward, cos; but hold up your head,
so; and let the Idea of what you are be portrayed i' your
face, that men may read i' your physnomy, "Here, within
this place, is to be seen the true, rare, and accomplished
monster—or miracle—of nature" (which is all one). What
think you of this, cos?                              (1.3.91–109)

All the metaphors in Edward's flattery describe Stephen's nobility
as essentially a costume, a cheap gilding, draping, or ornamen-
tation of the self, and Stephen's failure to object to that characterization is predictable and revealing. The monstrous Stephen is
not only *in* a humor, he virtually *is* a humor: Cash later tells Cob
that a humor "is a gentleman-like monster, bred, in the special
gallantry of our time, by affectation" (3.4.20–21). For a man to
be in his humor is really for him to be in a melodramatic role that
aggrandizes his true nature and his true role in the world, miraculously to himself, monstrously to less interested observers. When
every man is in his own humor, but all are sharing the same stage,
the performers are doomed to a series of humiliating confronta-
tions. Like the jealous Kitely (4.8.77), they create a "monstrous"
world by attempting to enlist their fellow men in their private
melodramas.

Edward's suggestion that Stephen could be displayed (like a
sideshow creature) with either the title of monster or that of miracle, because they are the same, refers back more pointedly to the
Prologue's accusation that the popular appetite for miraculous theater
was actually an appetite for monstrosity over humanity. The fact
that both references were added in the Folio revisions supports
the notion that they were part of a deliberate and coherent critical
statement, and Jonson's complaint in *Discoveries* that bad writers
are often acclaimed as "Miracles" (VIII, 582, ll. 592–595) confirms
that the word was active in his critical vocabulary. The degradingly
false posture the spectators are compelled to ridicule in Stephen,
the allusion suggests, is really only a version of the postures they
had praised in earlier plays about warlike noblemen who paraded
in threadbare velvets, mouthed grand phrases, and waved their
tinsel swords. Edward is using the equation of miracle and monstrosity to slip an insult past Stephen, but Jonson is using it to
alert us, not only to the falsely theatrical quality of Stephen's

attitude, but also to the connection between the sort of theatrical excess condemned by the Prologue and the impulse to theatricalize the self exemplified by Stephen. The project of chastising the gulls within the play and the project of educating the audience about the play are again intertwined.

Stephen's only reaction to Edward's hollow panegyric on his merits is a promise to add another popular theatrical role, as a melancholic, to his role as a gallant:

> *Stephen* Why, I do think of it; and I will be more proud, and melancholy, and gentleman-like, than I have been, I'll ensure you.
> *Edward* Why, that's resolute Master Stephen! [*Aside*] Now, if I can but hold him up to his height, as it is happily begun, it will do well for a suburb-humor; we may hap have a match with the city, and play him for forty pound. (1.3.110–115)

Edward might as well be speaking for Jonson, who is profitably "playing" this same gull to his height of foolishness by making him "play" his absurdly inflated idea of himself. Melancholy is easily added to Stephen's traits because the addition suits Jonson's purposes as well as Stephen's. Melancholics in the period were frequently accused of assuming the trait superficially, to project a refined aesthetic sensibility; furthermore, as Burton's *Anatomy of Melancholy* suggests, the disease was often associated with too much reading. The role also had some specific and positive literary precedents; for example, the noblest figure, and the romantic victor, in Chapman's *An Humorous Day's Mirth* is the ostentatiously melancholic Dowsecer. In act 3, scene 1, Stephen proves as good as his word, and no better. He introduces himself to Wellbred as "somewhat melancholy, but you shall command me, sir, in whatever is incident to a gentleman" (69–71), then tells Matthew, "I am mightily given to melancholy" (78), and confidentially asks Edward,

> Cousin, is it well? Am I melancholy enough?
> *Edward* Oh, aye, excellent!
> *Wellbred* Captain Bobadill: why muse you so?
> *Edward* [*To Wellbred*] He is melancholy, too. (3.1.98–102)

The joke is pointed: such an explanation is no less and no more of a self-dramatizing fiction than Bobadill's claim that he was recalling his service in a noble siege.

Matthew feels obliged to tell Stephen that "I am melancholy myself divers times, sir, and then do I no more but take pen and paper presently, and overflow you half a score or a dozen of sonnets at a sitting" (3.1.80–83). He, too, is trying out for the role of Dowsecer, Chapman's romantic scholar-hero, only to find himself cast instead as Chapman's Labesha, the false scholar who is therefore a failed suitor. The fact that Matthew's poems are never written as exorcisms of a true inner passion but rather are plagiarized out of the writings of others reinforces the association of gentlemanly melancholia with derivative literary postures. Matthew's pose as a Petrarchan lover is never taken seriously by either the play or the other characters (1.4.65–70; 3.5.139–141). By the end of the play, that pose has been thoroughly discredited in both its literary and its amorous aspects. That Jonson intends this humiliation to reflect on bombastic literary traditions is clear enough from the fact that he shows Matthew extensively quoting and plagiarizing Kyd and Marlowe (1.5.43–59; 4.2.41–56), two grandiloquent authors whose huge popularity Jonson evidently resented.[17]

Jonson similarly employs Bobadill, whose life is a hollowly bombastic role, to praise old playwrights such as Kyd and old chestnuts such as *The Spanish Tragedy* over new ones: "I would fain see all the poets of these times pen such another play as that was!" (1.5.46–47). Such a foolish critical perspective, Jonson implies, corresponds to a general inability to distinguish real life from romantic literature. One reviewer criticized F. R. Benson's portrayal of Bobadill in a 1903 Stratford production as "a little bit too much like a burlesque of the bad bold pirate of transpontine melodrama," but Benson may have been on the right track. Bobadill insists that his sword is a real-life version of such romance weapons as "Morglay, Excalibur, Durindana" (3.1.144). He even converts his crude humiliation by Downright's cudgel into a supernatural romance in which he was "strook with a planet" or "fascinated, by Jupiter—fascinated; but I will be unwitched, and revenged by law" (4.7.125–126; 4.9.16–17). He wants to be seen as an adventuring soldier, but he is trapped in Jonson's version of Latin comedy, which keeps exposing him as a cowardly *miles gloriosus.* His military exploits are mostly fictions, constructed less skillfully than Brainworm's openly fictional soldier; his artful swordsmanship and his noble lodgings are mere verbal artifacts that collapse under the lightest touch of reality. As Jonas Barish suggests, "Years of poring over books on the duello have ended in his being able to mesmerize not only Matheo and Stephano but himself into a belief in his own valor."[18]

Kitely seems convinced that the play is a *commedia dell'arte* cuckolding story, and that he will enact the *Pantalone dei Bisognosi,* its victimized husband.[19] Again, the typecasting is done less by Jonson than by the Jonsonian character himself, and if we expect any fulfillment of the cuckolding plot, we are ourselves guilty of imposing a play we remember onto the more original satiric play we watch, an error that implicates us in Kitely's final embarrassment. By the sheer force of his conventional and perversely egocentric imagination, Kitely nearly fabricates such a tale out of the play's material. He is finally humiliated, not by any pliancy of his wife, but instead by the stubbornness of his author, who refuses to give Kitely's fears any justification or centrality. Realistic satire can attack Kitely only because of his unwitting allegiance to conventional melodrama. As Clement finally tells him, "Horns i' the mind are worse than o' the head" (5.5.70).

Kitely's offhand remark, in the final few lines of *Every Man In His Humor,* that he had once memorized "a jealous man's part in a play" (5.5.78) is merely the culmination of a long series of indications that Kitely has a cuckolding play in his head to which he subordinates all naturally perceived reality. Some psychological critics have attributed Kitely's obsession to a form of voyeurism which impels him to envision his wife in illicit embraces.[20] To me, the evidence suggests that Kitely is a compulsive spectator of theatrical activity, whether or not he is a compulsive voyeur of sexual activity. His delusions associate themselves with dramatic conventions at least as frequently and systematically as with any conventional neurotic syndrome. He complains that his houseguest Wellbred "makes my house here common as a mart, / A theater, a public receptacle / For giddy humor" (2.1.56–58), but it is Kitely's own humor that has made his world a *commedia dell'arte* stage. Kitely explains to Downright that if he banished Wellbred and his decadent followers, they would

> out of their impetuous rioting fant'sies,
> Beget some slander that shall dwell with me.
> And what would that be, think you? Marry, this.
> They would give out (because my wife is fair,
> Myself but lately married, and my sister
> Here sojourning a virgin in my house)
> That I were jealous!                           (2.1.103–109)

*Qui s'excuse, s'accuse.* Out of his own rampant fantasies Kitely has in fact earned this "slander." He is only too correct in his fear that, in trying to forestall his own disgrace, he is instead inviting and advertising it (2.1.114–119); his terror of cuckolding, and not cuckolding itself, is finally the focus of his public mortification. He puts the horns on his own head by imagining they are there, as indeed he does literally in the stage direction at 3.6.10. Even in stories where men falsely suspect their wives (again, *An Humorous Day's Mirth* provides one example), there is almost always someone who has attempted or impugned the women's virtue. In *Every Man In His Humor,* however, no one seems even to have considered the possibility of seducing Kitely's wife. His concerns are simply those of someone who has seen too many such plays:

> Why, 't cannot be, where there is such resort
> Of wanton gallants and young revelers,
> That any woman should be honest long.
> Is't like that factious beauty will preserve
> The public weal of chastity unshaken,
> When such strong motives muster, and make head
> Against her single peace? No, no. Beware
> When mutual appetite doth meet to treat,
> And spirits of one kind and quality
> Come once to parley, in the pride of blood:
> It is no slow conspiracy that follows.
> Well (to be plain), if I but thought the time
> Had answered their affections, all the world
> Should not persuade me but I were a cuckold.    (2.3.11–24)

That is true only because, in his mind, "all the world" is a stage.

The degree to which Kitely's rage is conventional for the theatrical cuckold is clear from the fact that several of his speeches parallel Othello's so strikingly that critics have speculated how a play published in 1601 (the parallels are in the Quarto as well as the Folio) could have parodied a play written in 1604.[21] What is being parodied, of course, is a set of standard theatrical markers of jealousy that Shakespeare would exploit in a less parodic spirit. By ingenious close reading, Kitely completely misinterprets his wife's innocent remarks (2.3.40–50), then writhes on his own misinterpretation much as Othello does: "Ah, but what misery 'is it to know this? / Or knowing it, to want the mind's erection / In such extremes?" (2.3.69–71). Ironically, Kitely only "knows" about his cuckold's horns because his mind has erected them. By the third act the anticipation becomes striking. Othello's "Why did I marry . . . O now, for ever / Farewell the tranquil mind!" (3.3.242–348) reflects Kitely's

> What meant I to marry?
> I, that before was ranked in such content,
> My mind at rest, too, in so soft a peace,
> Being free master of mine own free thoughts—
> And now become a slave?                    (3.6.14–18)

Kitely's expectation of cuckolding makes him misread his wife's description of Edward with a crude kind of literalism that reappears in Leontes as well as Othello.[22]

> *Dame Kitely*  Indeed, he seemed to be a gentleman of an ex-
> ceeding fair disposition, and of very excellent good parts!
> *Kitely*  [*To himself*] Her love, by heaven! My wife's minion!
> Fair disposition? Excellent good parts?
> Death, these phrases are intolerable!
> Good parts? How should she know his parts?
> His parts? Well, well, well, well, well, well!
> It is too plain, too clear.                    (4.3.30–37)

This is significant, not only in echoing standard motifs of theatrical jealousy, but also in marking such jealousy as essentially an act of naive misreading in which expectation overwhelms perception—the same sort of misreading Jonson provokes in his spectators.

Kitely is preternaturally alert to all the tricks by which theatrical adulterers arrange their encounters. He is convinced that Edward must now be hidden in the house, less because he has any evidence of such a scheme than because the search for the closeted adulterer is part of the mental script he feels compelled to perform:

> Aye, I thought so: my mind gave me as much.
> I'll die, but they have hid him i' the house,
> Somewhere; I'll go and search, go with me, Thomas.
> Be true to me, and thou shalt find a master.    (4.3.47–50)

Master Ford appears ridiculous in *The Merry Wives of Windsor* because he cannot find the hidden Falstaff; Kitely appears ridiculous in a more profound way, because there is no one there for him to find.

Kitely enlists his manservant Thomas Cash in the task of decoding and forestalling a wide range of standard cuckolding plots:

> Note every gallant, and observe him well,
> That enters in my absence, to thy mistress:
> If she would show him rooms, the jest is stale;
> Follow 'em, Thomas, or else hang on him
> And let him not go after; mark their looks;
> Note, if she offer but to see his band,
> Or any other amorous toy about him;
> But praise his leg; or foot; or if she say
> The day is hot, and bid him feel her hand,
> How hot it is; oh, that's a monstrous thing!    (4.8.68–77)

The only possibility he seems unable to entertain is the possibility that *Every Man In His Humor* is not a cuckolding story at all, that there is no code and nothing to forestall. Once again the word "monstrous" points us back to the Folio Prologue. As in Edward's description of Stephen, or Cash's description of humors, monstrosity corresponds to the imposition of melodrama on reality. The precedents of the word within the play convert Kitely's accusation of adultery into an unwitting confession of his self-dramatizing folly.

This kind of mentality can enlist every casual remark in the service of its fantasy, a fantasy so strong that it takes precedence over physical reality. When Dame Kitely expresses concern that Downright's quarreling might have proved dangerous, Wellbred replies dismissively that almost anything can sometimes be dangerous. But the example Wellbred gives only serves to upset Kitely further by inadvertently conjuring in Kitely's mind some famous stories of husbands brutally betrayed by their wives:

> *Wellbred*  Might, sister? So might the good warm clothes
>    your husband wears be poisoned, for anything he knows; or
>    the wholesome wine he drunk, even now at the table—
> *Kitely*  [*Aside.*] Now, God forbid: O me! Now I remember,
>    My wife drunk to me last—and changed the cup—
>    And bade me wear this cursèd suit today.
>    See if Heav'n suffer murder undiscovered!
>    [*To Bridget.*] I feel me ill; give me some mithridate,
>    Some mithridate and oil, good sister, fetch me;
>    Oh, I am sick at heart! I burn, I burn.
>    If you will save my life, go fetch it me.
> *Wellbred*  [*Aside.*] Oh, strange humor! My very breath has
>    poisoned him.                                          (4.8.15–26)

Like Leontes in *The Winter's Tale,* Kitely has drunk and seen the spider. He is suddenly Augustus, poisoned by the meal his wife Livia fed him, or Hercules, poisoned by the suit his wife Deianira gave him. He perceives as inevitable precisely what Wellbred was citing as absurd, and both extremes arise from the grandiose precedents for such a murder. The consciousness that can be "poisoned with a simile" (4.8.31) is an overly literary consciousness, not merely an overly jealous one.

The theatrical model for cuckolding so haunts Kitely's mind that he cannot conduct the business of his real life for fear that the play will begin. He dares not travel to meet a customer, because there is something ominous to him about the likely duration of his absence. I suspect this reiterated duration disturbs him because it was apparently the standard duration of an Elizabethan play, and he envisions "the two hours' traffic of our stage"[23] passing through his bedroom:

> Two hours? Ha? Things never dreamt of yet
> May be contrived, aye, and effected too,
> In two hours' absence; well, I will not go.
> Two hours; no, fleering opportunity,
> I will not give your subtlety that scope.
> Who will not judge him worthy to be robbed
> That sets his doors wide open to a thief

> And shows the felon where his treasure lies?
> Again, what earthy spirit but will attempt
> To taste the fruit of beauty's golden tree,
> When leaden sleep seals up the dragon's eyes?
> I will not go. Business, go by for once.
> No, beauty, no; you are of too good caract
> To be left so, without a guard, or open!
> Your lustre too'll inflame at any distance,
> Draw courtship to you as a jet doth straws,
> Put motion in a stone, strike fire from ice,
> Nay, make a porter leap you with his burden!     (3.3.10–27)

Even Kitely's jealous apostrophe to "opportunity" reflects an Elizabethan literary convention.[24] He is not a dragon, nor does anyone else mistake his wife for beauty's golden tree. What would be merely poetical exaggeration in a man whose wife was truly coveted (as are the wives in *The Devil Is an Ass* and Middleton's *The Changeling*) becomes an absurd display of egocentric and masochistic imagination in Kitely, whose wife is apparently not even desired, let alone seduced, by any of the play's other characters.

Kitely then vacillates repeatedly over whether or not to go about his business: "Nor will I go. I am resolved for that. / Carry'in my cloak again—Yet, stay—Yet do, too. / I will defer going, on all occasions" (3.3.39–41). This alternation, which continues for a number of lines, and the similar dithering about explaining his fears to Cash, which fills up the rest of the scene, are standard devices of Bergsonian humor: Kitely becomes a puppet of his conflicting compulsions. But Jonson draws significance from this comic device by showing that Kitely cannot resolve his choice because he is trying to weigh two entirely separate worlds of possibility against each other for likelihood and consequences. There is no rational system for weighing ordinary reality against theatrical fantasies, and so his practical and melodramatic perspectives can only alternate, not negotiate:

> I am a knave if I know what to say,
> What course to take, or which way to resolve.
> My brain (methinks) is like an hourglass,
> Wherein my'imaginations run like sands,
> Filling up time; but then are turned, and turned,

So that I know not what to stay upon,
And less, to put in act.                         (3.3.47–53)

The two meanings of "acting" are mutually exclusive for him, as they are for Hamlet.

What is funniest about Kitely's long (and similarly vacillating) presentation to Cash is that he is agonizing over a revelation that will presumably mean nothing to Cash, who is likely to react with neither the melodramatic loyalty Kitely desires, nor the melo-dramatic disloyalty Kitely fears. Cash's inability to understand his master's concerns parallels the play's unwillingness to respect those concerns; Kitely's text is coherent only in the context of his own mind, or of a different sort of literary work. Several editors have been puzzled by the clear echoes of Shakespeare's *King John* (3.3.19–58) in Kitely's dithering speech.[25] Perhaps the parallel to a momentous royal decision enacted on the stage a few years earlier would have underscored the triviality and the theatrical derivation of Kitely's concerns. His reluctance to trust Cash may arise from another cautionary literary precedent. If Kitely has one clear dramatic ancestor, it is Hermino in Bentivoglio's *Il Geloso*.[26] What interests me particularly about the parallel is the way Jonson chooses to break it. Hermino's great mistake is confiding his jealousy to Truffa, who is actually a pimp, and enlisting Truffa's help in guarding his wife. It is as if Kitely, who so often seems like an echo of Hermino, were specifically trying to avoid Hermino's error. But Jonson consistently rebuffs his characters for expecting real life, and therefore the realistic world of Jonsonian comedy, to follow such established literary patterns. Again, what finally humiliates Kitely is Jonson's refusal to respect the theatrical precedent: the fact that Cash is not a Truffa exposes Kitely's prudence as self-dramatizing folly.

The confrontation between Cob and Tib in act 4, scene 4, is a systematic parody of what are already parodies; its closest analogue is the puppet show in *Bartholomew Fair*. The scene begins with Cob expressing his terror, based like that of Kitely on a ridiculous misinterpretation of his wife's words, that he has suddenly acquired the cuckold's horns. In fact, the mutual sexual mistrust of Cob and Tib, like the conjugal fears of Kitely and the parental fears of Old Knowell, may derive partly from literary precedent rather than real evidence: if *Every Man In His Humor* were *commedia dell'arte,* Cob and Tib would indeed be adulterers, and their house a brothel.[27] That same overly conventional understanding of the plot is what draws the Kitelys and Old Knowell there in such confident outrage. The squabble between Cob and Tib quickly degenerates into misplaced soldierly oaths and empty soldierly threats of the sort we have seen in Bobadill, against whom Cob then threatens the same sorts of legal reprisals Bobadill had threatened against the choleric Downright. Cob next spouts mindless praise of Justice Clement, reiterates his Kitely-like insistence on isolating Tib, and composes a silly pair of closing couplets. Even Cob's fishy boast of his noble genealogy, apparently an ironic allusion to Nashe's *Lenten Stuff,* is also plausibly a burlesque of Stephen's attempts to portray himself as a gentleman. Cob and Tib thus expose the other characters as role-players by assuming the various roles more rapidly, randomly, and clumsily than the others. The noisy, pointless arguments involving these poor imitations of the poor imitations force us to recognize that the play itself has become a jumble of unsuccessful poses and poseurs, waiting for some masterful figure to bring order out of their chaos.

Chaos breaks out openly in several of the subplots six scenes later, and what generates this hilarious series of misunderstandings is the clash of various conventional expectations. Each of the victims of the superior plotters arrives at Cob's lowly house expecting to find the culmination of his special play, only to encounter people who insist on incorporating him into their own. Knowell believes he has found the den of iniquity where his prodigal son must be doing all sorts of prodigal things, Kitely and his wife believe they have found each other's adulterous trysting place, and Cob believes he has discovered his wife's seducer, but none of them are right. Each assumes he has finally caught up with his play's malefactor, only to be cast as the malefactor of someone else's play. All they can do is eye one another suspiciously and shout at one another in righteous indignation. Typical is Knowell's conviction that Tib's squabble with Dame Kitely over her husband's whereabouts is

> but a device, to balk me withal.
> *[Enter Kitely.]*
> Soft, who is this? 'Tis not my son, disguised? (4.10.26–27)

This is a wonderful moment of misprision, in which Old Knowell responds to cognitive dissonance not by accepting the mundane truth, but instead by postulating yet another conventional dramatic maneuver in order to sustain his fantasy. The foolish characters are not victims of each other's "devices," so much as victims of their own insistent devisings.

The real victimizers are the witty characters, who use the confusion to gain the advantage in their personal struggles, and Jonson himself, who uses the same confusion to establish the superiority of satiric city-comedy over more standard modes of Elizabethan drama. The abortive performances of formulaic comedies at Cob's house serve to distract everyone who might prevent Edward from marrying Bridget: his father, her brother, and her less worthy suitor. Brainworm has deliberately staged the fantasies of these fools so that Edward can successfully perform a version of classical New Comedy in the space they have been induced to vacate. By the same trick, Jonson has cleared space in the comic genre for himself. Of course, by the time Jonson writes *Every Man In His Humor*, New Comedy is itself old hat. He can hardly claim that his wily-servant plots really eliminate the conventionality and implausibility he attacks in his rivals' plays. But the classical model does offer him, in a symbolic and chronological way, the distance he so clearly craves from the degraded world of his theater and his fellow playwrights. Throughout his life, Jonson asserts his superiority over his rivals by asserting his superior intimacy with classical literature, to which he attributes the status of a higher truth; it is hardly surprising, then, that he adapts classical comedy in order to claim that he is writing something more real and valuable than the works of his competitors.

Edward and Wellbred are certainly not wholly immune to the allure of self-dramatization. Their inclination to cast themselves in conventional literary forms jeopardizes their plans from the start of the play (1.3.50–54).[28] But though Wellbred's speeches at moments become dangerously stylized, he regularly reverts to an ironic distance from his courtly pose, puncturing his own inflated praise with indirect taunts and his own inflated tone with obscene puns, as in his exchange with Bridget about what "touches" her concerning Edward, who "hath vowed to inflame whole bonefires of zeal at his heart" in her honor. Bridget responds in kind, placing Wellbred on an uneasy margin between the role of chivalric wooer and that of farcical pander: "this motion of yours savors of an old knight-adventurer's servant a little too much, methinks"

(4.8.97–116).[29] Clearly these are people with enough theatrical awareness, and enough of a debunking instinct, to survive in the world of Jonsonian comedy.

Yet, while Edward's marriage to Bridget is allowed to succeed at center stage near the end of the play, it is not really the central or final interest of *Every Man In His Humor*. That status is reserved for Brainworm and his relationship to Clement. Brainworm outdoes the other wits by sustaining a closer alliance with Jonson's programs of classical revival and contemporary satire. He conceives of himself as the wily servant of classical New Comedy, and Jonson allows him to succeed in that role, partly because the role itself consists largely of strategic and self-conscious role-playing.[30] Brainworm is not merely a better actor than the others; he is also more alert to the possibilities of becoming a playwright. The play repeatedly invites us to associate Brainworm with his creator.[31] When he first disguises himself, as a soldier, he laughs "to see myself translated thus from a poor creature to a creator; for now I must create an intolerable sort of lies, or my present profession loses the grace" (2.4.1–3). But clearly he is a creator in a nobler sense as well, a liar only in the Platonic terms (referred to in Prospero's letter in the Quarto version of *Every Man In His Humor*) that categorized poets as liars.

Brainworm resembles the gulls in that he reenacts conventional literary motifs, but he resembles Jonson in that he self-consciously exploits those motifs; he rewrites them, instead of being rewritten by them. He has adeptly "writhen"—perhaps with a pun on "written"—"himself into the habit of one of your poor infantry," a role that was evidently popular among beggars as well as on the stage during the period (3.5.7–13).[32] Brainworm thus shows himself as skillful an "artificer" as one who had "been a weaver of language from his infancy for the clothing of it" (3.5.20–24). Soon Brainworm undertakes another "act" (4.6.53), this time by stealing the costume of Formal, a device which he—and Jonson—successfully adapt from *The Jests of Peele* and *The Blind Beggar of Bednal Green*. Brainworm humiliates Formal by thus forcibly altering his costume, much as Jonson humiliates his gulls by forcibly shifting their roles (5.3.107–5.4.8). At the end of the fourth act, Brainworm reappears in yet another guise, this time playing a sergeant, as he—and Jonson—adapt a trick from *The Blacke Bookes Messenger*.[33]

The play invites us to associate Brainworm, not only with the general idea of the playwright, but also with Jonson's specific program for mortifying popular theater on behalf of satiric realism. Brainworm announces that he has disguised himself to protect Edward, for fear that otherwise "we may wear motley at the year's end, and who wears motley, you know" (2.4.7–12). The remark has caused the play's editors considerable consternation, but Jonson may be playing on the fact that "motley" referred either to the costume of a disgraced servant or to the costume of a professional fool.[34] The analogy between Brainworm's role in serving the Knowells and Jonson's role in entertaining his audience converts the distaste for wearing motley into a significant critical statement. If Brainworm fails to defend the interests of his future master Edward from his repressive father—the standard project of the wily servant in classical New Comedy—he may be relegated to a lowlier livery. In the same way, if Jonson fails to escape into rejuvenated New Comedy through a successful wily-servant plot, he may be relegated to writing the lowest and most conventional forms of comedy, and in that sense to wearing the motley of the stage fool. So, like Brainworm, Jonson poses as the servant of the older generation's plots, but is secretly using his apparent participation in those plots as a way of subverting them, on behalf of a new generation of comedy.

When he is assigned to "perform this business" of diverting Old Knowell, Brainworm assures Wellbred that his "nimble soul has wak'd all forces of my fant'sy by this time, and put 'em in true motion" (4.5.1–8). He succeeds in this motion-making (from behind his disguise) largely by casting Edward as the wayward son Knowell proudly envisions himself rescuing. Like Jonson himself, Brainworm thrives by improvising on the melodramatic expectations of his audiences. When Knowell stumbles across a hole in the disguised Brainworm's story, Brainworm effectively fills it with an explanation directly out of *Doctor Faustus*:

*Knowell*   But how should he know thee to be my man?
*Brainworm*   Nay, sir, I cannot tell; unless it be
   By the black art! Is not your son a scholar, sir?
*Knowell*   Yes, but I hope his soul is not allied
   Unto such hellish practice: if it were,
   I had just cause to weep my part in him,
   And curse the time of his creation.            (4.6.17–23)

Knowell accepts this outlandish explanation without hesitation because it fits with his proud role as the protector of his scholarly son from a terrible temptation and a terrible fate. Once this crisis is past, Brainworm reverts to playing in a milder but no less seductive way on Knowell's fantasy:

> But, sir, thus much I can assure you, for I heard it while I was locked up, there were a great many rich merchants' and brave citizens' wives with 'em at a feast, and your son, Mr. Edward, withdrew with one of 'em, and has 'pointed to meet her anon, at one Cob's house, a water-bearer that dwells by the Wall. Now there your Worship shall be sure to take him, for there he preys, and fail he will not.                                        (4.6.38–44)

As soon as Knowell stalks off on this noble mission, Brainworm imagines him sitting at Cob's house

> three or four hours, travailing with the expectation of wonders, and at length be delivered of air: oh, the sport that I should then take to look on him, if I durst! But, now, I mean to appear no more afore him in this shape. I have another trick to act yet.                    (4.6.49–53)

Here is the starkest sort of distinction between the man who wanders blindly through real life in the expectation of theatrical wonders, and the man who uses a more self-conscious theatricalism to exploit that naive theatrical appetite for our sport and his profit. When Knowell first falls for Brainworm's disguise and reveals his own mission, Brainworm wonders, " 'Slid, was there ever seen a fox in years to betray himself thus?" (2.5.129–130). Jonson's comedies are in fact full of characters (including the "fox" Volpone) who are just clever enough to delude themselves in this fashion.

Even Brainworm, however, like the great conspirators in *The Alchemist* and in *Volpone,* proves only clever enough to entangle himself beyond his powers of extrication. His plot, like that of *Every Man In His Humor* as a whole, and like those of Subtle and Mosca in later works, finally reaches such a degree of complexity that he can only throw away all disguises and plead for acceptance on the merit of his wit. (In this, Brainworm also closely resembles Lemot in *An Humorous Day's Mirth*). Justice Clement's role in judging this plea, and in presenting and perfecting this new sort of play fits well with the common supposition that he is Jonson's surrogate, a representation of the triumphant playwright upon his own stage.[35] One can allegorize the play into a commentary on its own creation, as critics often allegorize Shakespeare's *The Tempest:* Brainworm, like Ariel, is the creative spirit, energetic and protean, while Clement, like Prospero, shapes that spirit into intelligible moral comedy. The tone, of course, is different, but the transaction appears to be similar. Like the traditional satirist, Clement holds a mirror up to those he intends to embarrass and reform. His judicial skill involves a kind of inverse *sprezzatura:* he is artful in a way that reveals the artfulness (in a bad sense) of the other characters. His martial costume allows him to demonstrate how hollow an act Bobadill's soldierly pose had been (5.1.39–5.2.20). His poetic pose—"I will challenge him myself, presently, at *extempore*"—demonstrates the hollowness of Matthew's poetical pretensions (5.5.9–33). But he is careful to spare poetry as a whole from this deflation, using a favorite adage of Jonson's in defense of the poet (5.5.36); he is an enemy of the misuse of the literary arts, not an enemy of those arts themselves. G. B. Jackson complains that Clement typifies the weakness of Jonson's normative figures, who, instead of being "engaged in the same type of action as the others in a more desirable way (like Viola, Theseus, and Rosalind) . . . are simply not engaged in the same type of action."[36] This objection disappears if we recognize that Clement is indeed offering a healthier version of the action—indeed, the acting—that the lesser figures undertake less productively.

The play, however, allows a slightly different interpretation of Clement's role, one that permits the identification of Brainworm with Jonson. There can be little question that Clement, like Jonson, essentially authorizes and marginally participates in the plot of *Every Man In His Humor.* But that may indicate that he represents Jonson's ideal audience rather than Jonson himself.[37] Brainworm essentially completes the plot on his own. What he asks of Clement is merely what Jonson implicitly asks of his audience: hearty approval of his New Comic plot and its rejection of more conventional moralistic schemes. Facing imprisonment by Justice Clement, Brainworm reveals his true identity and spells out for all his victims the course of "the day of my *metamorphosis,*" emphasizing its success in the marriage of Edward to Bridget (5.3.54–82). It is as if

Jonson were turning to his audience and pointing out that, though
he has demolished various popular comic patterns, he has nonetheless performed the standard business of comedy: exposing hypocrisy, punishing and reforming fools, and propelling young love
past various obstacles into marriage. Neither Brainworm nor Jonson, however, can evade that fact that they have accomplished
these standard comic tasks in rather unorthodox ways. By throwing off his disguise and then begging forgiveness for his faults
directly from his judge, Brainworm behaves very much like a
standard Elizabethan epilogue. It is now up to Justice Clement, as
it will be to Lovewit in *The Alchemist,* to endorse acts of theater
that are undertaken in clever ways and toward good ends: "Thou
hast done or assisted to nothing, in my judgment, but deserves
to be pardoned for the wit of the offense" (5.3.104–105). At the
same time, it is up to Jonson's audience to offer forgiveness on
the same grounds.

Clement's conduct, furthermore, exemplifies the attitude Jonson's play attempts to inculcate in its audience. He is able to play
such roles as poet and soldier more effectively than Matthew or
Bobadill, without losing (as they do) his ironic awareness of the
mere theatricality of his poses. Certainly the wild whimsicality of
Clement's judgments (particularly in the Folio version) more resembles the vagaries Jonson recognized in his audience than it does
his ideal image of himself as a judicious critic. Clement finally tells
the failed self-dramatizers what Jonson wants his audience to shout
at future performances of more conventional plays:

> Come, I conjure the rest to put off all discontent. You,
> Mr. Downright, your anger; you, Master Knowell, your
> cares; Master Kitely and his wife, their jealousy.
>
> (5.5.66–68)

To put off these discontents is to put off the roles in roaring plays,
prodigal son stories, or *commedia dell'arte* cuckolding plots, by
which these characters have lived; to take these men out of their
humors is to take them out of their formulaic plays, which Jonson
has here subsumed. Jonson has in effect put these words into his
spectators' mouths, compelling them by ventriloquy to demand
the new kind of play Jonson has just offered them; through Clement's judgment, Jonson arms his audience with a sort of pre-scripted
and prescriptive heckling. Clement calls every man back out of

his self-dramatizing humor, and in doing so he calls an end to the conventional plays in which each man was acting. Once they dispense with such hackneyed performances, only Jonson's mode of comedy will remain.

Brainworm, the plotter of New Comedy, will reign over this purged stage, under the genial sufferance of Clement, who has the final words. These words are both an invitation and an analogue to the applause Jonson seeks from his audience. Clement bestows on Brainworm the affection, and predicts the canonization, that Jonson seeks for his upstart invader into the genre of popular drama:

> Here is my mistress—Brainworm! to whom all my addresses of courtship shall have their reference. Whose adventures this day, when our grandchildren shall hear to be made a fable, I doubt not but it shall find both spectators, and applause. (5.5.82–85)

When the spectators begin their applause, this prophecy is instantly fulfilled. The play about redeeming life from its bondage to theater and theater from its bondage to convention here weaves the two liberations into a unitary celebration. The lasting worth of the play lies in its insistence on creating its own sort of fable; it will survive, not as part of a convention, but precisely because it can claim to have made its own convention. The audience, in applauding this triumph, will in effect be applauding themselves (in the person of Clement) for having sufficient wit to appreciate this invigorating expedition into the unpredictable. This is one final indication that *Every Man In His Humor* has been shaped by Jonson's two interlocking missions: to alert the audience to the conventional follies they tend to act out instead of employing their wits, and, by identifying those follies, to alert the audience to the possibility of a drama quite different from the melodramatic routines they had come to expect on the Elizabethan stage.

Edward sarcastically lauds Matthew's verse in the final scene as less a badly performed plagiarism than "A parody! A parody! With a kind of miraculous gift to make it absurder than it was" (5.5.26–27). The same words—the earliest use of the term "parody" cited by the Oxford English Dictionary—could be applied, as sincere praise, to Jonson's play. He captures alive the melodramatic "monsters" that (as the Prologue complains) were threatening to overrun

Elizabethan drama and leads them in triumph through his own more realistic territory; the stage that had once been their home becomes their menagerie, with all their absurdities on display. Like Justice Clement, Jonson outdoes Matthew at his own practice by performing it with more self-conscious wit: Jonson's thefts from his fellow playwrights are spent to ransom humorous creatures such as Stephen—and, by analogy, the naive members of the audience—who have made themselves "monsters" by confusing their real lives with the "miracles" of conventional drama (1.3.108–109). In *Every Man In His Humor* Jonson uses his "miraculous gift" for parody to free the theater from its bondage to its own entrenched illusions. His pockets are stuffed with shreds from the works of other authors, not because he lacks a voice of his own, but because he can make himself heard most clearly by temporarily mimicking voices more familiar to his audience. His characters, who seem to be a random gathering of humors, are in fact a strategic array of dramatic commonplaces, and his parodies coalesce at the end of *Every Man In His Humor* into a systematic defense of satiric city-comedy.

# CHAPTER TWO

# Every Man Out of His Humor

## THE LIMITS OF
## SATIRIC COMEDY

*Every Man Out of His Humor* (1599) is a very peculiar play, and several of its peculiarities help to reveal the workings of Jonson's parodic strategy. Three unusual traits of *Every Man In His Humor* recur in this sequel in more extreme forms. First, Jonson does not attempt to achieve any convincing unity either of plot or of tone in the play, as if the conflicts, discords, and irrelevancies were themselves the point. Second, the delusions and affectations of the humorous characters are of an insistently bookish character; Jonson repeatedly associates their humors with literary roles, and distinguishes the superior characters by their superior alertness to literature and role-playing. Third, those delusions and affectations are strategically arranged to compel the audience to recognize and approve Jonson's new satirical mode of comedy if they are to avoid a degrading identification with the fools on stage.

*Every Man Out* is not, however, as streamlined a weapon against dramatic convention as its predecessor. Its loose structure offers Jonson the opportunity to mortify a large number of conventional plots and characters by decentering them in his play, by signaling their presence only to neglect them. But the effect is now centrifugal rather than centripetal, because those conventional motifs seem to be merely discarded, rather than actively conquered as they are in *Every Man In*. The argument against the old patterns is somewhat vitiated because, while they are eradicated by Jonson's satiric plot, they are not systematically subsumed by it. The sequel does not build to any significant triumph like that of Brainworm and Clement in *Every Man In,* and (like the late comedies) it depends largely on an Induction and on choral interruptions to carry its critical message. Despite spasmodic efforts to do so, it fails to offer any substantial and consistent definition of the term "humor." Again Jonson's comedy is discernibly directed against self-dramatizing impulses, and against the naive forms of drama then in favor with Jonson's rivals and audiences. It pushes that campaign so relentlessly, however, that it runs up against the self-limiting nature of the parodic strategy. At the end of the play the satiric manipulator stands, not gloating in the midst of his profits, but bewildered on the brink of the dramatic and moral void his victories threaten to generate.

Even before *Every Man Out of His Humor* properly begins, Jonson sets up a cynically wise controlling figure as his surrogate, blurs the boundary between his play and the audience's reality, and blackmails that audience into endorsing the play. The supposed playwright Asper introduces his new play, also called *Every Man Out of His Humor,* by carefully demarcating what may look to us like an absurd distinction—between his "real" identity and his role as a humors character—and by indirectly but sternly warning that the audience will humiliate themselves rather than him if they fail to appreciate his comedy:

> Now, gentlemen, I go
> To turn an actor and a humorist,
> Where (ere I do resume my present person)
> We hope to make the circles of your eyes
> Flow with distilled laughter: if we fail,
> We must impute it to this only chance,
> "Art hath an enemy called Ignorance." (Induction, 213–219)

Whether or not Jonson himself took the role of Asper, and departed with this defiant quotation from his critical mentor Horace, he has given the playwright-figure lines that prepare us to understand *Every Man Out of His Humor* as a defense of Jonson's approach to comedy.

Asper says he is offering the play to "Such as will join their profit with their pleasure" (202), and the classical principle of mixing *dulce* with *utile* has special force in Jonson's parodic comedies, because our amusement is an active ingredient in the moral cure, not merely a sugar coating on the pill. The laughter in the theater and the lesson about the theater depend on each other: we laugh at the fools' disastrous efforts to stage their self-aggrandizing melodramas, and we learn from seeing how absurd such poses appear in any realistic context.

The pattern of the action in *Every Man Out of His Humor* is not always sufficient to convey Jonson's critical argument, however, and he therefore supplements that pattern with choral commentary. In the characterizations Jonson offers in the front of the printed versions of *Every Man Out of His Humor,* he describes Cordatus as "the author's friend; a man inly acquainted with the scope and drift of his plot" (98–99). The weakness here is that Cordatus is not part of the play proper, and so cannot use his superior intimacy with Jonson's plot to triumph over the deluded characters. Instead of showing us a new sort of play in an old sort of form and letting us learn from the betrayal of our expectations, Jonson has Cordatus warn us in advance that the play will be

> strange, and of a particular kind by itself, somewhat like *Vetus Comoedia:* a work that hath bounteously pleased me; how it will answer the general expectation, I know not. (228–230)

Although this is at once coy and heavy-handed, it does make clear that Jonson is determined to innovate and afraid that his innovation will be misunderstood and disliked. The hedging about whether his play is *Vetus Comoedia* or sui generis, and about whether he wants to prepare or to ambush expectations, indicates an ambivalence toward the parodic strategy that characterizes the entire play.

Cordatus then offers a long speech on the history—indeed the genealogy—of comedy, which is Jonson's way of justifying his own rebellion against the comic tradition he inherited in England. Cordatus rejects conventional rules on the grounds that each great writer of comedy, from Susario to Plautus, has introduced some radical innovation:

> I see not then but we should enjoy the same licence or free power, to illustrate and heighten our invention as they did; and not be tied to those strict and regular forms, which the niceness of a few (who are nothing but form) would thrust upon us.

> *Mitis*   Well, we will not dispute of this now: but what's his scene?
> *Cordatus*   Marry, *insula fortunata,* sir.
> *Mitis*   Oh, the fortunate island? Mass, he has bound himself to a strict law there.
> *Cordatus*   Why so?
> *Mitis*   He cannot lightly alter the scene, without crossing the seas.
> *Cordatus*   He needs not, having a whole island to run through, I think.                    (257–268)

Jonson uses the veiled reference to England[1] to allow himself to assert indirectly what he asserts directly in other plays: that all the material of true comedy can be found in a small modern urbanized world, without undertaking the monstrous voyages of romance. Playwrights err toward exotic settings for the same reason that self-dramatizing people make fools of themselves at home: neither group understands how much comedy is generated when people melodramatically misread their ordinary lives.

In the middle of the play Jonson uses Cordatus to remind us of the sort of conventional comedy Jonson resists writing. Mitis warns Cordatus of "another objection, signior, which I fear will be enforced against the author":

> That the argument of his comedy might have been of some other nature, as of a duke to be in love with a countess, and that countess to be in love with the duke's son, and the son to love the lady's waiting-maid: some such cross wooing, with a clown to their serving-man; better than to be thus near and familiarly allied to the time.
> *Cordatus*   You say well, but I would fain hear one of these autumn-judgments define once *quid sit comoedia?*
>                                                            (3.6.166–176)

He has just heard exactly that, but in a form that shows how much absurd convention, and how little true ethical edification, an Elizabethan audience would accept in a comedy. Barton has described Mitis' summary as an "alarmingly prescient account of *Twelfth Night,*"[2] much as Kitely's speeches are often disquietingly prescient of Othello. In both cases the correlation seems to suggest how skillfully Jonson preempted the essential material of conventional drama, material Shakespeare was obliged to rescue from the realm of parody to which Jonson had banished it.

Jonson further assaults the conventions of the genre and the complacencies of the audience by altering the standard boundaries, as well as the standard content, of Elizabethan comedy.[3] The play begins before it begins: Jonson blurs the boundary between his play and the audience's reality, as in *Poetaster* and *Cynthia's Revels,* by having his choral characters begin to speak *"After the second sounding"*—in other words, before the Prologue is due. The effect would of course have been considerably more disorienting in the theater than it is on the page. When the supposed Prologue finally does arrive, he declines to add anything to what Cordatus, Mitis, and Asper have already said (277–298): the implication is that these supposed spectators have unwittingly written themselves into the play they thought they were judging. The chorus thus mediates between audience and play, and does so in a way that warns the audience not to be too critical, because this chorus is as prepared to watch and criticize the audience as it is to watch and criticize the play:

> And Mitis, note me, if in all this front,
> You can espy a gallant of this mark,
> Who, to be thought one of the judicious,
> Sits with his arms thus wreathed, his hat pulled here,
> Cries miaow, and nods, then shakes his empty head,
> Will show more several motions in his face
> Than the new London, Rome, or Niniveh.      (158–164)

The accusation is pointed: such a spectator is not only playing a role with set actions, costumes, and lines, but he is inadvertently acting out the most naive sort of drama—a medley of puppet shows—in his effort to dismiss Jonson's play as naive. Those who do not appreciate Jonson's attack on ignorant, self-aggrandizing roles are condemned to repeat those roles. Asper calls such conduct "monstrous" (177): as throughout *Every Man In His Humor,* that word is associated with bad theatricality, with hollow dramatic poses.

The same word appears in Asper's bitter attack on poetasters. Asper laments

> the monstrousness of time,
> Where every servile imitating spirit,
> (Plagued with an itching leprosy of wit)

In a mere halting fury, strives to fling
His ulcerous body in the Thespian spring,
And straight leaps forth a poet!                    (66–71)

Although Asper, playing the role of a standard biting satirist, may
not be entirely in a position to throw stones at such derivative
poets, his accusation nonetheless serves Jonson's purposes. The
poetasters' efforts to transform themselves into something grandly
literary is merely another manifestation of the self-dramatizing
impulse Jonson attacks throughout his comedies, an impulse that
poisons the flow of literary transmission.

Asper suggests that his play will specifically attack people who
try to give their petty affectations some stature and justification
by calling them humors. He vows to "scourge those apes; / And
to these courteous eyes oppose a mirror, / As large as is the stage
whereon we act" (117–119). This is a standard gesture, distinguishing the audience of a satire from the objects of that satire,
but Jonson makes it a tenuous distinction. He seems to be promising to mock the pretentious imitators by imitating them—itself
a paradoxical project—and his wording comes suspiciously close
to suggesting that, in showing such follies, the stage will be merely
imitating the audience. The mirror regression threatens to become
infinite here, since what the stage claims to be imitating is the
tendency of audiences to mirror in their lives the humorous affectations they have seen on the stage.

The juxtaposition of Asper's complaint about those who imitate
poets with his complaint about those who "ape" humors suggests
that Jonson's real targets were the playwrights who adopted his
"humors" theme without understanding its critical purpose. Perhaps Jonson, who was becoming accustomed to subsuming parodically the conventions of others, now felt obliged to reclaim one
of his own. *Every Man Out of His Humor* is partly Jonson's way
of telling city-comedy playwrights who were making mechanical
use of his motif—particularly Marston, I suspect—that they should
get out of his humors. When Mitis reacts to Asper's tirade with
a warning that "this humour will come ill to some," Asper struggles to restrict the definition of the word "humour" (73–117); Jonson may be simultaneously struggling to restrict what he saw as
misuses of humors comedy.

Asper insists that a momentary trick of language or clothing is not a humor; only a fundamental and consuming mood, and the style it generates, deserves that title. But Jonson realized that such superficialities as speech and costume, whether or not they correspond to any imbalance of the bodily fluids known as humors, can be important symptoms of a self-dramatizing tendency. In *Every Man In His Humor* Jonson implicitly offered one definition of a humor, as an aggrandizing literary role in which a person casts himself, and (as if in a masquerade) that person's tricks of speech and costume help reveal the role he has in mind. (The Epilogue to Dekker and Middleton's *The Roaring Girl,* ll. 28–29, similarly defines a "humourous" brain as one that anticipates conventional "scenes.") This association of humors with self-dramatization outflanks and exploits Asper's definition, just as Jonson's version of *Every Man Out of His Humor* outflanks and exploits Asper's version. Jonson's more complex definition generates a more extensive and self-conscious form of comedy. He uses the play-within-the-play motif to expose the delusions of people who try to enact traditional literature within their lives, and a traditional satirist is not immune. When, in the middle of the Induction (l. 51), Asper suddenly realizes that he is being watched as part of the play, he in effect finds himself suddenly trapped inside a script that he thought he had written and had yet to begin performing; he is a little like Alice through the looking-glass, discovering that what she thought of as her independent and volitional life is actually only a contingent part of the Red King's dream. Jonson is that superior dreamer, and what he steals from Asper is literally his authority, perhaps because Asper is himself susceptible to the unconscious literary posing that Jonson intended to attack. Jonson asserts his dominance, and Asper's susceptibility, by the way he positions Asper's play within *Every Man Out of His Humor:* the fact that Asper prepares to play Macilente without knowing that he is already playing a similar role establishes Jonson's control. The satirist himself is satirized—or at least the conventional sort of satirist is exploited to help Jonson argue for the superiority of a new kind of satiric city-comedy.

To facilitate that argument, Jonson shows us three or four separate characters striving for the controlling position as his surrogate playwright, each a recognizable embodiment of one conventional image of the satirist. Asper is the forthright railer, a figure of grand moral indignation. Macilente is the envious conniver, a version

of the melancholic scholar. Carlo Buffone is the scurrilous epigrammatist, a carelessly abusive social parasite.[4] Shift may qualify
as a satiric coney-catcher. This prismatic division has generally
been perceived as a sort of moral scale, with Asper's noble spirit
placing him above Macilente's envy, Macilente's intellectualism
placing him above Buffone's buffoonery, and Buffone's comic
spirit placing him above Shift's petty maneuverings. But Jonson
is evaluating modes of satire here, not merely ranking individual
personalities, and Macilente comes closest to representing Jonson's
own satiric practice. At the time of *Every Man Out,* Jonson was
at least as much a bitterly competitive man of letters and author
of nasty epigrams as he was a crusading moralist. Even Buffone,
though eventually rebuked, has more of a direct role in chasing
fools out of their humors than Asper does, and Macilente seems
more in touch than either of them with the spirit and principles
of early Jonsonian comedy. This may help to explain why Jonson
refuses to convert him completely back to Asper to complete the
story frame (5.11.68–71).

Asper's flaws become more visible when we recognize *Every
Man Out of His Humor* as a play partly about the foolishness of
conventional literary poses. From his first lines Asper echoes all
the standard motifs and flourishes of the morally indignant satirist:
he seems to have read too much Juvenal, and in fact his first lines
are an unacknowledged quotation of that master.[5] One study sees
Asper as a direct descendant of Bohan, the powerful satirical
spokesman of Greene's *James IV*,[6] but perhaps it is Asper himself
who is trying to model Asper after such righteous figures. His
slightly embarrassed discovery that he is addressing a theatrical
audience is a commentary on the unconsciously literary pose he
has been striking (51–59). As in Marston's satires, the pose of
satirist risks being dismissed as yet another "humor."[7]

Indeed, Asper's bludgeoning style of moral instruction seems
designed to exalt Jonson's subversive tactics by contrast. Considering the bitterness of Jonson's later outbursts against popular
audiences and public morals, we can understand Asper as the author's dangerous alter ego, an embodiment of the more direct
satiric attack Jonson has barely managed to sublimate into his
parodic maneuvers against naive dramatists and dramatizations.[8]
This sort of distancing representation appears, I will argue, in such
suppressed critics as Surly in *The Alchemist,* and Busy and Overdo

in *Bartholomew Fair*. In fact, Asper often resembles Chrysogonus in Marston's *Histriomastix,* a character evidently designed as a satire on Jonson himself. Jonson may be using the railing Asper to distance himself from the negative way he had been perceived and portrayed, and using Asper's play (which lacks the ironic commentary of the story frame) to distance his critically alert dramaturgy from its reputation as mere negative satire.

Jonson uses the doubling of roles to reinforce this point. The playwright-character Asper in Jonson's *Every Man Out of His Humor* plays the manipulative character Macilente in his own slightly shorter play of the same title. This arrangement allows Jonson to remind us that he is sparing us the harshness—the asperity—of direct satire that may be in his heart, and replacing it for the course of this play with a strategy that merely encourages fools (in the audience as well as on stage) to announce themselves. It is an oddly passive sort of assault. As Jonson's humors play nears it denouement, Buffone tells us that Macilente is hovering over the various gulls, "plotting some mischievous device, and lies a-soaking in their frothy humours like a dry crust, till he has drunk 'em all up" (5.4.22–24). Macilente's method of plotting, in other words, is the same as Jonson's—both men strategically absorb the various humors surrounding them—and contrasts sharply with the overt attacks of Asper, whose "strict hand / Was made to seize on vice, and with a gripe / Squeeze out the humour of such spongy natures" (Induction, 143–145). The jealousy that propels Macilente's schemes may not be as admirable as the ethical alertness that arouses Asper's tirades, but jealousy (of the popularity of what he viewed as less worthy rivals) is very much what shapes the parodic structure of Jonson's comedies. The combination of scorn and envy Macilente expresses toward the fools around him who thrive in their expensive costumes resembles Jonson's exasperation toward the success of the naive, gaudy plays he both includes and attacks in his own.[9]

Since Macilente embodies and exploits Jonson's satiric perspective on life's imitation of art, he is portrayed as too clever to become enthralled with his own role as an embittered social commentator. At times, like Asper, he does sound like a conventional railing malcontent, a combination of sources from classical, medieval, and Elizabethan literature (1.1.16–28; 2.4.6–16, 161–166).[10] Macilente's self-introduction is largely a literary allusion, as Cordatus points out (1.1.33–35). However, Macilente usually modifies his own allusions in ways that acknowledge (and therefore limit) his susceptibility to hollow literary poses. At such moments he becomes a character visibly in transition from the condition of a Jonsonian gull to that of a Jonsonian manipulator, writing his way out of (instead of into) his own humor. He first appears quoting classical Stoicism, as Asper did classical satire, but Macilente seems more conscious than Asper that grand literary poses are often compromised by human reality:

> *Viri est fortunae caecitatum facile ferre.*
> 'Tis true; but, stoic, where, in the vast world,
> Doth that man breathe that can so much command
> His blood and his affection?                                    (1.1.1–4)

When Macilente does quote Juvenal, the passage he quotes is less part of his role as satiric malcontent than it is a satiric commentary on that role: *"Nil habet infelix paupertas durius in se / Quam quod ridiculos homines facit—"* (3.6.24–25). "Unhappy poverty has no more bitter ingredient than that it makes men ridiculous."[11]

The third of these satirists, Carlo Buffone, embodies the crude wit of personal attack. His favored genre should therefore be the epigram, but in fact he uses literary modes to attack his enemies with as little discrimination as an ape picking up objects to throw at an intruder. He has a reputation for destructive similes (Induction, 341–343; 2.1.7–8), but he is also capable of staging a crude puppet show (5.4.44–81) that anticipates the one in *Bartholomew Fair,* and, like Shakespeare's Pistol, of echoing phrases from hackneyed Elizabethan revenge tragedies (3.6.13–14).[12] Buffone is not naive about incorporating literature into his life; he is simply very careless. If Macilente is a character in transition from a Jonsonian gull to a Jonsonian hero, Buffone is the opposite, a literary manipulator who loses control of his weapons. When Cordatus begins to orate in place of the Prologue, Buffone condemns "these fustian protestations," only to replace them with his own. He takes over from the previous failed Prologues, makes fun of the author of the play (who sounds more like Ben Jonson than like Asper), and tells the audience (as do so many of Jonson's choral figures) that "their best way, that I know, is, sit still, seal up their lips, and drink so much of the play in at their ears" (332–334). Ironically, Buffone himself is finally the one whose lips are forcibly sealed up (by Puntarvolo, at 5.6.73) for failing to control his satiric impulses, suggesting that he has become the sort of presumptuous audience he earlier condemned.

Buffone's last articulate words are an echo of a famous Shakespearean line—"*Et tu, Brute!*"—that a classicist such as Jonson would gleefully have dismissed as a fatuous literary invention.[13] It is fully appropriate that, after this self-aggrandizing quotation of a melodramatic misquotation, and after wishing to imitate a famous incident on the Elizabethan stage by wishing for "one of Kemp's shoes" to throw at Puntarvolo (4.8.127),[14] Buffone is beaten "out of [his] humor." As a punishment for imagining that he is the satirist-hero in a work of his own composition, where he can attack his enemies with impunity, Buffone is humiliatingly silenced and excluded from the remainder of the play. His downfall thus offers the audience some of the same emotional satisfactions as Malvolio's humiliation in *Twelfth Night,* but also some of the same intertextual interest as Jaques's exile in *As You Like It.*

The petty chiseler Shift is arguably a fourth, and least attractive, form of the satirist. Jonson allows him only very narrow successes, because Shift uses his cynical insights for only the most selfish and narrow-minded sorts of predations. Cordatus describes him as "a whole volume of humour, and worthy the unclasping" (2.6.164–165), but that does not mean that Shift gullibly confuses his reality with literature. Shift may be an anthology of literary poses, but it is an anthology composed to sell to a wide readership of gulls seeking affirmation of their various humorous delusions. He knows that Sogliardo's literary translations of their friendship are ridiculous, but plays along with the wealthier man's allegorical identity as Countenance to gain his much-needed countenance (5.3.1–6). Like Brainworm in *Every Man In His Humor,* Shift strikes a standard pose as a mendicant war veteran (3.6.37–73), not because he believes in it, but because he suspects that the standard bluster is precisely what will convince and impress Brisk enough to get his money. Shift does not succeed as Brainworm does, however, either in his plots or in his play for our admiration. This is partly because he is a less buoyant figure, but also, in a larger sense, because *Every Man Out of His Humor* is less willing than its predecessor to accept a happy ending in the style of New Comedy as the rightful culmination of its satiric project.

The other characters are easy marks for Jonson and his on-stage

satirists, precisely because they have dragged their romantic notions of themselves into a hostile genre, which Jonson identifies
with reality. These gulls cannot see through their self-aggrandizing
literary fantasies because they are not satirists; or, to put it the
other way, they cannot be satirists precisely because they are too
deeply invested in more romantic genres. Jonson demonstrates
that these are shallow fantasies by trapping them in a parodic
context; or, to put it the other way, Jonson generates a parodic
context by populating it with fantasies that prove shallow. Without
the milieu of satire, the conventional poses would not be demonstrably naive; without the demonstrated naiveté of the poses,
their function on the stage would not be parodic. Jonson's peculiar
mode of comedy, and the peculiarities of his individual characters,
make sense of each other.

Recognizing the self-dramatizing tendencies of the greedy farmer
Sordido, for example, reveals several apparently awkward and
inconsistent scenes as skillful pieces of intertextual orchestration.
Indeed, the faults critics have perceived in the Sordido scenes typify
the faults they have perceived in *Every Man Out of His Humor* as
a whole, but in both cases these supposed defects—flat characterization, fragmentary plotting, a violent yoking together of ridicule
with melodrama, and misleading hints of a conventional course
of events—make sense as part of Jonson's parodic strategy. They
are systematic attacks on the standardized expectations of both the
characters and the audience. Though these peculiarities may not
make for a crisp, appealing theatrical experience, they nonetheless
make a significant critical statement, if the audience is prepared to
recognize them as deliberate failures at conventional dramaturgy.
Robert Witt complains that Sordido's attempted suicide "gives the
impression that the main action is interrupted for the performance
of another play."[15] Barton argues that Sordido's repentant speech
"comes close to sounding plausible. But, again, Jonson cannot
maintain a serious attitude towards this conversion."[16] My point
is that Jonson has no intention of making Sordido's adventures a
central or serious part of his play, because they constitute a trite
sort of drama that Sordido is attempting to impose on that play.
These transplanted scenes are attacked by the body of Jonson's
satire as fiercely and reflexively as a human body attacks a transplanted organ. The Sordido scenes do not show any uncertainty

or ambivalence on Jonson's part; what they show is that Jonson is a clever and ferocious defender of his dramatic territory.

Sordido seems to pride himself on his role as the miserly villain of the piece, and the fact that he is transformed into a positive moral exemplar (instead of destroying the hero or being destroyed by him) is a first rebuke to his conventional expectations. He presents himself as a figure straight out of the early morality plays, an embodiment of Avarice, and his glee at exploiting the hunger of others is expressed in revealingly theatrical terms: "they hiss at me, whilst I at home / Can be contented to applaud myself, to sit and clap my hands, and laugh . . . " (1.3.113–115). He stalks around the stage with his weather almanac, which he seems to mistake for Faustus' book of magic, calling it

> this dear book: not dear for price,
> And yet of me as dearly prized as life,
> Since in it is contained the very life,
> Blood, strength, and sinews of my happiness.
> Blessed be the hour wherein I bought this book,
> His studies happy that composed the book,
> And the man fortunate that sold the book.
> Sleep with this charm, and be as true to me
> As I am joyed and confident in thee.          (1.3.51–59)

Sordido's confidence is misplaced, and when the book proves false in its predictions, and good weather renders his hoarding futile, it also reveals the falseness of his book-learned idea of himself. He will not be permitted to become a powerful but self-damning speculator like Faustus: the ruination of his speculations in the grain market also ruins his speculations about his own dramatic identity.

His self-dramatizing impulses are undaunted by that defeat, however, and he turns immediately to the conventional response of misers on the Elizabethan stage to the loss of their fortunes. Like similar characters in plays by Fletcher and Middleton, and in a Lodge and Greene collaboration, he attempts to hang himself as a martyr in the cause of villainy.[17]

> *Sordido*  'Tis time that a cross should bear flesh and blood,
>     since flesh and blood cannot bear this cross.

> *Mitis*   What, will he hang himself?
> *Cordatus*   Faith, aye; it seems his prognostication has not
>    kept touch with him, and that makes him despair.
> *Mitis*   Beshrew me, he will be out of his humour then,
>    indeed.                                                          (3.7.6–11)

But again the play's climate betrays Sordido's dramatic prognos-
tications as much as England's climate betrays his agricultural ones.
He is virtually compelled out of the miserly role that best suits
his humor, then out of a subsequent performance as Despair,
carrying unavailingly (like representations of that deadly sin in
Spenser and elsewhere) a noose.

After the farmers interrupt his moment of glorious despair,
Sordido condemns his suicidal impulse as a "wretched humour . . . that / Makes me thus monstrous in true human eyes,"
and again the words "humour" and "monstrous" point toward
bombastic theatrical traditions. Instead of becoming a truly human
being himself, however, Sordido resorts to yet another highly
conventional role, as the miraculously redeemed miser, a role he
assumes with an appropriate shift into blank verse. Perhaps he
now envisions himself as the sort of miser whose reformation is
so prominent and satisfying in works such as *The Mad Pranks and
Merry Jests of Robin Goodfellow, Wily Beguiled, Englishmen for My
Money,* and *The Hog Hath Lost His Pearl*.[18] But Sordido's moral
transformation suffers from decentering. The miracle play of his
life is an early and unimportant development in the satiric play he
inhabits, and he disappears entirely from its second half.

Sordido's conversion (like that of the villains in Shakespeare's
*As You Like It*) has been condemned as an unrealistic piece of
dramatic convenience; even Jonson's on-stage spectator Mitis ad-
mits that "your author hath largely outstripped my expectation
in this scene" of Sordido's salvation (3.8.68–69). But that conversion is really only a shift from one sort of conventional pattern—the suicidal miser-villain—to another conventional pattern
that is even less suited to Jonson's comic universe. The moral
miracle has been dragged in, by Sordido as much as by Jonson,
from a different sort of work, and that is where his rescuers promise to put it: "I'll get our clerk to put his conversion in the *Acts
and Monuments*" (3.8.56–57).[19] Jonson may therefore have intended
this scene to disturb readers in much the way it has. If he wanted

us to perceive that Sordido is merely echoing stock lines from didactic conversion stories, then he would have made the conversion speeches "oddly stilted and artificial," as Barton has called them, and the entire conversion scene "flat and unrealistic," as Randolph Parker has called it.[20]

Another character enslaved to his literary self-conceptions is the would-be gentleman Sogliardo. Whether or not one gives any credence to the eccentric theory that Sogliardo represents Shakespeare, and that the portrait of Sogliardo therefore represents a direct attack on a dramatic rival,[21] the attack on Sogliardo's hollow aspirations certainly implies an attack on a naively theatrical way of understanding human selfhood. In introducing himself as a man in search of a gentlemanly identity, Sogliardo virtually introduces himself as a character in search of a humors author:

> Nay, look you, Carlo: this is my humour now! I have land and money, my friends left me well, and I will be a gentleman, whatsoever it cost me.
> *Carlo*   A most gentleman-like resolution.
> *Sogliardo*   Tut, and I take an humour of a thing once, I am like your tailor's needle, I go through; but, for my name, signior, how think you? Will it not serve for a gentleman's name, when the signior is put to it?     (1.2.1–8)

All Sogliardo seems to care about is how he will appear in the dramatis personae at the front of the tragicomedy of his life. The fact that Carlo Buffone's subsequent advice on how to gain this status is drawn largely from Erasmus' *Colloquies* may exemplify Jonson's parodic strategy rather than (as is commonly assumed)[22] Jonson's proclivity for simple plagiarism: the *Colloquies* were well enough known in Elizabethan London that the audience could have perceived Buffone as merely feeding Sogliardo the printed words his sick appetite prefers to real substance. The advice on how to become a gentleman comes from a source as literary as the ones that probably provided Sogliardo with his romantic idea of becoming a gentleman in the first place. Certainly Buffone's speeches portray gentility as very much a conventional role, with its assigned props, cues, lines, costumes, even "humours" (1.2.17–19, 33–83); it is what one critic calls "the histrionic approach to gentility."[23] When he reports that Sogliardo has resorted to heraldry to confirm his gentlemanly identity, Buffone's comparison sug-

gests that a coat of arms can be as degrading, and as theatrical, a
costume as a coat of motley:

> *Puntarvolo*   What? Has he purchased arms, then?
> *Carlo*   Aye, and rare ones, too: of as many colours as e'er
>   you saw any fool's coat in your life. I'll go look among
>   yond bills, and I can fit him with legs to his arms—
> *Puntarvolo*   With legs to his arms! Good.          (3.2.23–27)

The jest is "good" because it suggests how thoroughly Sogliardo
is attempting to replace his entire natural self with a grand social
role.

Sogliardo can manage neither friendship nor courtship without
a literary role to give them shape. He and Shift affirm their intimacy less by action than by allusion:

> *Sogliardo*   Aye, he is my Pylades and I am his Orestes: how
>   like you the conceit?
> *Carlo*   Oh, it's an old stale interlude device: no, I'll give you
>   names myself; look you, he shall be your Judas and you
>   shall be his elder tree to hang on.
> *Macilente*   Nay, rather, let him be Captain Pod and this his
>   motion; for he does nothing but show him.
> *Carlo*   Excellent: or thus, you shall be Holden and he your
>   camel.
> *Shift*   You do not mean to ride, gentlemen?
> *Puntarvolo*   Faith, let me end it for you, gallants: you shall
>   be his Countenance and he your Resolution.     (4.5.52–62)

Sogliardo is pleased by this translation of their roles into allegory.
The satiric nature of the suggestions is lost on him, because he
hardly cares what sort of a role he occupies, so long as it has
literary associations.

The literary appetite that distorts Sogliardo's friendship also
cripples his courtship. When Macilente urges him to approach
Lady Saviolina "most naturally and like yourself," Sogliardo offers
to "begin to her in tobacco"; if Saviolina grants him an audience,
he will perform the bits of stage-business he has accumulated for
his role as gentleman. Macilente, evidently despairing of correcting
the gull, then outlines a conventional set of wooing lines and
gestures for Sogliardo to memorize (5.1.44–55). In recommending

Sogliardo to Saviolina, Puntarvolo tries to make this imitative instinct a virtue:

> *Puntarvolo*  But that which transcends all, lady; he doth so peerlessly imitate any manner of person for gesture, action, passion, or whatever—
>
> *Brisk*  Aye, especially a rustic or a clown, madam, that it is not possible for the sharpest-sighted wit in the world to discern any spark of the gentleman in him, when he does it.                                              (5.2.32–37)

Brisk's rejoinder reveals that Sogliardo's supposed successes as an actor are really failures of his overall simulation of a gentleman.

The irony is doubled when Lady Saviolina proves so devoted to the role her name offers her as a perspicacious woman of the court that she claims to recognize the spark of aristocracy in Sogliardo despite his rustic "act" (5.2.60–69).[24] They are made for each other, because they share a blindness to the difference between a performance and reality; since neither of them can see that he is merely a clown playing a gentleman, she is exposed as merely a fool playing a wise woman. In insisting that she can perceive the gentility under Sogliardo's apparent rusticity, Saviolina is trying to cast herself as a figure of courtly insight by reenacting a standard scene in Elizabethan literature. Both Erasmus in *Sir Thomas More* and Bacon in *Friar Bacon and Friar Bungay* must prove their powers of discernment by recognizing a true nobleman through his disguise as a commoner;[25] Joan la Pucelle undergoes a similar test in Shakespeare's *1 Henry VI*. When the scene fails to play out the same way in *Every Man Out of His Humor,* Macilente has chased Saviolina "out of [her] humour" by excluding her from the ennobling conventional role she wished to play (5.2.88–113). Like Jonson, Macilente goes a step deeper into theater to reveal the faults of theater; the feigning of Sogliardo's feigning exposes the feigning of Saviolina.

Only a sophisticated audience, though, will appreciate the true nature of this comedy. When Brisk and Puntarvolo, with cruel glee, praise the trick for putting Saviolina "most miserably out of her humour," Macilente complains that "this applause taints it, foully" (5.3.7–10). A dull audience that merely gloats over Saviolina's humiliation similarly taints the better part of Jonson's comedy, which is essentially a demand for more sophisticated theatergoing. Several critics have wondered how a playwright as uproariously funny as Jonson often is can endorse the Aristotelian precept that comedies should not provoke too much laughter (*Discoveries*, VIII, 643–644, ll. 2629–77). Macilente's complaint suggests an answer: the laughter is healthy only if it reflects a chastening insight into the flaw of self-delusion that opens Saviolina to ridicule. On a larger scale, critics have wondered how to reconcile Jonson's greatness as a comic playwright with his outspoken disdain for the popular theater. My theory of the parodic strategy suggests that, paradoxically, Jonson's dramatic energy was largely generated and structured precisely by his mistrust of drama; and he must have been aware that an ignorant audience could at any careless moment reclaim him as their own, as Brisk and Puntarvolo here attempt to reclaim Macilente.

Saviolina tries to pattern herself according to other exalting literary models as well. The noblewoman wittily repelling her fawning suitors at court is a standard figure in Greene and Lyly, and several of Saviolina's attempts at wit are imitations of specific jests performed more successfully by Iffida in *Euphues*.[26] Brisk concedes that Saviolina is "a little too self-conceited, and 'twere not for that humour, she were the most-to-be-admired lady in the world" (4.8.50–52). Her self-conceited humor is not merely excessive pride; it is also the remaking of the self out of received literary conceits. She is not simply a poseur but specifically a plagiarist:

> *Brisk*    . . . she does observe as pure a phrase and use as
>   choice figures in her ordinary conferences as any be i' the
>   *Arcadia.*
> *Carlo*  [*Aside*] Or rather in Greene's works, whence she may
>   steal with more security.                    (2.3.201–204)

Jonson again attacks pretensions in terms of a naive subservience to books, and underscores the point by having both the foolish Fungoso and the evil Sordido speak obsessively of their own books in the seven lines that follow.

Deliro, like Sogliardo, is a figure whom Macilente attempts (with only moderate success) to rescue from a destructively literary understanding of courtship. Deliro has trapped himself in the pose of Petrarchan lover, and can be jolted back into reality only by evidence that, if he insists on treating his marriage as a literary subgenre, it is more likely to mimic the cuckolding plot of a fabliau than the sentimental constancy of a love lyric. He tries to live out every cliché of romantic courtship, treating his wife as if he were indeed her servant and she his goddess, and as if her momentary disfavor were indeed to be avoided at any price. His loving complaint to Macilente about his cruel mistress is revealingly formulaic in its alliterations, its quibbles, and its grotesquely subservient posture:

> *Deliro*  Strew, strew, good Fido, the freshest flowers, so.
> *Macilente*  What means this, Signior Deliro? All this censing?
> *Deliro*  Cast in more frankincense, yet more; well said.
>   Oh, Macilente, I have such a wife!
>   So passing fair, so passing far unkind,
>   But of such worth and right to be unkind,
>   Since no man can be worthy of her kindness.
>   . . . . .
>   As though this dull gross tongue of mine could utter
>   The rare, the true, the pure, the infinite rights
>   That sit, as high as I can look, within her!
> *Macilente*  [*Aside*] This is such dotage as was never heard.
>                                                   (2.4.25–40)

Macilente must never have heard much of the period's inferior love verse. He strives to teach the doting husband, who crowds Fallace's walks with flowers, that the high-poetical game of courtship must give way to the realities of marriage. But he can shake Deliro's determination to perceive life as if it were art only by showing him something that cannot be reconciled with his script: his worshiped Fallace embracing the courtier Brisk, in an effort to fulfill her own hackneyed romantic fantasy.

Even after this clash of contradictory scripts destroys one illusion, Macilente knows his pupil is still in danger, because Deliro (like Fungoso and Sordido) has virtually forgotten how to function without a literary model:

> *Macilente*  Nay, why do you not dote now, signior? Methinks you should say it were some enchantment, *deceptio visus* or so, ha? If you could persuade yourself it were a dream now, 'twere excellent: faith, try what you can do,

signior; it may be your imagination will be brought to it in
time; there's nothing impossible.          (5.11.8–14)

Macilente's sarcastic suggestion is doubly incisive as a way of
diverting Deliro from what might well be his next piece of cuck-
oldly folly. It points again to the general psychological pattern
called cognitive dissonance, which impels people to misperceive
reality rather than alter the scripts they have developed to explain
and exalt their experiences. But it also points to a specific unflat-
tering literary model that Deliro would be following in yielding
to such a forgiving interpretation. In works such as *Greenes Vision,*
Boccaccio's *Decameron,* and Chaucer's "Merchant's Tale," husbands are persuaded that the infidelity they truly witnessed was
merely a dream or a hallucination.[27] Macilente thus uses Deliro's
self-dramatizing impulses to alert him to a real danger. Even when
Deliro is forced to face the truth about his marriage, however, his
literary conventionality remains undaunted. His rage as the supposedly cuckolded husband—"Out, lascivious strumpet" (5.11.14)—
is almost as derivative, hackneyed, and misinformed as his raptures
as a Petrarchan wooer had been.

Fallace, too, confuses reality with romantic literature. The high-
poetical terms in which she describes herself indicate that Deliro's
delirious visions have distorted her self-perception:

No, I am like a pure and sprightly river,
That moves for ever, and yet still the same;
Or fire, that burns much wood, yet still one flame.
                                        (2.4.113–115)

Only a fatuously narcissistic reader would see herself reflected in
such worshipful similes. Even her adulterous desires seem to be
mediated by literary tradition: "I have heard of a citizen's wife has
been beloved of a courtier," she tells herself, and retreats into a
locked chamber to examine her fantasy without any interference
from reality (2.6.122–125). She would have been most likely to
hear of such a thing in any number of popular Elizabethan works—
ballads and proto-novels as well as plays—that resembled popular
romance novels of the twentieth century. In fact, when she finally
has an opportunity to spin out her tale of loving service to her
paramour, she prefers Lyly's words to any of her own: "Oh,
Master Brisk (as 'tis in *Euphues*) 'Hard is the choice when one is
compelled either by silence to die with grief or by speaking to live

with shame' " (5.10.30–32). Jonson, of course, finally permits her neither of these melodramatic courses.

Puntarvolo is the most overtly self-dramatizing of the characters. We are told that his "humour" is to turn his homecomings into a carefully scripted romantic drama in which he plays a visiting knight (2.1.112–2.2.72; Nick Stuff uses a similar device to spice up his conjugal relations in *The New Inn*). Carlo Buffone rightly describes this as an exercise in spectating on the self—he says that Puntarvolo's wife "should let down a glass from the window" to show Puntarvolo that he is himself the noble knight she is awaiting (2.2.62)—and rightly dismisses the entire ritual as

> A tedious chapter of courtship, after Sir Lancelot and
> Queen Gueneuere? Away. I mar'l in what dull cold nook
> he found this lady out, that, being a woman, she was
> blessed with no more copy of wit but to serve his hu-
> mour thus? (2.3.60–63)

Again, a "humour" is essentially a stale bit of literary imitation. While performing this fore-play, Puntarvolo even lapses into a hackneyed Petrarchan love lyric (2.3.24–31), a form of poetry which Jonson frequently satirizes as mere hollow posturing. Buffone remarks that Puntarvolo's chivalric scene is "a thing studied and rehearsed as ordinarily at his coming from hawking or hunting, as a jig after a play" (2.2.30–32); in other words, it is merely a natural extension of the role-playing that is Puntarvolo's entire life. Like Asper earlier, Puntarvolo's wife is embarrassed to discover she has been watched, but Puntarvolo himself makes a revealingly smooth transition into his usual affected speech as a brave warrior devoted to singular oaths and epithets (2.3.21–23, 78–98).[28]

Puntarvolo's ridiculous plan for an adventurous voyage with his loyal dog seems to be taken from Shakespeare's *Two Gentlemen of Verona,* and Jonson's satiric attitude toward such sentimental arrangements is suggested by Macilente's remorseless poisoning of the poor animal.[29] Macilente covers his misdeed, furthermore, by playing into Puntarvolo's assumption that others are as obsessed as he is by his grand wager: "Upon my life, he hath stolen your dog, sir, and been hired to it by some that have ventured with you" (5.3.22–23). Puntarvolo can much more easily accept that his plans have turned into an elaborate conspiracy than that they have been mooted, either by the playwright-figure Macilente's cruel trick of poisoning, or by the playwright Jonson's analogous cruel trick of decentering. The play-world simply refuses to care about what Puntarvolo cares about.

The language in which Puntarvolo phrases the indentures for the wager, Gifford and Baskervill have shown, constitutes "a burlesque upon the oaths taken by the combatants of romance."[30] What is particularly interesting is Baskervill's demonstration that courtiers in Jonson's time echoed these same conventions to lend some quaint prestige to their tournaments. In satirizing Puntarvolo's romanticized ventures and adventures, therefore, Jonson was satirizing contemporaries who actually attempted to exalt themselves by living out the superficial conventions of chivalric romance. Again Jonson was able to kill two birds with one stone: his burlesque of the romance tradition in literature and his satire on those who proudly incorporate such traditions into their lives reinforce each other.

Fungoso strives in a different way to build a new self out of books and plays. He pries money from his father to buy clothes under the pretext of buying books for his studies, a lie that is as revealing to us as it is deceiving to old Sordido: costumes are really only another example of book-learned formulations of the self. His letter pleads for money toward "that which is fit for the setting up of our name, in the honourable volume of gentility: that I may say to our calumniators with Tully, *ego sum ortus domus meae, tu occasus tuae*" (3.7.33–36). The book metaphor is significant—precisely what Fungoso wants is to project his own name into an ennobling volume—and his reliance on a line from a classical author contradicts the aspiration that line supposedly expresses, the aspiration to generate a fresh line of nobility out of himself through his own wit. Finally Fungoso is driven "out of those humours" (5.9.38) when his one feeble attempt at out-plotting the others backfires: hiding from the constable under the tablecloth merely obliges him to pay the tavern bill for the entire party (5.7.23–41).

Until this failure convinces him to "have done imitating any more gallants either in purse or apparel" (5.9.4), Fungoso remains in thrall to his imitating, costuming humor—that is, to theatricality itself. Fungoso recognizes that Fastidious Brisk is essentially "a very fine suit of clothes" (2.3.109), but his reaction is emulation rather than condemnation. He is so devoted to the idea that costume creates identity that he supposes his own sister might mistake him for Brisk when he appears in Brisk's garments (2.5.1–8). This foolish supposition connects Fungoso's dandyism to a confusion of reality with popular drama, since the failure of recostumed sisters and brothers to recognize each other is as commonplace in Elizabethan comedy as it is inconceivable in real life. Jonson emphasizes the connections further by allowing Sogliardo's speculations about the theater to interrupt Fungoso's speculations about a costume:

> *Fungoso*   Oh, and I might have but my wish, I'd ask no
> more of God now but such a suit, such a hat, such a band,
> such a doublet, such a hose, such a boot, and such a—
> *Sogliardo*   They say there's a new motion of the city of Nin-
> iveh, with Jonah and the whale, to be seen at Fleetbridge?
> You can tell, cousin?
> *Fungoso*   [*Aside*] Here's such a world of question with him,
> now.                                                    (2.3.127–134)

Its reference to naive stagecraft makes the interruption thematically much more relevant than Fungoso thinks it is. He is repeatedly humiliated (as well as impoverished) by his assumption that he is what he wears. His reflexive craving for the latest fashion is a standard Bergsonian comic device in its predictable repetitions, and it was a standard subject of ridicule in Elizabethan topical satire, but it also reveals a profoundly theatrical notion of human selfhood.

Subsequent scenes reinforce the connection between garments and literary fantasies of the self. Fallace tells the recostumed Fungoso, "Oh, you are a gallant in print now, brother," and he replies that "It's the last edition, I assure you" (2.5.15–17; cf. 2.6.11–12). In the next act Fungoso tells the tailor who is assembling his next costume that he will "sit i' my old suit, or else lie abed and read the *Arcadia,* till you have done" (3.5.24–25). One fantasy—the same implausible romance from which Lady Saviolina draws—will do until the next is ready; reading the *Arcadia* will serve as a sort of temporary prosthesis to his uncomfortably ordinary selfhood, until the grand new costume can generate a grand new identity. The fact that Fungoso always ends up wearing whatever Brisk has just stopped wearing may refer to the common use of secondhand clothes as costumes on the English Renaissance stage; when Fungoso tries to wear clothes, they keep turning out to be costumes, because he uses garments to try to change his entire unsatisfactory identity. When Fungoso promises to pay his tailor or else "never breathe again upon this mortal stage, as the philosopher calls it" (4.7.44–45), his use of the *theatrum mundi* commonplace is doubly significant. It is a secondhand literary topos, yet for him it is also a kind of living truth: he could not survive without his tailor because he lives as if his whole world were a stage on which costume chiefly determined and maintained identity.

Like Stephen in *Every Man In His Humor* (1.3.37–42), Fungoso expects the indifferent world to be as entranced by his fantastical new outfit as he is himself (2.5.11–20); it is another version of Jonson's technique of humiliating his gulls by decentering their egotistical fantasies. Fungoso excludes himself from the joys of the comedy, not (like a Malvolio) because he has been directly injured in the comic solution, but simply because that solution has not focused on his concerns. While the rest of the play-world savors its complicated crisis, Fungoso cannot escape his obsession with his costume:

> *Macilente*   . . . Come, signior, your looks are too dejected, methinks: why mix you not mirth with the rest?
> *Fungoso*   By God's will, this suit frets me at the soul. I'll have it altered tomorrow, sure.
>
>               [*Exeunt*]                              (5.2.118–121)

The momentary pause as these characters move aside to allow Shift to enter and begin a new scene must have been an uneasy interval for the sort of spectators who were anathema to Jonson— the gallants who (like Fitzdotterel in *The Devil Is an Ass*) came to the theater only to scorn the play and to display their gorgeous new outfits, as if they were the show and not merely the audience. They could hardly afford to exalt their suits and their glum disdain at Jonson's comedy over the general laughter here without announcing themselves as versions of Fungoso. As in the Induction (158–184), Jonson grants the wish of such spectators to become the show, but he systematically deprives them of any sympathetic audience. Jonson defeats this set of competitors for control of the stage much as he defeats rival playwrights: by placing a demeaning version of their concerns up on the stage, and humiliating that representative by decentering as well as by direct satiric attack.

When Brisk enters with his own new suit and, like Fungoso, expects everyone to be as fascinated by it as he is (2.6.1–37), it becomes hard to choose between the two fools. An obsession with costume is not the only evidence of Brisk's overly literary understanding of himself, however. Like Osric in *Hamlet,* Brisk is so devoted to the role of courtier that he seems to have no spontaneous words, gestures, or motives beyond the formal outlines the role dictates. Macilente dismisses Brisk's encomium on the virtues of a courtier's life as "not extemporal" (4.8.29), and in the dramatis personae (32–33) Jonson describes him as an "affecting courtier" who "speaks good remnants." Some of those remnants are traceable: several critics have seen in Brisk a reflection of the Elizabethan author Samuel Daniel, and Brisk's compliment to Saviolina at 3.9.94–98 is a commonplace which he seems to have taken from Shakespeare's Romeo.[31] But Brisk's most prominent flaw is the theatrical assumption he shares with his imitator Fungoso, the assumption that clothes make the man—in other words, that costume makes the character. Just as Sogliardo had virtually replaced his natural limbs with the coat of arms by which he cast himself as a gentleman (3.2.23–27), and Fungoso revealingly boasts of having "as good a body in clothes as another" (4.7.18–19), so Brisk, too, exists more as costume than as person.[32]

Brisk describes the cause of his duel with Luculento in absurdly self-aggrandizing literary terms ("the same that sundered Agamemnon and great Thetis' son"), and narrates the conduct of that duel as if it were a battle between costumes rather than between bodies:

> Sir, I missed my purpose in his arm, rashed his doublet sleeve, ran him close by his left cheek, and through his hair. He again, lights me here (I had on a gold cable hatband, then new come up, which I wore about a murrey French hat I had), cuts my hatband (and yet it was massy, goldsmith's work), cuts my brims, which by good fortune, being thick embroidered with gold-twist and spangles, disappointed the force of the blow: nevertheless, it grazed on my shoulder, takes me away six purls of an Italian cut-work band I wore . . . [I stabbed]

through the doublet, through the shirt, and yet missed
the skin. He, making a reverse blow, falls upon my em-
bossed girdle (I had thrown off the hangers a little before), strikes off a skirt of a thick-laced satin doublet I
had (lined with some four taffetas), cuts off two panes,
embroidered with pearl, rends through the drawings out
of tissue, enters the linings, and skips the flesh.

(4.6.64–94)

The story continues from head to toe, including the spurs, boots,
and stockings, making it a parody of the epic costuming of such
warriors as Agamemnon and Achilles: instead of the elaborate
dressing anticipating the battle, an elaborate undressing actually
replaces it. All Brisk tells us about the wound he finally receives
is that he bound it "with a piece of my wrought shirt." The mock-
heroic character of the fighting combines with the overemphasis
on costumes to ridicule Brisk's self-dramatizing tendencies.

Macilente's visit to court allows him to offer a reductive satiric
perspective on Brisk's vanity, much like the perspective Jonson
himself offers on the other vain characters. Again the satire depends
on decentering. Instead of allowing Brisk to continue depicting
himself as the attractive focal point of the court, Macilente portrays
Brisk from the perspective of the women he pursues there, and
when they notice him at all they dismiss his courtships as merely
another set of fantastic imitative "humours" that invite mockery:

> *Macilente*   Alas, the poor fantastic! He's scarce known
>     To any lady there; and those that know him
>     Know him the simplest man of all they know:
>     Deride and play upon his amorous humours,
>     Though he but apishly doth imitate
>     The gallantest courtiers, kissing ladies' pumps . . .   (4.2.25–30)

The ladies "play" along with him, but their cynical perspective
alters the genre: like Jonson, they subsume his elegant romance
into a dismissive comedy. Brisk suddenly becomes a less sympathetic version of the Don Quixote who, in the second part of
that novel, falls into the hands of the cruelly cooperative lord.

The most stark example of Jonsonian decentering is visited upon
the characters Orange and Clove, who are thrown momentarily
into the brew merely for the spice of it:

> *Mitis*   What be these two, signior?
> *Cordatus*   Marry, a couple, sir, that are mere strangers to the
> whole scope of our play; only come to walk a turn or two,
> i' this scene of Paul's, by chance.                    (3.1.14–17)

With this piece of dramatic absurdism, Jonson goes a step beyond
the Rosencrantz and Guildenstern of Shakespeare, toward those
of Tom Stoppard. Orange and Clove are not Prince Hamlet, nor
were meant to be, but they can hardly know how infelicitously
their creator has positioned them. Jonson injects them into the
play with this commentary as a teasing reminder of the dramatist's
power to choose among the potential characters and plots his scene
offers.

   This exclusion of Orange and Clove from the real business of
the play is made all the more humiliating by the fact that they are
nothing if not performers. Cordatus reports that Orange is merely
a collection of catchphrases and feigned laughter at jests he cannot
understand, while Clove generally poses for hours "in a book-
seller's shop, reading the Greek, Italian, and Spanish; when he
understands not a word of either: if he had the tongues to his suits,
he were an excellent linguist" (3.1.20–29). In his hollow devotion
to books and costumes, learning by rote lines he cannot comprehend, Clove is a condensation of the self-dramatizing follies of the
play's other foolish characters.

   The two reappear briefly a few scenes later, attempting to fool
the other characters with a theatrical performance, but Jonson's
drama makes fools of them instead. They try to control what their
audience will hear them saying, but Jonson humiliates them by
allowing us to overhear the planning of, and the reaction to, their
grandiloquence:

> *Clove*   Monsieur Orange, yond gallants observe us; prithee,
> let's talk fustian a little, and gull 'em: make 'em believe we
> are great scholars.
> *Orange*   Oh Lord, sir.
> *Clove*   Nay, prithee, let's; believe me, you have an excellent
> habit in discourse.
> *Orange*   It pleases you to say so, sir.
> *Clove*   By this church, you ha', la: nay, come, begin: Aris-
> totle in his *Daemonologia*, approves Scaliger for the best
> navigator in his time: and in his *Hypercritics,* he reports him

to be heautontimorumenos: you understand the Greek, sir?
*Orange* Oh God, sir.
*Macilente* [*Aside*] For society's sake, he does. Oh, here be a
couple of fine tame parrots.

(3.4.5–18)

"Fustian" and "habit" are words for clothing as well as language,
and Jonson conflates the two categories throughout *Every Man Out
of His Humor* to suggest the constitutive elements of a theatrical
self. Orange's lame responses were evidently the faddish conver-
sation-fillers at court; Jonson points out the mere theatricality of
such standard lines by yoking them with Clove's more obviously
inflated rhetoric and fictionalized information. Several critics, alerted
by a subsequent reference to "Plato's *Histriomastix*" (3.4.26), have
discerned a parody of Marston in the turgid style of Clove's remarks.[33] Whether or not Jonson is attacking Marston specifically
here, he is certainly demonstrating the way he can turn naive
dramatic bombast against itself, by controlling the perspective
from which we view it. Macilente's satiric asides subvert the efforts
of gulls such as Clove to impress us, in much the same way that
Jonson's parodic structure subverts the efforts of his melodramatic
rivals (such as Marston) to impress us.

Finally Macilente, who has had the last word against so many
of these self-dramatizing characters, has the last word against his
own dramatic identity as well. Having chased all the foolish characters out of their humors, he finds he has run out of humors to
chastise, and therefore out of his own humor as a humors dramatist. As the last literary poses are dropped, Jonson's own literary
mission loses its motive. If *Every Man Out of His Humor* is essentially a collection of targets, it has little left to offer once the targets
have all been destroyed. What remains is the man who hit those
marks so unerringly, but as the Induction suggested, the role of
satirist is not in itself a very healthy or appealing one. Jonson has
deconstructed a variety of literary mythologies, and (like many
deconstructionist critics) he is finally obliged to turn his analytic
weaponry inward and deprive himself of any decisive conclusion.
His parodic strategy depends on a plot structure that is essentially
self-consuming; the Jonsonian satirist, both envying and loathing
the trite but popular creations of his rivals, is a green-eyed monster
that mocks the meat it feeds on, and continues to waste away.[34]

As soon as the last fool has been satirically disabused, Macilente (like Sordido earlier, when his role shifted) falls from his rollicking prose into a weary blank verse, populated by negatives:

> Why, here's a change! Now is my soul at peace.
> I am as empty of all envy now
> As they of merit to be envied at.
> My humour, like a flame, no longer lasts
> Than it hath stuff to feed it, and their folly,
> Being now raked up in their repentant ashes,
> Affords no ampler subject to my spleen.
> I am so far from malicing their states,
> That I begin to pity 'em. It grieves me
> To think they have a being. I could wish
> They might turn wise upon it, and be saved now,
> So heaven were pleased: but let them vanish, vapours.
> Gentlemen, how like you it? Has't not been tedious?
>
> (5.11.48–60)

Although the tone turns suddenly more casual at the end, the speech as a whole anticipates the farewell of Prospero. Macilente the actor asks for our approval as he retreats to his role as Asper the presenter and hints at his identity with Jonson the author. He even anticipates Prospero's transformation from malice to pity and Prospero's musings on the ontological transience of the role-players around him—a topic at least as relevant to Jonson's vindication of his dramatic strategy as it is to Prospero's (or Shakespeare's) farewell.

What Macilente confronts here is a problem that haunts Jonson throughout the comedies. The endings of these plays have often provoked otherwise respectful critics to complain that Jonson resolves neither plot nor morality in any satisfactory way—that is, any conventional way.[35] Such repeated and conspicuous failures should suggest that Jonson had other fish to fry; in fact, the accusations of failure may indicate Jonson's success in exposing, if not in altering, the complacencies of his audience. Many of the comedies proceed less as a development of a melodramatic situation than as a stripping away of various conventional situations that threatened to dominate the plot; the endings are therefore less a narrative resolution of the plays' actions than an increasingly explicit acknowledgment of Jonson's dominant presence and per-spective.[36] These developments can hardly be expected to appeal to an audience less interested than Jonson in his own struggle for literary ascendency and generic *Lebensraum*. There is more inher-ent dramatic tension in the series of attempts by characters to pull the sword from the stone, so to speak, and thereby to demonstrate their sovereignty over the course of a play, than there is in the flourishing of that sword over those fallen opponents by Jonson and his surrogate in the final act. Even where benevolent characters such as Clement or Lovewit preside, they preside over dramatic ghost-towns. No matter how effectively Jonson may have hu-miliated our conventional dramatic appetites and roused our crit-ical intellects, we may still feel let down when criticism (however well integrated into the dramatic structure) replaces drama (how-ever badly wounded by the implied criticism) before the play is actually over.

Jonson could not evade the fact that, in offering only false end-ings and non-endings, he was directly refusing to give the cus-tomer what the customer wanted. Dryden defines *catastasis* as "the Counterturn, which destroys that expectation, imbroyles the ac-tion in new difficulties, and leaves you far distant from that hope in which it found you."[37] No one (as Dryden was aware) does this better than Jonson, but he needs to convince his audience to accept this betrayal as a benevolent act of education. The success of Jonson's fifth acts generally depends on the success of his entire experiment in generic engineering, and vice versa: he tries to con-vert us into a Clement or a Lovewit by showing the inferiority of other plays, and tries to show the inferiority of those plays by offering us the perspective of Clement and Lovewit. But in the absence of such a figure offering the unlikely combination of au-thority, wit, and benevolence, where could these stories lead? By the same token, without the intervention of Jonson's own benev-olent authorial wit, what would be the future of the mode of comedy he had invented?

Macilente's speech is evidence that Jonson was well aware of the problem, and at the end of *Every Man Out of His Humor* Jonson implicitly acknowledges that he is still in quest of a lasting solution. His temporary solution is to ask for our sympathy with his di-lemma and our assent that the undoing of theatricality is a more appropriate ending to a realistic comedy than any decisive judgment. He does so by offering the model responses of Cordatus and Mitis to Macilente's weary question, "Has't not been tedious?":

> *Cordatus* Nay, we ha' done censuring, now.
> *Mitis* Yes, faith.
> *Macilente* How so?
> *Cordatus* Marry, because we'll imitate your actors, and be out of our humours. Besides, here are those, round about you, of more ability in censure than we, whose judgments can give it a more satisfying allowance: we'll refer you to them. (5.11.61–67)

This is a calculated challenge to the audience. Under a courteous guise, it warns them that unless they drop the proud poses and conventional expectations they brought to the theater, and give the play their wholehearted approval, they, too, are mere fools who have not yet seen their way out of their humors, despite all the efforts of Macilente and Jonson to redeem them. The last one out of his humor is a rotten egg.

At the same time it offers the audience an opportunity to identify themselves with the wiser characters by appreciating the satiric movement of Jonson's comedy. For once, it is acceptable to "imitate your actors," not only because the actors have now dropped their roles in Asper's *Every Man Out of His Humor,* but also because the characters they played in Jonson's *Every Man Out of His Humor* have learned to stop imitating melodramatic actors. Asper returns for a half-hearted Epilogue still dressed as Macilente, and he implicitly asks us to share his reasonable attitude—not the attitude of a Fungoso or a Brisk—toward that discrepancy of costume:

> Well, gentlemen, I should have gone in and returned to you as I was Asper at the first: but, by reason the shift would have been somewhat long, and we are loth to draw your patience farther, we'll entreat you to imagine it. (5.11.68–71)

We are in effect being trusted to understand that both Asper and Macilente were merely roles, and that there is a real person—perhaps Jonson himself—behind them both. To protest against this disillusioning announcement is to announce a kinship with the play's gulls, who are victims of their naive hunger for standard theatrical illusions.

In his final words, Asper-Macilente declares himself "out of humour for company," and asks approval largely on the grounds of his distance from the company of more standard and approved plays and playwrights:

> Marry, I will not do as Plautus, in his *Amphytrio,* for all this, *summi Iouis causa, plaudite:* beg a plaudite, for God's sake; but if you, out of the bounty of your good liking, will bestow it: why, you may, in time, make lean Macilente as fat as Sir John Falstaff.   (5.11.72–78)

This is a typical Jonsonian farewell. He cannot wave to his audience without simultaneously thumbing his nose at his more popular competition. The reformations of characters in the play are covert (and subversive) pleas for a reformation in the attitudes of the audience, so that the theater will begin to sustain its subtle satirists as well as its outlandish clowns.

What Jonson still needs to discover is some positive basis for demanding that sort of support, some positive moral value in satiric wit beyond its ability to avoid the popular patterns of stupidity. The initial performance of *Every Man Out of His Humor* evidently included one figure whose role-playing Jonson had neither the desire nor the power to deflate, whose noble stature was not susceptible to exposure as an affectation. The original version of the play (reprinted in the Quartos with a spirited defense of its propriety) showed Macilente's envy suddenly obliterated when he encounters Queen Elizabeth, who was probably both present in the audience and represented on the stage. Wit thus found a use in praise, and pretensions could be contrasted with authentic glory. The eagerness with which Jonson seized upon this focal point at the end of the play suggests how desperate he was for any such solution.

The opportunity that the Queen's involvement offered to Jonson could not be recreated, however. Usual circumstances and principles of decorum forbade it, and Jonson eventually surrendered the original conclusion even in the printed versions of *Every Man Out of His Humor*. Perhaps Jonson became so fond of the court masque as a literary form partly because it allowed him to employ truly noble actors, and thereby to explore the relationship between human beings and their grand roles in a positive light. Both the material and the structure of satiric city-comedy necessarily emphasize the negative. Jonson and his superior characters could amuse themselves and exploit their lesser rivals by exposing hackneyed conventions, but what was the ethical purpose for which the alertness of the audience and the integrity of drama had to be maintained? What was it that he wished to write on the blank of the stage, once he had erased the works of his rivals?[38] What was he going to sell to an audience he had taught not to buy fool's gold, not to be dazzled by all that glitters in the expectant imagination? How could he end his plots in a way that would be satisfying without being overly pat, happy without being overly romantic, ethical without being overly moralistic? How could he give pleasure without reinforcing unhealthy complacency?

These are the questions raised by the strikingly peculiar course of *Every Man Out of His Humor,* which pursues to their logical extremes the devices and principles established in *Every Man In His Humor.* Never again would Jonson edge quite so close to the theoretical limits of his satiric method, nor would he again invite his audience quite so close to his artistic self-doubts. Many of the plays that follow are more compact and delightful, precisely because they avoid brooding on these questions, but none of them raise more open and interesting questions about the parodic strategy that gives them their shape.

# CHAPTER THREE

# *Volpone*

## SURPRISED BY MORALITY

The plays following *Every Man Out of His Humor* reflect Jonson's discomfort with his role as satiric city-comedian. They express implicitly the fear Macilente had voiced, that there may be no viable moral center between foolish self-dramatization and bitter attacks on that foolishness—except within the decorous confines of the court. Indeed, at this stage in his career Jonson seems eager to get out of the business of playwriting altogether, hoping to support himself instead by writing masques on commission and by currying favor with the wealthy and powerful, whereby he would become something like an official moralist.[1] *Cynthia's Revels* (1600) and *Poetaster* (1601) have an air of wish-fulfillment about them. The royal Cynthia assigns Crites to write a masque exposing the folly of all the corrupt—and overly theatrical—courtiers who had underrated and abused him. Like Jonson and his surrogates in the humors plays, Crites humiliates his less worthy, less self-aware competitors by rewriting the fifth act of their play. Similarly, Caesar in *Poetaster* authorizes Horace (with Virgil at his side) to judge and punish his literary rivals in the final act.

These fantasies allow Jonson largely to abandon his parodic strategy in favor of more direct attacks on his rivals and on the diseases of society. The escalating War of the Theaters may also have forced Jonson to forsake his guerilla tactics—infiltrating his opponents' territory, destabilizing their systems of authority, courting their loyalists with ingenious propaganda—in favor of open combat. There is certainly parody in these plays, but mostly of a traditional and explicit kind. The mockery of rivals is no longer conducted through the betrayed expectations of the audience; Jonson's fools often represent the rivals themselves, rather than their literary creations. Ordinary plagiarism is at issue more often than the witless translation of literary models into life. This is by no means to pass judgment on the inherent worth of these plays, but simply to explain why others are preferable for the purposes of this study.

With *Eastward Ho* (1605), Jonson returns to his technique of subsuming rather than berating his rivals, but the fact that he wrote this comedy in an extensive collaboration with Chapman and Marston makes it a problematic case for my argument. Certainly the play shows significant traces of the parodic strategy. Like *Every Man In His Humor* and *The Alchemist, Eastward Ho* deflates a variety of grand self-dramatizing projects, primarily by making them collide with each other one stormy day. A woman named Gertrude, who at several points seems to confuse herself with Shakespeare's Gertrude, rides off blithely and proudly to occupy the castle of her new husband, Sir Petronel Flash, only to find an empty field. With that royal fantasy evaporated, she promptly casts herself into a fairy tale and a Greek myth, with no better success (5.1.67–96). Sir Petronel, meanwhile, thinks he is escaping on an adventure to the New World, but discovers that he has been shipwrecked, not on the shores of France (as he grandly supposes, and as the heroic Godfrey truly is in Thomas Heywood's *Four Prentices of London*), but simply on the Isle of Dogs a little way down the Thames. The usurer Security, disastrously misreading the portent of his name, oversecurely allows his wife to join Sir Petronel's voyage, then pursues them shouting, "A boat, a boat, a boat, a full hundred marks for a boat," as if he were Richard III defying usurpation instead of an old fool fearing cuckolding (3.4.4–5). The goldsmith Touchstone envisions a fate for his son that is clearly derived not from reality but from such plays as *The Legend of Whittington, The Story of Queen Elenor,* and *If You Know Not Me, You Know Nobody,* a fate he predicts will be "played i' thy life-time by the best companies of actors, and be called their get-penny" (4.3.65–66). Even Touchstone's moral exhortation to the audience at the end of the play might as easily have been delivered (as Barton remarks) "by the prophet Oseas in the Lodge and Greene collaboration *A Looking Glass for London and England* (1590), or by the actor entrusted with the Prologue to Gascoigne's *The Glass of Government* (1575)."[2] The noble poses of virtually all the characters in *Eastward Ho* ring false in histrionic ways.

The play as a whole, however, functions more as ordinary burlesque than as Jonsonian parody. The central prodigal son story is ridiculed by caricature rather than by decentering, by exaggeration of its generic signatures rather than by rewriting those signatures into a context that renders them absurd. By making the moralistic ending too pat and perfect to be believable, the authors point up the absurdities of many sententious citizen-comedies and prodigal son stories, but there is no heuristic betrayal of the audience's expectations, no evolving dialogue at the center of the play between old and new modes of drama. If, in the final act, the noble son Golding's astonishing generosity had rendered him vulnerable to one final swindle, if the noble father Touchstone's forgiveness had proved unwelcome to the villains, if the play itself had turned away bored from the exalting moral transformations, then *Eastward Ho* would have constituted a thoroughly Jonsonian attack on the conventions. Naturally I like to believe that, had Jonson been writing the play by himself, it might have followed such a course, but the argument can only be circular; such suppositions are as impossible to prove as they are conveniently impossible to disprove.

*Volpone* (1606) has long been established as one of Jonson's most praised and performed plays, but many aspects of it still trouble its critics and audiences; an understanding of Jonson's parodic strategy resolves a number of these problematic points. As in the humors plays, the various characters are led astray largely by overconfidence in the flattering scripts they have written (or rewritten) for themselves. What is new in *Volpone* is the degree to which the satiric manipulators delude and injure themselves in the process of deluding and injuring their gulls. Jonson's audience, meanwhile, is rebuffed for confidently awaiting either the victory of virtue that culminates most popular comedies, or else the victory of satiric wit that culminates so many other Jonsonian comedies.[3] Behind his ostensible purpose in punishing the rogues, which is to disarm the moral critics of the theater, there may also be other purposes, including the experimental repression of his own roguish allegiances, and the renewed assertion of control over his audience by betraying in a new way their expectations.

Several objections have commonly been raised to this harshly moralistic ending. Critics have complained that the severe sentences meted out to Mosca and Volpone trap the play in a generic no-man's-land, by signaling at various moments that it may be comedy, tragedy, or satire. Edward Partridge, for example, comments that "the tone seems closer to tragedy than comedy," and that even if we ignore the tone, we will likely remain confused about the sort of play we are watching: "Is it satire, burlesque, farce, comedy of humours, melodrama?"[4] Northrop Frye cites the play as an anomaly in being "a kind of comic imitation of a tragedy";[5] C. G. Thayer tries to redeem the play by claiming that the tragic undertones are merely illusory.[6] My suggestion, of course, is that Jonson is again exploiting the clash of generic expectations, both to generate a new sort of comedy and to force the audience to recognize that innovation.

Barton locates the confusion in a conflict between the moralism that governs the outlines of the plot and the picaresque appeal that governs our reactions to the immoral hero: "The Epilogue to *Volpone* is there to remind us that there are fictive criteria for judging scoundrels, older and more universal than the severities of Venetian law. Volpone cannot be forgiven within the play. No Justice Clement will pardon him, like Brainworm, 'for the wit o' the offence' (*EMI*, 5.3.113–114). But the Fox, like Face, can rely on the spectators to acquit him."[7] Is it true, however, that Volpone "cannot be forgiven within the play"? To adapt the famous theological paradox, can a playwright create a fate he cannot redeem? Face, after all, is forgiven within *his* play.[8] Why does Jonson want to create this sharp discord between the spectators applauding Volpone in his appearance as the Epilogue, and the severe sentence passed against him a few lines earlier?

The strain we feel at the end of *Volpone* is Jonson pulling back on the bridle of his own satiric spirit; he projects into the audience his own dilemma as a comic moralist.[9] The surprisingly blunt exposure and punishment in *Volpone* pits the indulgent conventions of satiric comedy, in which wit is the sole criterion for success, against the forces of conventional moralism that were exerting renewed pressure against the popular theater. Justice Clement is temporarily off duty, and a more authoritative and authoritarian version of Justice Overdo is filling in for him. In his Epistle to the play, Jonson announces that his "special aim" is "to put the snaffle in their mouths that cry out: We never punish vice in our interludes" (109–110). This does not necessarily mean that Jonson intends simply to accede to that complaint; he may instead be enlisting his audience's support for the notion that a narrow sort of moralism does not belong in interludes. What is imprisoned at the end of the play, but escapes into the Epilogue, is an aspect of comedy that conspires with the cruel, selfish, cynical exuberance of the spectators. Volpone and Mosca betray each other, but in a deeper sense they are both betrayed by Jonson's decision to stop indulging the amoral exercise of wit that triumphs in so many of his other comedies. The lead characters and the audience alike confidently await the vindication of the clever exploitative plot, only to have it explode as badly as the more naive plots.

Surely I am not alone in wondering why Mosca refuses to accept half of Volpone's fortune, when his insistence on a total triumph practically forces Volpone to seek out vengeful countermeasures; or why Volpone chooses a countermeasure that essentially assures him of a fate far worse than poverty, even for such a greed-driven personality. Neither of them can conceive that their play could really end so bluntly and brutally, any more than the audience can, perhaps because they all share the same set of expectations about Jonsonian comedy. Alexander Leggatt has argued that what he calls "The Suicide of Volpone" results from Volpone's compulsion to perform, control, and finish a complete dramatic action.[10] Leggatt's examples clearly demonstrate the nature of the compulsion—"theatricality is the key to their essential failure"[11]— but Volpone does not seem to me fully conscious that he is merely playing, nor fully prepared to accept the actual ending of his play. Volpone's announcement of his true identity at the end of the play may indeed be "a flourish of defiance" like those of Webster's Duchess of Malfi or Shakespeare's Richard III,[12] but the result is a long, dull, painful penance, not a glorious final conflagration. Critics have long striven to identify the literary sources of *Volpone* and to understand how Jonson translates them into Volpone's speeches and schemes. They have also struggled to explain why someone as clever and generally disillusioned as Volpone makes such grave errors in predicting the reactions of Celia and Mosca at crucial points in the plot. Combining the questions leads to some plausible answers: Volpone deludes himself by expecting his story to conform in full to its literary precedents. He is a creature of mediated desire and imagination—it shows in his sexuality as well as his greed—and the primary mediator is literature. *Volpone* is another case of a Jonsonian character becoming a victim when real life stubbornly refuses to imitate conventional art.

Volpone apparently believes exactly what many critics now believe: that his story is essentially a retelling of old beast-fables about the clever fox who outwits the birds of prey and finally entraps them by feigning death. These parables resemble the typical satiric city-comedy, with the clever figure feeding himself fat on the self-defeated gulls. Volpone, disguised as a court sergeant to taunt Corvino further, evidently understands himself as the moralizing spokesman at the end of such a fable:

> Methinks
> Yet you, that are so traded i' the world,
> A witty merchant, the fine bird Corvino,
> That have such moral emblems on your name,
> Should not have sung your shame, and dropped your cheese,
> To let the fox laugh at your emptiness.           (5.8.9–14)

What Volpone is gloating over is the fulfillment of a standard little literary piece in which his is the triumphant role. He does not—cannot—recognize that Jonson may decline to sustain the parallel all the way to the end. The moldy tale in which Volpone has cast himself with too much confidence, vanity, and literary-mindedness, becomes instead a different story, "called mortifying of a fox" (5.12.125), as Volpone himself ruefully acknowledges.

The fox plays dead to draw his victims, whereas for most of the play Volpone plays merely dying. Critics generally dismiss this discrepancy as unimportant, but it may explain why Volpone finally pushes his scheme beyond manageable limits and gives out that he is dead. The bold move that is a fatal blunder for Volpone may have seemed promising to him because it is precisely the winning move for the fox in the source-story on which he senses that his life is based. Once again Jonson twists a conventional story, not merely to make it his own, but also to rebuke a character who confuses his life with art. As Subtle discovers in *The Alchemist,* even the strongest cynical wit must guard constantly against falling into the same self-dramatizing complacency he has been exploiting.

This understanding of Volpone's self-dramatization may explain more than his basic tactic and his fatal error. R. B. Parker has shown that a wide range of Volpone's actions have plausible analogues in stories of Reynard the Fox. Jonson's audience, Parker argues convincingly, "would *almost certainly* have recognized behind the play the familiar episodes of the fox feigning sickness and death to lure scavengers and catching the crow's wife; the fox's attempt at rape, and double trial before a venal and savage court, where his defense is a plea of age and an attack on his accuser's chastity; and the combination of fox as false doctor and lecherous preacher behind the episode of Scoto the mountebank."[13] The problem is that (except in the metatheatrical sense suggested by the Epilogue) Volpone does not finally escape his grim fate, as Reynard somehow always escapes his. The discrepancy may be Jonson's trick on both his character and his audience.

Discussions of *Volpone* often begin at the beginning, with Volpone's famous panegyric to gold (1.1.1–27). Critics sift through the various literary echoes in the speech for evidence that the play is essentially another condemnation of greed, that it is a subversive celebration of appetitive values, or that Volpone suffers from a perversion of his religious or sexual instincts. To me, the flood of conventional motifs suggests a man searching for a satisfactory role in which to cast himself. In an interesting echo of Barabas from *The Jew of Malta,* Volpone acknowledges himself as a miser, but the fate that generally awaits such characters is so unappealing that he tries (with temporary success) to translate it into the more exalting roles of worshipful saint and devoted romantic lover, with gold as his god and his paramour. He also employs a wide range of classical allusions to give his miserly posture the dignity it conspicuously lacks in so much early English literature.[14]

Mosca amplifies Volpone's interest in Celia with the most hackneyed sort of romantic imagery (1.5.107–122), as if he knew that Volpone could not resist writing himself wholeheartedly into this sort of bawdy tale. Volpone consciously assumes the role of Scoto of Mantua in order to make contact with Celia, but his subsequent seductive song to her betrays his carelessness about the interplay of literature and life. It is quite lovely in its way, but dangerously secondhand; he relies on a literary precedent from Catullus that merely serves to foreshadow the ill-fatedness of his corrupt schemes, sexual as well as financial.[15] Even when expressing his most powerful private desires, Volpone is a puppet to conventions familiar to readers of such works as *The Faerie Queene, Mucedorus,* and the plays of Marlowe: "whenever a male creature—be he natural, simple, or good, be he ugly, lustful, or absolutely evil—whenever he speaks passionately to a supremely beautiful woman, he must pull out all the stops and speak gorgeously, often in a catalog of delights."[16] Volpone's careless reading, furthermore, has led him to miscast his play. He assumes that Celia will prove to be like Lucrezia in Machiavelli's *La Mandragola,* a typical wife in the world of Italianate satire who is entirely willing to be seduced away from her worthless husband. What he offers to Celia is a sensual version of the technique used successfully by the satiric manipulators in Jonson's earlier comedies: he promises her a life of virtually infinite role-playing, a set of participatory literary allusions which they will consciously control to maximize their own pleasure (3.7.206–245). It is merely his bad luck that the play seems to drift unexpectedly out of the gravitational field of satiric comedy, and into that of sentimental melodrama.

Barton's response to these fatal errors of Volpone's is instructive:

> Volpone's reckless insistence upon spreading the news of his death, installing Mosca as heir, and walking abroad in the habit of a Commendadore to taunt his disappointed victims, is indeed an attempt to regain ascendancy and control. Had he truly known Mosca, he would never have risked it, any more than even a superficial understanding of Celia would have allowed him to assume that she could be "collected" as unresistingly as a diamond, or a piece of embossed plate.[17]

My suggestion is that both these mistakes make sense, not simply as Volpone's failures to read the character of people around him, but as failures induced by a tendency to read those people as if they were characters in the conventional works to which Volpone so often alludes. Once again, what to us is genre, to the characters is gestalt; Volpone's world-view makes it virtually impossible for him to imagine his plots effectively resisted or subsumed.

Volpone's performance as Scoto of Mantua helps to mark him as a surrogate of Jonson, mocking his competitors for "their moldy tales out of Boccaccio" (2.2.51), but there is a distinct suggestion that Jonson is now mocking his own cynical performances as well as his rivals' naive ones. Eventually Volpone discovers that, though he started off as a theatrical manipulator, he has himself become trapped playing an unanticipated and undesirable part. His double role as corpse and as sergeant (the latter performed in precisely the manner Jonson dismisses in *Bartholomew Fair* as a hackneyed convention for stage constables)[18] becomes increasingly inconvenient, but he finds he cannot drop it without confessing all his villainies. When he lies uncomfortably trapped in the courtroom, Volpone fears that his role as a cripple will become real and permanent (5.1.1–10), a fear that soon proves prophetic in the court's poetically just sentence (5.12.117–124). He failed to see what was coming only because he understood his world as a satiric genre that privileges cynical predations, rather than an equally familiar genre that enforces poetic justice.

A similar explanation resolves some oddities in the conduct and the fate of Mosca. Just as Volpone imagines himself the triumphant fox of the fable, so Mosca envisions himself as the all-conquering wily servant of New Comedy and of the satiric city-comedies based on that classical model. Leggatt has recognized that the struggle between these two for control of Volpone's fortune is really a contest between playwright-figures: "The parasite becomes a rival creator, devising a new play in which he is the hero and Volpone is his dupe . . . The rapid bargaining between Volpone and Mosca in the final scene is not just over Volpone's estate; it is a fight between two rival artists, each trying to end the play on his own terms."[19] The self-infatuation in Mosca's famous soliloquy (3.1.1–33) is filtered through conventional literary formulas of worship. The speech begins with a divine genealogy and then builds a classic catalogue of qualities, in a Neoplatonic manner, closing with an epigrammatic definition.[20] As his plot progresses, Mosca asks his master to "applaud my art," even while hoping to avoid the sort of punitive "epilogue" that punished Volpone's strategic role-playing as Scoto of Mantua (2.4.32–38). Leggatt notes that Mosca may be echoing Kyd's Hieronimo in "fitting" Volpone for this part at 5.3.113, and that Mosca later perceives "something artistically right in cheating Volpone. He does not merely justify his action; he finds a title for it . . . 'this is call'd the Foxe-trap' (5.5.18)."[21] That title seems to be derived from Hamlet's "Mouse-trap,"[22] which is a noble enough precedent. But by pursuing a plan merely because it seems to fit a standard artistic pattern, Mosca is virtually assuring his doom in the context of Jonson's iconoclastic plotting.

Mosca's fate is particularly bitter, however, because the pattern he relies on is essentially Jonson's own, in which the sharpest predatory wit—often a wily servant—ends up triumphant. Like Volpone, Mosca is finally defeated less through his own weakness than through a paradoxical betrayal by his creator, who is experimenting with a sternly moralistic ending. When Volpone calls an end to all the playing by throwing off his disguise as the sergeant, all the other roles—Volpone as a dead or dying man, Voltore as a victim of diabolical possession, Mosca as a magnifico—collapse too. In Jonson's other comedies, characters who try to end the play by casting off their own masks fail to crush the theatrical and picaresque spirit as they had planned; when Surly in *The Alchemist* and Justice Overdo in *Bartholomew Fair* throw off their disguises, they succeed neither in ending the play nor in punishing the rogues. The plays would have been very different if these censorious figures had succeeded: in fact, they would have been, like *Volpone,* betrayals of the resilient spirit that so often characterizes Jonsonian comedy. If Jonson does manage (as his Epistle had promised) "to put the snaffle in their mouths that cry out: We never punish vice in our interludes," it is only by putting the irons on the legs of the characters who assumed that such critics were right, and that theirs would prove to be another amoral Jonsonian world.

Through most of the play Volpone and Mosca control their gulls by the same principle that functions in the other comedies: they exploit the fact that people would rather misperceive reality than surrender their self-aggrandizing fantasies. Like Clement and Brainworm or Lovewit and Face, they are exploiters of cognitive dissonance. Mosca comments that each of the legacy hunters

> Is so possessed and stuffed with his own hopes
> That anything unto the contrary,
> Never so true, or never so apparent,
> Never so palpable, they will resist it—       (5.2.23–27)

While Voltore daydreams happily about the new role, costume, and name he supposes he is about to acquire, Volpone and Mosca delight themselves (as do the coney-catchers in the earlier plays) by envisioning the moment when this inflated image will collide with the degrading reality of the situation (1.2.97–113).

Volpone's manipulative performance as Scoto of Mantua provokes Corvino into a rage, precisely because it threatens to make
Corvino's house a *commedia dell'arte* stage, and himself the conventional pantaloon of that cast:

> No house but mine to make your scene?
> Signior Flaminio, will you down, sir? down?
> What, is my wife your Franciscina, sir?
> No windows on the whole Piazza, here,
> To make your properties, but mine? but mine?
> Heart! ere tomorrow I shall be new christened,
> And called the Pantolone di Besogniosi
> About the town.                                    (2.3.2–9)

Later he rages at Celia because she made herself "an actor" in this
scene (2.5.40). But Mosca distracts Corvino with the notion that
he could be understudy to the role of magnifico now played by
the supposedly dying Volpone. The prostitution of his wife suddenly becomes, in Corvino's eyes, merely a piece of stage business
peripheral to this grand transformation. Volpone will get what he
wants, not so much through his virtuosity as an actor in the role
of mountebank, as through Mosca's virtuosity as a reviser of plays.
Corvino can only stumble from one script to another. Even when
he finds out the truth, his impulse is to resort (like Sordido in
*Every Man Out of His Humor*) to a conventional representation of
his despair, "with a rope and dagger / To visit all the streets"
(5.2.93–94).

Celia and Bonario provoke the greatest confusion among the
critics of *Volpone* and generate what is probably the most striking
and interesting instance of Jonson's parodic strategy in the play.
The extreme and apparently authentic virtue of these characters
makes them anomalous in the world of satiric city-comedy. Are
we to take them as the sole remaining locus of true virtue, or as
yet another naive and pretentious target of satire? The question is
impossible to resolve, as the protracted critical disagreements suggest, because these characters are one thing on their own terms,
and another within the dramatic context Jonson imposes on them
(just as they are transformed from heroes to villains by the little
play of demonic possession in the Venetian courtroom). What
critics have tried to resolve by analyzing personality traits can only
be understood by analyzing generic conventions: these are exiles

from the world of sentimental melodrama, which is the only place their sort of virtue has any real relevance or force.[23]

The fate of these characters has disturbed readers of *Volpone* in revealing ways. Coleridge's oblique objection took the form of a suggestion that "a most delightful comedy might be produced, by making Celia the ward or niece of Corvino, instead of his wife, and Bonario her lover."[24] Since then, critics have repeatedly puzzled over the fact that Jonson neglects to steer Celia and Bonario into the romantic union that would conventionally have been their lot.[25] It often seems as if Celia and Bonario themselves expect their life trials to be resolved as they would be in such a comedy. In this, however, Jonson shows them to be deluded. Those who call on the heavens for aid in *Volpone* will meet some rude surprises, and though they may survive, they will never be allowed to fulfill the roles that they rather grandly assign themselves. Jonson thus again turns our conventionalized expectations of romantic theater against us, to remind us that life is not much like such plays.[26] If we try to perceive Celia and Bonario entirely as heroes, the play calls us fools; if we try to perceive them entirely as fools, the play calls us rogues. The discomfort felt by readers is natural under such circumstances, and what it reveals is the effectiveness of Jonson's parodic strategy. We can escape the dilemma only by recognizing the generic novelty of Jonsonian comedy.

Celia is not inherently a simpleton; that would take all the critical edge off the parody. Critics such as Thayer dismiss her as "an idiot, an eloquent Dame Pliant"—something of an oxymoron—whose speeches are a "parody of the sort of thing one might expect from a young woman named Celia."[27] But why shouldn't a virtuous young woman named Celia expect to be allowed to say such things? She is guilty, not of stupidity per se, but (like so many of Jonson's victims) merely of misunderstanding the nature of the world and the plots she inhabits. The eccentric perspective of her extreme and conventional virtue causes her repeatedly to misread the plot. Because she is constitutionally incapable of fathoming the greed and cynicism of the schemes enmeshing her, Celia misinterprets her husband's urgings (as Mistress Fitzdotterel in *The Devil Is an Ass* misinterprets the advances of Pug) as evidence of a conventional plot to test her doubted fidelity. Corvino's actual plot is of course quite different—virtually the opposite (3.7.24).

As Volpone attempts to rape her, Celia's repeated, almost automatic pleas for divine rescue sound very much like an actor repeating a cue waiting for a saving entrance. And that is very much what they are. She keeps calling on heaven to stand up for the right (Bonario joins in this practice at the trial), because that is what would happen in a traditional story of threatened innocence. But here, as in a much grimmer way in *King Lear,* the lack of any divine response to these repeated calls is an exploitation of the audience's desires and expectations, used to remind us yet again that the real world does not work in the reassuring manner of the play-worlds we are used to witnessing.

Celia begs to be allowed to "take down poison, / Eat burning coals, do anything," rather than submit to sexual dishonor. She tells Volpone that she is his "martyr," and goes on spouting—with perfect sincerity—the classic clichés of female virtue (3.7.94–107). Celia behaves, in other words, just as a conventional heroine should behave. But no one—not her seducer, her husband, her god, or her author—seems to be impressed. The world of satiric city-comedy is like the world of the Venetian court: it is a place "where multitude and clamor overcomes," and where calling as witnesses "our consciences" and "heaven, that never fails the innocent" is therefore equivalent to having "no testimonies" at all (4.6.15–19). Celia is a victim of genre displacement, as well as of a rapist. One critic repeatedly refers to her as "a comic Lucrece."[28] That odd epithet raises some intriguing questions. Could there be such a thing? How would it feel to be Lucrece, and be trapped in a comedy?

Bonario looks at Mosca's outrageously insincere show of sad humility and tells himself, "This cannot be a personated passion," probably because it is exactly the sort of behavior that occurs sincerely in the sentimental melodramas that populate Bonario's mind as if they were the real world (the echo of Benedick's "This can be no trick" suggests the nature of his delusion). Bonario's histrionic entrance to prevent the rape can only be characterized as corny:

> Forbear, foul ravisher! libidinous swine!
> Free the forced lady, or thou diest, impostor.
> But that I am loth to snatch thy punishment
> Out of the hand of justice, thou shouldst yet
> Be made the timely sacrifice of vengeance,

Before this altar, and this dross, thy idol.
Lady, let's quit the place, it is the den
Of villainy; fear nought, you have a guard;
And he ere long shall meet his just reward.      (3.7.267–275)

This play is not an allegory, nor do its speeches end in rhymed couplets; these anomalous signals of a more exalted genre reinforce the impression that the virtuous couple and their sentiments are badly out of place in this play.[29]

Some critics claim that the grand speeches of these two innocents ring false merely because of our jaded modern sensibilities. Alan Dessen argues that, "despite the post-Jonsonian clichés evoked by both the terminology and the situation" of Bonario's intervention, his speech is meant to be taken as a straightforward assertion of the play's true values:

> Before objecting to Bonario . . . the modern reader should both recognize the traditional dramatic formulas and appreciate how they are being transformed. Jonson's audience would not have been aware of the conventions of nineteenth-century melodrama but would have had as part of their dramatic heritage various contests between Heavenly Man and Worldly Man or various stock situations in which Good Conscience or God's Merciful Promises rescues Innocent Humanity or Youth from the clutches of the Vice.[30]

But what would Jonson make of such traditions, or those who adopt them without discrimination? Bonario, in his proud naive indignation, is far more likely than Jonson to throw himself wholeheartedly into those morality conventions.

Other critics argue that Jonson wants us to recognize these two as merely more skillful hypocrites. This suggestion of an unalloyed satire is, to me, no more convincing than Dessen's idea of a straightforward allusion to the morality play, but the discrepancy suggests how provocative a generic conundrum the play poses. Jonson has given these characters lines that would, in the proper context, sound perfectly appropriate, but here do not; even though they are not subjected to any open derision, the noble protestations sound silly. It is in this delicate middle ground that Jonson's parodic strategy thrives.

One other aspect of *Volpone* that has long troubled critics, editors, and directors—the questionable integration of the Would-Be subplot into the play as a whole—has been rendered considerably less problematic by Jonas Barish's insightful commentary. He shows that the English follies of this couple often generate useful parallels, in both plot and theme, to the Venetian vices in the main plot.[31] What I wish to add to Barish's argument is the idea that, as their family name suggests, the Would-Be's provide further examples of Jonson's attack on self-aggrandizing literary delusions. If at times their story seems irrelevant to the center of the play, that may itself be Jonson's point. The Would-Be subplot is a would-be main plot.

Lady Politic acknowledges that she derives her behavior from *The Courtier* (4.2.35), and her speech is an obsessive chain of literary allusions (3.4.75–95). Characteristically, Jonson attacks this affectation indirectly, through the framing of the plot, as well as by direct ridicule. Lady Politic's ability to mistake the Englishman Peregrine for a Venetian courtesan, because she believes Mosca's hints that her life is becoming a standard story of Italianate sexual connivance, is symptomatic of her self-dramatizing tendencies. She is too enthralled with her role as the righteous detective to notice how little Peregrine resembles such a courtesan, and there is no way for her to recognize that Mosca's advice is merely a ploy in the main line of the story, to which her marital problems are extremely peripheral.

Sir Politic, too, feeds his melodramatic fantasies on the mere detritus of the main plot. He is obsessed with clothing and scripted behavior (4.1.8), and his grandiose schemes resemble not only those generated by the "projectors" of the other comedies, but also those triumphantly executed by figures such as Gresham in *If You Know Not Me, You Know Nobody*. Pol is absorbed in such outlandish schemes and tales that Peregrine is left wondering, "Does he gull me, trow—or is gulled?" (2.1.24). The answer, of course, is both: Sir Pol is so enthralled with his imaginary intrigues that he starts believing his own lies. What his diary reveals is that he takes the painfully banal events of his daily life and writes them down in books ("quotes" them) as if they were indeed the makings of an international spy thriller (4.1.128–147). In letting us know that we would not be interested in reading Pol's closely guarded diary, Jonson is partly letting us know why he has forestalled Pol's efforts to make the play into a political melodrama and to cast himself as its Machiavellian protagonist.

That does not mean, however, that Sir Pol cannot be useful in another genre. Peregrine concludes that Pol "would be a precious thing / To fit our English stage," were it not that everyone would dismiss him as an exaggeration (2.1.55–60). He finally decides to punish Pol by pretending that these dangerous melodramas are actually occurring, that Pol's spy fantasies have been misread as real by real spies. Pol's reaction is to confess, too late, that he drew all of his politic schemings "out of play-books" (5.4.41– 42). His fate (analogous to that of Volpone) is to find the world all too willing to play along with his role, in a way that makes him confront its negative aspects. The tortoise shell in which he conceals himself was a Renaissance symbol of Polity,[32] and his refuge there is yet one more example of his effort to cloak himself in grand literary terms (in this case, allegorical terms) that finally serve only to humiliate him. Peregrine speculates that his "coun- terplot" (4.3.24) may frighten Sir Pol into actually fleeing on the sort of exotic adventure he has boasted about: "Yes, and ha' his / Adventures put i' th' book of voyages, / And his gulled story registered for truth?" (5.4.4–6). By twisting around the relation- ship between life and literary fantasy, the punishment will ironi- cally fit (and even, in a sense, undo) the crime. After Pol is humiliated, one witness describes the scene as "a rare motion to be seen in Fleet Street," and Sir Pol moans that he "shall be the fable of all feasts, / The freight of the *gazetti,* ship-boys' tale / And, which is worst, even talk for ordinaries" (5.4.82–84). He has become a renowned literary figure, as he had hoped, but not exactly in the way he had hoped. In the context of Jonson's parodic comedy, the effort to play an exalting literary role is once again a sure path to humiliation.

Peregrine's uncertainty about whether Pol is a coney-catcher or a coney is a natural result of the fact that Pol deludes himself with his own self-important fantasies. But Peregrine's fear that he is being tricked enmeshes him in this same pattern of error: he, too, ends up misreading Jonson's plot. Some critics assume that Per- egrine is the wise hero of the play,[33] but his one decisive action is a misreading of a misreading, rather than a perfect moral insight. When Lady Pol mistakes him for her husband's supposed cour- tesan, Peregrine misinterprets her behavior as evidence that *she* is a courtesan, and Sir Pol her pander. So when Peregrine punishes Sir Pol for this supposed moral crime, it is hardly the triumph of the all-knowing satirist exploiting folly. It is instead the delusion of another victim, witty though he is, of Jonson's control of the plot. Like Mosca, Peregrine is a plausible version of Jonson's usual triumphant satiric wit, against whom this play finally turns the tables of parodic betrayal: the clever characters eventually become the prey of the very devices that had privileged them in earlier Jonsonian comedies, and earlier in this comedy.

Again the observations of the critics are revealing; they generally see Peregrine as a Jonsonian hero who inexplicably forfeits the heroic role. J. A. Bryant observes that while Peregrine may be the only plausible candidate in *Volpone* for the role of Jonson's standard "crusading reformer," his susceptibility to an "improbable fiction" of his own making shows that "Peregrine has now become afflicted with a blindness more serious than that of Sir Politic, who is at least halfway aware that his fantasies are merely fantasies and under pressure can repudiate them." Peregrine "plays his part briefly and vanishes into obscurity with questions about his fate unanswered. Readers seem not to have cared greatly."[34] In other words, Jonson here uses his techniques of parody and decentering to repudiate his own sort of hero. Barton observes that Peregrine is "just like the man whose follies he has undertaken to punish," in that "he imagines a sinister plot where there is none."[35] In *Volpone* everyone is susceptible to the self-dramatizing disease, wits as well as fools, victimizers as well as victims.[36]

If Peregrine had exposed Sir Pol's schemes as mere self-inflation, exposed the fraud of Volpone and his co-conspirators, punished them merely with shame and impoverishment, and bestowed the ill-gotten fortune on Celia and Bonario, the play might have been much more satisfying. The Jonsonian hero would achieve his usual moral and practical sovereignty, the two plots would be unified, the fate of the evildoers would be just without marring the comic atmosphere, and the romantic couple would be vindicated. But Jonson chooses to challenge us, not merely satisfy us. Specifically, he challenges the moralistic critics mentioned in the opening Epistle. *Volpone* tells them that a strictly ethical conclusion in Jonsonian comedy will not take the conventional and comfortable form envisioned by Celia and Bonario, because the real world does not work that way, and Jonson will not yield his realism to any pleasant literary formula. If his critics demand a moral ending, they will receive it only in the harsh discordant form of the court's official sentences, and they will have to decide whether they really prefer that to the comic spirit that survives in Volpone's Epilogue.

The striking oddities of *Volpone* are functioning parts of Jonson's evolving parodic strategy. Things that do not fit are, for the most part, not intended to fit. The Would-Be subplot is, in this sense, not nearly so extraneous as it might have seemed. The characters of Celia and Bonario are indeed anomalous, but it is an anomaly that forces us to confront our unthinking responses to various generic contexts. The ending of *Volpone* may seem too sternly punitive as a response to the witty plotters who, for the most part, merely allowed the wickedness of the fortune hunters to punish itself; the play, as a result, may give confusing generic signals, announcing itself at various moments as comedy, tragedy, and satire. But that confusion contributes to Jonson's attack on the complacencies of the audience, including any assumption that the victory in Jonson's comedies always goes to the strongest predatory wit.

# CHAPTER FOUR

# *Epicoene*

## FROM SATIRE TO FARCE
## TO IMPROVISATIONAL COMEDY

*Epicoene, or The Silent Woman* (1609) consists essentially of a series
of plots subsuming each other.[1] The three most skillful plotters,
however, finally agree to share the authorial "garland" (if a little
unevenly) (5.4.199–203), and in so doing they replace formulaic
and potentially grim models of satire with a more modern, pleasant, and sophisticated sort of comic improvisation. The play subordinates the relentless bitterness of formal verse satire, embodied
by Morose, to the energy of abusive farce, stage-managed by
Truewit, which yields in turn to the witty coup contrived by
Dauphine. Morose thinks of himself as a sort of lonely satiric
Diogenes, searching the folly-ridden world, not for a single honest
man, but rather for a single silent woman. But because there is
no such thing (in the play's conventional sexist joke) as a silent
woman,[2] Morose's plot is superseded by other plots that humor
his fantasy toward their own ends.

No audience, of course, is likely to be deluded into believing
that Morose is the authorial spokesman, though some critics have
argued that he does speak for an important aspect of Jonson's own
intolerant psyche.[3] But an audience could easily mistake the farceur
Truewit for that spokesman, a misprision shared not only by a
number of critics,[4] but also by Truewit himself. Just when the
audience begins to feel complacent in its recognition of the plot
as a series of cruelly humorous punishments of folly, with Truewit
as master of ceremonies, Jonson shifts his ground yet again. Through
Dauphine, and through Dauphine's delicate plot to assure his in-

heritance, Jonson asserts the infinite adaptability of the dramatic illusion and the ultimate sovereignty of the witty illusionist. Dauphine takes control of his financial legacy in a way that asserts Jonson's analogous seizure of control over his dramatic legacy: *Epicoene* is a theatrical trick of transformation that takes the literary riches of Jonson's satiric ancestors and spends them on his own cavalier pleasures.

In an influential study Barish has argued that *Epicoene* is compromised by the conflicting nature of its literary allusions.[5] He sees the play as Jonson's effort to write a pleasant Ovidian story, a conscious project repeatedly undermined by Jonson's subconscious affinity for the harsher Juvenalian viewpoint. More recently, John Ferns has shown that neither the Ovidian nor the Juvenalian viewpoint is privileged in *Epicoene,* and that neither viewpoint is consistently associated with a single character. What unifies the allusions is the ironic distance the gallants always maintain from their sources, expanding the passages from Juvenal and compressing those from Ovid in equally comic ways.[6] This squares very well with my own theory that what matters in Jonsonian comedy is less the nature of a character's literary sources than that character's ability consciously to manipulate those sources, rather than subconsciously to be manipulated by them. So the playful detachment with which the gallants in *Epicoene* echo the ancients is precisely what marks them as the heroes of the play, and what allows them to exploit those for whom literature is an absolute script for life, as Juvenalian satire seems to be for Morose.

Nonetheless, each of the gallants does have a specific plot in mind, and until those plots are reconciled into the play that is *Epicoene*, they repeatedly discomfit each other. At first Truewit focuses overconfidently on a straightforward plot to save Dauphine's inheritance: he will frighten Morose out of marriage by paraphrasing Juvenal's warning from the *Sixth Satire*.[7] When he boasts to Dauphine and Clerimont about how eloquently he has dissuaded Morose, Truewit is surprised that they do not "applaud" him for performing so well on their behalf (2.4.15). They are unenthusiastic simply because they have other plays in mind. Dauphine has let Clerimont in on enough of his secret that Clerimont supposes the play will culminate in a standard *charivari*—a raucous ritual that sometimes made its way onto the medieval stage,[8] consisting (according to Cotgrave's 1632 dictionary) of "an infamous (or infaming) ballade sung, by an armed troup, under the window of an old dotard married, the day before, unto a young wanton, in mockery of them both."[9] When he learns a little more about the plot, Truewit concurs with Clerimont's belief that their enforcement of such conventional boisterous mockery on Morose will be "a jest to posterity, sirs, this day's mirth" (2.6.25). The echo of the title of Chapman's *Humorous Day's Mirth* could be inadvertent on Jonson's part, but more likely it is a sort of Freudian slip Jonson imposes on Truewit to reveal the derivative theatrical character of his expectations. The jest of *Epicoene* will indeed live to posterity, but only because it insists on going a step beyond the popular entertainment that Truewit envisions.

Jonson's audience is invited to share Truewit's and Clerimont's half-informed deduction about the nature of the play, to believe that Jonson is content to create his dramatic legacy by repeating old comic forms. Only by revealing Epicoene's transsexual disguise at the end does Dauphine reveal that he has been one level deeper into plot and theatrical artifice than the rest of them; Jonson, by the same device, has been one step ahead of *his* audience. Because of the Elizabethan traditions of transvestite disguise on the stage, the audience would presumably have ignored the fact that the actor playing Epicoene was a boy. Throughout his comedies Jonson teaches his audience to mistrust theatrical conventions, by betraying those conventions and the characters who rely on them. Epicoene's disguise, impenetrable precisely because of the conventions of its context, adds a new dimension to that tactic. This silent woman is both the device and the emblem of the invisible plot, which turns out to be the masterplot of *Epicoene, or The Silent Woman*. The crude pleasure of punishing and humiliating a stock target yields to a more modern—that is, Augustan—sort of delight in the witty conquest of an inheritance. Dauphine's particular technique may be another literary inheritance, derived from Aretino's *Il Marescalco* and perhaps from Plautus' *Casina*,[10] but its purpose within the play looks ahead to the next generation of comedy, that of the Restoration.

Jonson thus uses the process of his plot to unsettle the inert literary heritage of his audience; he "refunctions" the convention of transsexual casting and the motifs of earlier literature. As Dauphine's revelations alter the context, the audience learns not to lean too heavily on literary monuments in the future, because they are not the stable supports they might apear to be. Barton observes that "in *Epicoene,* far more than in either of its two predecessors, these memories [of the noble past] are literary. The comedy is riddled with the names of long-dead classical writers: Homer, Pindar and Plato, Aristotle, Thucydides, Anacreon, Plutarch, Livy, Virgil, Ovid, Catullus, Juvenal, Horace, Martial, Tacitus, Seneca and many more. They are talismanic names, even though irrelevant and degraded in context."[11] That is a significant "even though"; the problem again is that characters misapply established literature to contemporary reality. Barton argues that the gallants are harshly judged by this mass of moral literature; my qualification is that they, and others, are condemned only when they fail to bring a modern alertness to bear on their reading of the ancients. To live one's life in utter obeisance to this literature would be typical Jonsonian folly, not glorious virtue. When Truewit (playfully?) reproves Clerimont for his luxurious idleness, Clerimont dismisses the criticisms, not by refuting them, but by describing them as merely a hollow bit of literary quotation: "Foh! Thou hast read Plutarch's *Morals* now, or some such tedious fellow, and it shows so vilely with thee, 'fore God, 'twill spoil thy wit utterly" (1.1.56–58). Truewit takes his revenge later by attacking Dauphine for allowing the literature of romance to displace any sexual romance in his real life: "you must leave to live i' your chamber, then, a month together, upon *Amadis de Gaul* or *Don Quixote,* as you are wont, and come abroad where . . . a man shall find whom to love, whom to play with, whom to touch once, whom to hold ever" (4.1.50–56). This would normally be a worthwhile warning. But Dauphine has evidently learned from Cervantes the kind of ironic, parodic distance on literary solemnities that Truewit could never glean from Plutarch, and it is precisely this distance that allows Dauphine's more modern plot to displace Truewit's old-fashioned one.

Truewit advises Dauphine to win a woman by a temporary theatrical indulgence of her self-dramatizing fantasies: "Admire her tires, like her in all fashions, compare her in every habit to some deity, invent excellent dreams to flatter her, and riddles; or, if she be a great one, perform always the second parts to her" (4.1.104–106). Truewit, then, does have much of the arsenal of a Jonsonian coney-catcher; at a number of points in the plot he seems wiser and more humane than Dauphine, who lusts after the horrible Ladies Collegiate and would cut off John Daw's arm for the sake of a jest. The still-unresolved controversy about whether Truewit thus establishes himself as the true hero of *Epicoene* reflects Jonson's strategic manipulation of his authorial power. Jonson grants Truewit attributes that would indeed mark him as the hero of many satiric city-comedies, yet deprives him of the authority that might ordinarily arise from his successful exploits of wit by framing the story around Dauphine's plot instead. Like Mosca before him and Subtle after, Truewit finds himself trapped in a play which adds one more twist to the parodic formula that would normally exalt him as its author-surrogate.[12]

The central struggles of the play all take place in oddly bookish terms that suggest a parodic rewriting of eminently serious works. Allusions to forgery, to false authorship, appear repeatedly and, at first glance, superfluously. Dauphine complains that Morose "will disinherit me" because "he thinks I and my company are authors of all the ridiculous acts and monuments are told of him." Truewit replies with a vengeful plan to "make a false almanac, get it printed, and then ha' him drawn out on a coronation day to the Tower-wharf, and kill him with the noise of the ordnance" (1.2.8–15). Along with the controversial thefts from the classics by Truewit and Dauphine, these references establish deceptive authorship as a major theme of *Epicoene*.

Unhealthy bookishness is most prominent, of course, in the fools. Sir John Daw is introduced as "a fellow that pretends only to learning, buys titles, and nothing else of books in him" (1.2.70–72). The pun on "titles" is significant: Daw is, in other words, a sort of false bookshelf, a hollow box purfled with impressive titles and bindings. When Daw recites his poetry in act 2, scene 3, the witty gentlemen mockingly mistake it for the work of Seneca or Plutarch, and Daw angrily dismisses the writings of nearly all the great classical authors. The only ones Daw will praise are not authors at all, but rather titles he mistakes for the authors' names:

> *Dauphine*  Why, whom do you account for authors, Sir John Daw?
> *Daw*  *Syntagma juris civilis, Corpus juris civilis, Corpus juris canonici,* the King of Spain's Bible.
> *Dauphine*  Is the King of Spain's Bible an author?
> *Clerimont*  Yes, and *Syntagma*.

*Dauphine*   What was that *Syntagma,* sir?
*Daw*   A civil lawyer, a Spaniard.
*Dauphine*   Sure, *Corpus* was a Dutchman . . . [*Aside.*] 'Fore
   God, you have a simple learned servant, lady, in titles.
(2.3.71–85)

This whole exchange renews the pun on "title" in a way that underscores Daw's tendency to confuse people with literary works. The question of whether Daw will "live by his verses" thus becomes not only a standard piece of commentary on the place of professionalism in the arts, but also another hint that Daw's empty literary pretensions reflect a false literary vision of the course his life will take.

It is intriguing, therefore, that this scene ends with Daw reciting a poem that seems to predict the entire plot of *Epicoene:*

> Silence in woman is like speech in man,
> Deny't who can.
> . . . . .
> Nor is't a tale
> That female vice should be a virtue male,
> Or masculine vice, a female virtue be:
> You shall it see
> Proved with increase,
> I know to speak, and she to hold her peace.   (2.3.111–119)

Jonson has Daw write these lines without permitting him to understand what they mean in the context of Dauphine's plot; Daw misinterprets them as a narrative of his successful seduction and impregnation of a woman, rather than as a formulation of the central paradoxes that structure *Epicoene.* This typifies his general error, and the errors of so many Jonsonian victims who notice the elements of the plot surrounding them but misshape them into something that suits their own egotistical fantasies, leaving themselves unprepared to cope with the master wit's more ingenious satiric structure. When Daw agrees that kicks can hardly hurt or humiliate "a man that reads Seneca" (4.5.259–261), and especially when he volunteers to have his left arm cut off, as long as he can retain the right one and his life "for writing madrigals" (4.5.109–110), we get an indication of how far Daw will go in substituting a literary identity for a real one.

The behavior of Amorous La Foole is similarly suggestive. He is introduced to us as a man who "does give plays" but has so little comprehension of this fashionable entertainment that he will salute "a lady when she is dancing in a masque, and put her out" (1.3.30–32). He is, in other words, a perfect candidate for the role of gull, because (like Bartholomew Cokes in *Bartholomew Fair*) he involves himself in the world of playing without any comprehension of the divisions between theater and real life. Like other Jonsonian gulls, La Foole takes pride in his name and in his literally foolish costume without recognizing the degrading implications of either: "I myself am descended lineally of the French La Fooles—and we do bear for our coat *yellow,* or *or,* checkered *azure* and *gules,* and some three or four colors more, which is a very noted coat and has sometimes been solemnly worn by divers nobility of our house" (1.4.36–40).

La Foole then sets about arranging his grand banquet, which he envisions as a triumphant affirmation of his nobility, but which, in the context of the previous speech and of the play in general, undergoes a generic debasement into an archetypal *festa stultorum*.[13] As Bryant observes, "the banquet that ought to bring these people together comes at the middle of the play rather than at the end and unites no one."[14] It is the playwright, of course, who decides what will be a middle incident in his play and what will be the ending; the characters, living out their own full lives, can only guess whether and where each part of their experiences will fit into the frame.[15] Jonson, through his on-stage surrogates, provides conventional signals that provoke and then betray La Foole's hopes of presiding over the comic resolution.

Clerimont easily draws Daw into his minor role in the plot against Morose by claiming that Dauphine has "discovered the whole plot" in which Daw (as Epicoene's slighted lover and La Foole's betrayed friend) is the noble victim, and by painting a scenario in which Daw would emerge triumphant (3.3.1–33). A similar theatrical fantasy enmeshes La Foole, a promise of "a pestling device" that "will pound all your enemy's practices to powder and blow him up with his own mine, his own train" (3.3.92–94). Both gulls are lured into the overarching scheme of the gallants by the notion that they will themselves be out-plotting a plotter. As Dauphine comments,

> Tut, flatter 'em both, as Truewit says, and you may
> take their understandings in a purse-net. They'll believe
> themselves to be just such men as we make 'em, neither
> more nor less. They have nothing, not the use of their
> senses, but by tradition.          (3.3.84–87; cf. 4.5.86)

This trait is ultimately what makes Jonsonian gulls vulnerable (Mosca makes the same point in *Volpone*, 5.2.23–28), and they transmit that vulnerability to the literary "traditions" they mistakenly credit. The sort of script the gulls proudly follow as if it were holy scripture is discredited when it cannot defend them from Jonsonian satire.

Truewit's scheme for further humiliating these two fools would have looked oddly familiar to Jonson's audience. "It seems clear," one critic comments, "that Jonson was remembering the mock-combat between Viola and Andrew Aguecheek in *Twelfth Night* when he devised the encounter between Daw and La-Foole in Act Four, each one falsely persuaded through the malice of a third party of the fury and terrifying swordsmanship of his adversary."[16] Perhaps the audience is meant to suspect that Truewit, looking for a showy device to turn these hypocrites against each other, remembers the same literary precedent. Both of the cowards must try to maintain noble postures while undergoing a demeaning sort of punishment, and then are lured into mutual forgiveness when Truewit offers them the hackneyed model of Damon and Pythias which Jonson would later parody so savagely in *Bartholomew Fair*. They are then finally disgraced, in a less crude but no less effective way, by Dauphine's superplot, because their boasts as seducers are undone when the bride they claim to have enjoyed turns out to be a boy. In other words, they are easily lured into scenarios that they believe will affirm their "manly" poses, and just as easily crushed by a strategic revision of those scripts.

Tom Otter, too, is introduced as a creature living in a world of theatrical lines, roles, and props:

> An excellent animal, equal with your Daw or La Foole,
> if not transcendent, and does Latin it as much as your
> barber. He is his wife's subject; he calls her Princess,
> and at such times as these follows her up and down the
> house like a page, with his hat off, partly for heat, partly

for reverence. At this instant he is marshalling of his
bull, bear, and horse . . . he has been a great man at the
Bear Garden in his time, and from that subtle sport has
ta'en the witty denomination of his chief carousing
cups.                                                           (2.6.48–57)

His wife, Mistress Otter, actually composed their prenuptial agreement as a script in which her role is regal. When he resists her
banishment of his carousing cups, she demands, "Is this according
to the instrument when I married you? That I would be Princess
and reign in mine own house, and you would be my subject and
obey me?" (3.1.27–30). Mistress Otter, like Deliro in *Every Man
Out of His Humor,* is determined to impose the clichés of Petrarchan
courtship onto the realities of marriage. Clerimont's scheme for
convincing her to accept the cups is appropriately literary: he will
merely remind her of the grand mythological conjunctions of great
women with bulls and bears. This idea pleases Otter so much that
he vows to "have these stories painted i' the Bear Garden, *ex Ovidii
Metamorphosi*" (3.3.114–115). Life and art seem headed toward an
infinite regression of mutual imitations.

In a fit of honesty, Otter points out that his wife is less a unitary
person than an assembly of costumes and makeup (4.2.87–96).
Like an actress playing a noblewoman, she depends on her "excellent choice phrase" to make her into "the only authentical courtier that is not naturally bred one, in the city," as the gallants
sarcastically note (3.2.24–26). She frequently dreams about the
Lady Mayoress—uneasy wish-fulfillment dreams, quite possibly
derived from the various citizen-comedies (such as *The Shoemakers'
Holiday*) in which a citizen's wife achieves that status. She also
evidently believes that fantastic desires and classical authors translate into her waking reality: she told the latest such dream to Lady
Haughty, who "expounded it out of Artemidorus, and I have
found it since very true" (3.2.51–55). The ultimate expression of
her narcissistic fantasies occurs when she overhears her husband
dispraising her and calls him "Thou Judas, to offer to betray thy
Princess!" (4.2.110–111). This blasphemous comparison is really
only a logical extension of Mistress Otter's willingness to read
herself proudly into any story she knows.

Otter and his wife might have been adequate as characters in
one of the humors plays, but Jonson has moved beyond a simple

series of attacks on such fragile fantasies. Clerimont is finally "glad we are rid of him," and Truewit agrees that "His humour is as tedious at last, as it was ridiculous at first" (4.2.137–139). The Otters and their absurd marriage remain peripheral to *Epicoene,* never permitted to make a bid for control of its central plot, perhaps because Jonson has decided to focus on the superiority of collaborative male friendship to morose male isolation, rather than focusing again on the follies of ordinary social intercourse.

Female collaborations receive much less sympathetic treatment than male ones. The Ladies Collegiate are no more successful than the Otters in shaping the play to their wishes and their credit. They envision themselves as something like a female version of Shakespeare's Gentlemen of Navarre, but in this case when sexual desire overshadows academic pretenses, the result is dehumanizing rather than humanizing. These are bad actors, not only in their intellectual pretensions, but even in the cosmetic makeup they wear. Truewit eloquently defends the wearing of such makeup, but as Judd Arnold writes, "the Collegians have all put on their artifices 'the wrong way.' "[17] This embarrassing misuse of cosmetics corresponds to the way the other fools wear their own artifices: they try to play roles which might look impressive on the right person and in the right sort of drama, but here are incongruous, ugly, and degrading.

Morose hardly seems like heroic material for any genre, but in fact many of his assumptions and attitudes would make considerably more sense and carry considerably more moral weight if he inhabited a different sort of literary work. He first appears as a sort of casting director for the play of his life, which he envisions as a dumbshow, with himself as the only speaking chorus:

> Cannot I yet find out a more compendious method than by this trunk to save my servants the labor of speech and mine ears the discord of sounds? Let me see. All discourses but mine own afflict me; they seem harsh, impertinent, and irksome. Is it not possible that thou shouldst answer me by signs, and I apprehend thee, fellow? (2.1.1–5)

The fact that this servant is called simply "Mute" in the dramatis personae is a latent joke on this suggestion that the play be converted into a dumbshow, a joke brought to life when Truewit addresses him as "Mute" in the following scene.[18]

Several excellent critics have seen Morose in a different light: as a degraded figure of the Jonsonian satirist, full of tirades on the stupid impertinencies of all those around him, hiding in horror from the ways of the world.[19] Delight in silence and withdrawal from society are hardly Jonsonian traits, however. Perhaps, more precisely, Morose represents a verse satirist who has stumbled into the world of Jonsonian comedy. From this perspective Morose's demand for silence appears as egoism of a very particular kind: not fully recognizing the transition from verse satire to satiric drama, he is naturally affronted to hear anyone but himself speak. Jonson may be doing to the figure of the verse satirist what he does to characters from other conventional modes of Elizabethan literature, lifting them into the noisy chaotic world of realistic city-comedy, which stubbornly refuses to function in the way they expect, and which thereby exploits, exposes, and punishes their egoism. In fact, when Morose envisions the ultimate torment, contemporary plays and playhouses appear prominently (4.4.11–16). Even the loose-flowing prose of *Epicoene* is an affront, not merely to Morose's inbred resistance to letting his mind "flow loosely" (5.3.44), but also to the verse form common to Elizabethan satire.

*Epicoene* thus serves to defend the territory and the autonomy of satiric city-comedy against the claims of conventional satire, just as *Every Man In His Humor* defended satiric city-comedy on its other border, against the claims of conventional drama. The entire project of converting satire from its usual narrative mode to an appealing dramatic mode poses serious problems, particularly since the satirist is the sole speaker, and an essentially unattractive one, in the narratives.[20] After years of trying to eradicate the resulting problems of structure and tone, Jonson may have decided instead to embody them starkly in the person of Morose, where he could vent his frustration by attacking them directly. Jonson had, of course, managed at times to create tolerably likeable satirists who knew how to share the stage with others, but only with great strain and under special circumstances. What Morose needs to become a Jonsonian spokesman is an ideal audience such as Crites found in the divine Cynthia, and Macilente found in Queen Elizabeth. Perhaps Morose is seeking such a figure in marrying his own ideal woman, Epicoene, but the joke is that she abruptly refuses to be either an audience or a positive moral exemplar: she talks instead of listening, and talks mostly about her own superficial appetites. It is as if Jonson were describing allegorically, through the progress of the plot, his own false starts in the struggle to create a healthy satiric drama.

Certainly Morose's speech is an ungainly amalgam of hollow, bookish, mismanaged rhetorical conventions.[21] Barish describes Morose's courtship of Epicoene as an "absurd attempt to translate an amatory conceit into a literal event . . . the speaker is airing courtly clichés he has found in love poems but never heard from a human voice."[22] In that sense, he is quintessentially vulnerable to Jonson's parodic strategy. When he discovers that he has married a real woman, willful and loquacious, rather than a dumbshow heroine, Morose merely shifts to a new literary gestalt, translating his rather ordinary predicament into a grand mythology: "I have married a Penthesilea, a Semiramis" (3.4.50–51; see similarly 3.5.35 and 4.2.115). The real plot, of course, is rather less romantic and more urbanely satiric than that. He has married, not a dumbshow player, not an Amazonian queen, not even an ordinary woman, but a disguised boy. Morose thinks in grand old-fashioned literary terms that demonstrate how unprepared he is to deal with the modern comedy of manners he actually inhabits. He insists that "he has married a Fury" (4.1.7–10), calls down the plagues of Egypt on the barber to repay him for arranging the marriage (3.5.55–57), and describes the voluble Mistress Otter as "that Gorgon, that Medusa," from whom he must hide (3.7.20).

The punishment fits the crime in this regard, because Morose's effort to assume authority over the play as conventional choral commentator submits him to a relentless hailstorm of authoritative booklearning: a crowd of observers allude to, and threaten to read from, the writings of Pliny, Paracelsus, Doni, Seneca, Plutarch, Aristotle, Becon, and Greene (4.4.51–94). Morose now seems to cling to some hope that he will be able to escape from this marriage in the desperate manner of "Morosus" in the Sixth Declamation of the fourth-century Greek rhetorician Libanius, who asks permission to kill himself in a highly similar predicament. But again Jonson offers a significant name and a traceable literary precedent only for the purpose of deluding both the character and the audience. Dauphine's extra twist to the plot (apparently derived, as suggested earlier, from Aretino and Plautus) renders ludicrous any serious expectations, even while in some ways deepening the defeat Morose suffers. Not even the perverse happy ending of the Aretino story (in which the old man ultimately prefers a boy as his bride) survives to mitigate the defeat of Morose's quest for control.

Truewit gloats over the skillful way the naive plots of Morose and Daw have been subsumed into the spousal of the supposedly silent woman:

> *Haughty* And Jack Daw told us she could not speak.
> *Truewit* So it was carried in plot, madam, to put her upon this old fellow, by Sir Dauphine, his nephew, and one or two more of us; but she is a woman of an excellent assurance, and an extraordinary happy wit and tongue. You shall see her make rare sport with Daw ere night.
> *Haughty* And he brought us to laugh at her!
> *Truewit* That falls out often, madam, that he that thinks himself the master-wit is the master-fool. (3.6.38–46)

Truewit recks not his own rede; he too will be hoist with his own petard, when he learns that Epicoene is no more a talkative woman than she was a silent one.[23] The audience is likely to fall into the same trap, for several reasons. First, Truewit's name naturally encourages us to identify his perspective with Jonson's. Second, the "jest" (2.6.25) of the woman whose silence abruptly changes to shrewish clamor as soon as she is married was something of an Elizabethan commonplace; for example, the sixty-second jest in *A C. Mery Talys* (London, 1526) describes "The Dumb Wife Cured," and a similar event was enacted a few years before *Epicoene* when Honorea is cured in Haughton's *Grim the Collier of Croydon* (1.4.100–133). Third, as I suggested earlier, Epicoene's disguise, which Truewit crucially fails to penetrate, was essentially impenetrable to the audience as well, because a Jacobean audience would presumably have expected all female characters to look a little like a boy disguised as a woman. That expectation not only solves some practical problems of stagecraft for Jonson; it also symbolically abets his parodic strategy, because it is precisely the audience's passive acceptance of a stage convention that leaves it vulnerable to his and Dauphine's superplot. When the boy Epicoene throws off his disguise as a woman, the play *Epicoene* throws off its disguise as a play like Middleton's *A Trick to Catch the Old One*.

Truewit is not at all bad as a plotter; he is simply overconfident. He casts and costumes Otter and the barber as a parson and a lawyer, and he gives them lines to speak, telling Dauphine that if they fail in their roles "trust not my election" (4.7.40–47; cf. 5.3.2–4). Truewit similarly urges Dauphine to "trust my plot" to humiliate the gulls and to ingratiate Dauphine with the Ladies Collegiate: "here will I act such a tragi-comedy between the Guelphs and the Ghibellines, Daw and La Foole. Which of 'em comes out first will I seize on. You two shall be the chorus behind the arras, and whip out between the acts and speak" (4.5.17–30). When Dauphine complains that "This is thy extreme vanity now; thou think'st thou wert undone if every jest thou mak'st were not published," Truewit answers by having Clerimont tell the ladies that "it was Dauphine's plot" (4.5.221–224). This is truly a generous gesture, but it may also point ironically ahead to the fact that (in the form Jonson chooses to publish them) Truewit's plots finally *are* subordinate to, and subsumed by, that of Dauphine. In the speech that closes the play, Truewit concedes that Dauphine has "lurched your friends of the better half of the garland, by concealing this part of the plot" (5.4.199–200).

Although none of these gallants can claim to be Jonson's sole and perfect spokesman, the three of them together fill that role. What characterizes the play (and made it so pleasant to Dryden) is that a set of witty gentlemen interweave their efforts into a varied but finally unified action. The relentless novelty and apparent spontaneity that characterized the plotting of Jonson's earlier comedies, allowing him to use the audience's expectations against dramatic conventions, here seems less arbitrary, because it is apparently generated by the improvisational ensemble work of three clever men, rather than by the capriciousness or stubbornness of Jonson himself. Dauphine is the clear winner, but he is part of a team that sweeps the first three places. In his study of Jonson's cavalier heroes, Arnold praises the gallants of *Epicoene* for having "the self-assurance that can allow them to laugh at themselves and the intelligence to adapt to changing circumstances."[24] These are precisely the qualities they need in order to enjoy the comedy they all help to write, without becoming dangerously committed to any single preconception of its eventual course. (It is almost as if *Epicoene* were a representation of what the composition of *Eastward Ho* could ideally have been like.) What initially appears to be another competition of plots finally resolves itself (at least among the gallants) into a sort of *commedia dell'arte* piece, with the various *lazzi* decorating a pleasant path to a satisfying destination. It is, in this sense, a preparation for the opening scene of *The Alchemist,* where Jonson again presents three witty plotters and self-conscious performers—Subtle, Face, and Dol—all working together to take advantage of the gulls' conventional fantasies, and using any spare energy and ingenuity to battle each other for control of the conclusion.

# CHAPTER FIVE

# The Alchemist

## THE CONVERSION OF COMEDY

The gulls in *The Alchemist* (1610) surrender their money, their honesty, even their perceptions, in exchange for the conspirators' promise to fulfill their secret melodramatic fantasies. Jonson invites his audience to make the same mistake, and then rebukes them in a way that argues for the superiority of realistic satire. Finally, he encourages them to drop the role of gull and take up the role of Lovewit, sharing in Lovewit's material and intellectual triumphs by endorsing the schemes of Jonson, their own wily servant. Subtle's promises to convert lead into gold are actually a cover for his more realistic project of converting human follies into profit; Jonson's representation of that alchemical fraud is similarly a cover for an effort to transform the base drama of his time into something resembling its classical Golden Age.

The play strongly suggests a correspondence between Lovewit's house and the theaters of Elizabethan London.[1] Like those theaters, the house is officially closed when the frequency of deaths from the plague reaches a certain threshold. An onset of plague, the Argument tells us, has encouraged a group of "Coz'ners at large"—a characterization often applied to actors themselves—to form something like an Elizabethan theater company: "they here contract / Each for a share, and all begin to act. / Much company they draw, and much abuse," until "they, and all in fume are gone."[2] Along with the philosophers' stone, these author-actors melt away into thin air like Prospero's rough theatrical magic. The house of glories is merely a grimy shed once the enchantment of language has ceased to fill it (5.5.38–42).[3] The resemblance between the play's opening scene and the usual backstage frenzy just before a performance is suggestive: these are indeed actors trying to quiet their nervous bickerings (including squabbles over top billing and top salary) and to redirect their predatory attentions from one another to the anticipated paying audience. Even the location of the house, in Blackfriars (4.1.131), suggests a connection with the private theater the King's Men had taken over in 1608, where many of Jonson's and Shakespeare's works were performed.

As Jonson converts that stage into Lovewit's house, Face converts Lovewit's house into an overpopulated Jacobean stage. The nature of the profitable little plays Face produces suggests that Jonson is using the gulls' headlong pursuit of their fantasies to educate his audience about his parodic mode; we are invited to read satire, as if in a heavy-handed palimpsest, beneath the melodramas the characters attempt to write for themselves. Although Leggatt is doubtless correct that "behind the variety of motives the dupes profess is the lowest common denominator of greed,"[4] there is another low and common denominator: popular literature. The house is full of tales of the sort that packed Elizabethan theaters and bookstalls: not only coney-catching stories, but also versions of Marlowe's dramas of extravagant riches and supernatural pleasures, Sidney's and Middleton's stories of dynastic marriage, Shakespeare's and Spenser's adult fairy tales, even Deloney's chronicles of triumphant middle-class commercial diligence. The fact that an editor can nonetheless describe *The Alchemist* as "freer of debt to a previous model" than any other play of the period[5] suggests how thoroughly Jonson has assimilated all these literary precedents into an unprecedented type of plot.

The first visitor to the house is Dapper, and conspirators easily convince him that he is the star of a fairy tale, embraced by a doting Fairy Queen. Ten years earlier London audiences had laughed at the egotistical Bottom's easy acceptance of his ludicrous match with Titania in Shakespeare's *Midsummer Night's Dream*; now that same literary fantasy makes an ass of Dapper. Subtle "never heard her Highness dote till now," Face assures their eager victim. Muriel Bradbrook reports that "tradesmen wooed by the fairy queen" were one of the common devices by which Elizabethan comedies appealed to "the simple dreams of the unlettered audience," and one poetical soul, according to court records, was actually prepared to pay some Jacobean tricksters a considerable sum of money to arrange his marriage to the Queen of Fairy.[6] Dapper is just such a manipulable audience to Subtle and Face. A compulsive gambler is generally someone who (perhaps for oedipal reasons) perpetually pursues evanescent hints that he is favored by Dame Fortune, and once the conspirators have deduced what Dapper wants to believe about himself, they can control his perception of reality. Face claims that Subtle has divined that Dapper was "born with a caul o' your head" (a conventional predictor of good fortune), and when Dapper swears this is untrue, Face simply bullies him into believing it:

> How!
> Swear by your fac, and in a thing so known
> Unto the Doctor? How shall we, sir, trust you
> I' the other matter? (1.2.128–133)

Dapper should instead be asking the conspirators how he can trust them in the other matter when they are wrong about a thing so known to him as his own nativity. But the standard fantasy of the "family romance," here sustained by the plot device of the changeling and the context of a fairy tale, suits Dapper's childlike mind so well that it supplants his true personal history.

Dapper's imagination is so lacking in creativity, for all its activity, that Face can make him appreciate the benefits of the Queen's favor only by couching them in the terms of another standard sort of play:

> Her Grace is a lone woman,
> And very rich, and if she take a fancy
> She will do strange things. See her, at any hand.
> 'Slid, she may hap to leave you all she has! (1.2.155–158; cf. 5.4.53–56)

The young wastrel redeemed by the whimsical affection of a wealthy widow was a favorite subject in the comedies of Jonson's rivals.[7] Face reinforces the credence and appeal of the fairy tale, itself merely a literary convention, by conflating it with another literary convention.

As the gulling continues, Dapper's will to believe induces him to accept a stinking privy as "Fortune's privy lodgings" (3.5.79), a dead mouse as a delicacy from the Fairy Queen's private trencher (3.5.65), pickpockets as punitive fairies, a mugging as a purifying ritual, a whore as the Queen herself, and an instruction to "Kiss her departing part" (5.4.57) as evidence of her royal favor. Subtle and Dol each shift the play's blank verse briefly into rhyme to lend a properly poetical atmosphere (3.5.5–18; 5.4.30–31), and even the pinching that punishes Dapper for withholding a few coins is kept in line with literary precedents. The conspirators' accompanying cries of "Ti, ti, ti, ti" were evidently conventional noises for theatrical fairies, and the physical battery matches those described in *John a Kent and John a Cumber,* in Shakespeare's *Merry Wives of Windsor,* and in Lyly's *Endimion:*

> Pinch him, pinch him, blacke and blue,
> Sawcie mortalls must not view
> What the Queene of Stars is doing,
> Nor pry into our Fairy woing
>
> . . . . .
>
> For the trespasse hee hath donne,
> Spots ore all his flesh shall runne.[8]

What makes Dapper's pitiful cry near the end of the play so funny— "For God's sake, when will her Grace be at leisure?" (5.3.64)— is our recognition that this pathetic figure, whom we and the conspirators have long forgotten, has been clinging to his ridiculous dream all this time amidst the choking stench of the privy, and speaks up only in a mannerly way that seeks not to offend the goddess who offered him this lodging and this provender. The fact that he has been forgotten and must shout his plea from somewhere backstage is part of the same joke as his specific delusion about the fairy queen: the play he imagines is simply not being performed on this stage on this day. Not even Lovewit's return can shatter his fantasy: when Dapper leaves Jonson's stage for the final time, the fairy tale is still running vividly (and expensively) on the stage of his mind (5.4.57–61).

The second gull to appear, Abel Drugger, is virtually the opposite of Dapper. Their names are similar in sound, and their gullibilities similar in extent, but where Dapper is the model of the young wastrel, Drugger is the model of the young worker, diligently striving to improve himself through commerce. So where the conspirators cast Dapper as the dashing young gallant, forever thriving at child's play, winning card games and fairy queens alike, they cast Drugger instead as the model of middle-class success, forever thriving in adult works. He is encouraged to imagine himself the hero of a Dekker play about virtue overcoming social rank, or perhaps more extensively, as the hero of a Deloney novel from the same period, about a hard-working young man propelling himself up through the social classes by his shrewd mercantile enterprises, and by the upward misalliance they permit. Where Dapper is supposedly allied to the Queen of Fairy, Drugger is promised alliance to the "rich young widow" next door (2.6.29–30). Face has evidently anticipated Drugger's dubiety and adapts it into another extension of Drugger's characteristic dream of social climbing:

> *Drugger*    No, sir, she'll never marry
> Under a knight. Her brother has made a vow.
> *Face*   What, and dost thou despair, my little Nab,
> Knowing what the Doctor has set down for thee,
> And seeing so many o' the city dubbed?          (2.6.50–54)

If this is a risky piece of satire on King James's selling of knighthoods, it is also an effective satire on the wish fulfillments that lesser authors were selling to the middle class.

From his first appearance, Drugger speaks in the humble, earnest, determined tones of one of Deloney's Horatio Algers beginning his upward journey:

> I am a young beginner, and am building
> Of a new shop, an't like your worship, just
> At corner of a street. Here's the plot on 't—
> And I would know by art, sir, of your worship,
> Which way I should make my door, by necromancy.
> And where my shelves? And which should be for boxes?
> And which for pots? I would be glad to thrive, sir.
> And I was wished to your worship by a gentleman,
> One Captain Face, that says you know men's planets,
> And their good angels, and their bad.          (1.3.7–16)

The polysyndeton of Drugger's speech seems to be a representation of his vision of a steadily building commercial success, and the tasks in which he wants to enlist Subtle's "necromancy" are ridiculously common and simple. Subtle agrees that he does know men's angels, and he is telling the truth, not only in his ability to recognize cozenable coins ("angels"), but also in his ability to recognize and thus manipulate the dominant spirits possessing each of the gulls. What Drugger supposes is the voice of his good angel is actually a reading from the popular literature of the time. Face, who knows exactly what conventional commercial virtues Drugger has been trained to value in himself, gains his victim's trust by mimicking that voice:

> This is my friend, Abel, an honest fellow,
> He lets me have good tobacco, and he does not
> Sophisticate it with sack-lees or oil,
> Nor washes it in muscadel and grains,
> Nor buries it in gravel underground,
> Wrapped up in greasy leather, or pissed clouts,
> But keeps it in fine lily pots that, opened,
> Smell like conserve of roses, or French beans.
> He has his maple block, his silver tongs,
> Winchester pipes, and fires of juniper.
> A neat, spruce, honest fellow, and no goldsmith.
>
> (1.3.22–32)

If this sounds like a commercial advertisement, it is because that is how Drugger enjoys picturing himself, standing with a friendly open face in front of all the finest products and all the latest equipment. The fate Subtle then predicts for him—"This summer / He will be of the clothing of his company, / And next spring called to the scarlet," with some greater fortune thereafter (1.3.35–37)— is the same ascension through peer and public ranks that characterized the hero's rise in Deloney's novels and in plays such as Dekker's *The Shoemakers' Holiday,* and was promised to the diligent Golding in *Eastward Ho*. Drugger will be "the honestest fellow" and "the goodest soul"—provided he brings Subtle "a new damask suit" and a pound of tobacco (2.6.72–79); the conspirators characteristically arrange things so that Drugger must pay them to confirm his secretly treasured image of himself. That image which would have been gloriously affirmed in one of the Lord Mayor's shows, becomes ridiculous in the context of satiric city-comedy. Near the end of the play Face sends Drugger off to acquire the costume of a Spanish nobleman and asks if he is well enough acquainted with the players to borrow one. "Yes, sir;" Drugger replies, "did you never see me play the Fool?" (4.7.69). He plays the fool here again in Lovewit's house in Blackfriars precisely because he does not realize he is still playing—and the irony would have been even sharper if Drugger was played by Robert Armin, the leading clown of the King's Men, as has been suggested. His effort to recast himself as a citizen-hero out of Middleton, Heywood, Dekker, or Deloney has only renewed his employment as a fool in Face's and Jonson's plays.[9]

The arrival of Kastril and his sister allows the conspirators to produce profitably some other conventional plays. Though apparently rustic and illiterate, Kastril carries within him a jumble of impulses that look suspiciously like the propelling motives of several late Elizabethan dramas. He aspires to be the "Roaring Boy" of many popular comedies and ballads, and he aggrandizes that role for himself by associating it with the tragic role of avenger, defending his family's honor as well as his own from the seductive wiles and the social slights of more urbane fellows. He has arrived seeking not only a roaring reputation for himself, but also a match for his widowed sister that will, he says grandly, "advance the house of the Kastrils" (4.4.88). Dame Pliant seems to envisage herself in such a comedy of dynastic marriage: when Subtle reads in her palm that she will soon marry "a soldier, or a man of art" who "shall have some great honor shortly," she tells her brother, "He's a rare man, believe me," suggesting that Subtle's fortune-telling has indeed matched her own dreams of the future (4.2.48–50).

The wrath of the Puritans also suffers from a literary taint. Ananias zealously fulfills the Biblical story to which his name alludes by refusing to trust all of his money to the grand scheme, and when he finds the Brethren cheated by their own greed, he curses from his book as much as from his heart. He places on Lovewit's theatrical edifice an absurdly reduced version of the curses visited on Pharaoh's Egypt: "may dogs defile thy walls, / And wasps and hornets breed beneath thy roof, / This seat of falsehood, and this cave of coz'nage" (5.5.113–115). Jonson's point may be that, even while pronouncing some of the standard Puritan accusations against theaters, Ananias is himself unwittingly involved in a dramatic pose, a pose that is less effective than Lovewit's because it is less conscious of its own theatricality.

His pastor, Tribulation Wholesome, is a more worthy ancestor to the great hypocrite of *Bartholomew Fair,* Zeal-of-the-Land Busy. Tribulation gladly interprets Subtle's abuses as merely part of a divine drama to test the Puritans with martyrdom in this world and thereby redeem them for the next:

> These chastisements are common to the Saints,
> And such rebukes we of the Separation
> Must bear, with willing shoulders, as the trials
> Sent forth to tempt our frailties.                    (3.1.1–4)

Busy chooses to perceive Bartholomew Fair as Vanity Fair only for the purpose of indulging gluttony. Tribulation's pious patience similarly conceals his real goal of monetary profit, and Jonson is openly scornful of the Puritan rationale that a holy end justifies worldly means. The term "hypocrite" was applied both to Puritans and to actors in Jonson's time, and here the two usages work together with devastating satiric effect.

Before either the Kastrils or the Puritans arrive on the scene, however, Sir Epicure Mammon has achieved levels of romantic and pietistic self-dramatization that they can never hope to equal. Even the role of public benefactor, which he may originally have assumed in order to conceal his selfish purposes from the supposedly pious alchemist, appeals so strongly to Mammon's conventional vanity that he becomes absorbed in it. His visions of great innovations are, paradoxically, precisely what prove him to be a disastrously conventional thinker. Subtle introduces him as a man who has been talking of the stone for the past month

> as he were possessed.
> And now he's dealing pieces on 't away.
> Methinks I see him ent'ring ordinaries,
> Dispensing for the pox; and plaguy houses,
> Reaching his dose; walking the Moorfields for lepers,
> And off'ring citizens' wives pomander-bracelets
> As his preservative, made of the elixir;
> Searching the 'spital, to make old bawds young;
> And the highways for beggars to make rich.
> I see no end of his labors. He will make
> Nature ashamed of her long sleep, when art,
> Who's but a step-dame, shall do more than She

In Her best love to mankind ever could.
If his dream last, he'll turn the age to gold.     (1.4.16–29)

When Subtle says, "Methinks I see him," he is mockingly evoking the ridiculously worshipful way Mammon envisions himself in these holy enterprises. The only thing turned to gold by the endurance of this dream will be Subtle's pockets. But the mental picture Mammon has of his own magnificent deeds is very much a mediated vision, shaped by Renaissance literature. The Elizabethan theater, as Bradbrook has demonstrated, was obsessed with the idea of restoring the Golden Age.[10] Mammon is indeed "possessed," by a naive misreading of the more grandiose writings of his era.

Mammon at moments seems to perceive himself as the kind of modern savior who appeared frequently in Jacobean poetry: the spiritual, scientific, or sensual creator of a new world for this new age. Jonson evidently considered such a figure an unhealthy literary fantasy.[11] Mammon's claim that he will have the power to "make an old man of fourscore a child" (2.1.53), already degraded by Subtle's earlier suggestion that Mammon will use the stone to "make old bawds young," clearly resembles the heroine's promise to "make the old man young" in Jonson's "Celebration of Charis" (1,l.20), a poetic sequence that satirizes the fatuous claims of Renaissance love lyricists. As Mammon first speaks, he reveals the accuracy of Subtle's parody, describing himself to Surly as the potential embodiment of all Renaissance aspirations, in exploration, wealth, pomp, and pleasure:

Come on, sir. Now you set your foot on shore
In Novo Orbe; here's the rich Peru,
And there within, sir, are the golden mines,
Great Solomon's Ophir!

. . . . .
                You shall start up young viceroys,
And have your punks and punkatees, my Surly.
And unto thee I speak it first, "Be Rich."     (2.1.1–24)

Mammon echoes the *fiat lux* of Creation here, but he is no better a God than he is a Redeemer.[12] Despite his richly festooned language, he cannot envision a world beyond the extremes of human greed and lust. Mammon, like everyone else, cannot serve both God and Mammon.

Mammon gradually becomes a recognizably Marlovian character, a Tamburlaine in his thirst for universal conquest, a Barabas in his absolute greed, a Faustus in his determination magically to reshape the world according to his desires.[13] The irony is that he plays the parts of these characters too well, especially that of Faustus. He unwittingly sells, if not his eternal jewel, at least his temporal ones, for a conquest of nature that can never quite lift him above mundane physical objects and mundane human appetites. Mammon's true potential is as limited as that of Faustus, who managed only to perform some slapstick violence and to acquire fresh grapes out of season. Face says that Mammon

> would ha' built
> The city new; and made a ditch about it
> Of silver, should have run with cream from Hogsden;
> That every Sunday in Moorfields the younkers
> And tits and tom-boys should have fed on, gratis.
>
> (5.5.76–80)

This version of Faustus' plan to erect a brass wall around Germany, and of Roger Bacon's similar project in *Friar Bacon and Friar Bungay*, is absurdly domesticated.[14] Mammon's instincts as a worldly sensualist thus mar not only his performance as a magnificent conjurer, but also his performance as a creating deity.

At the very least, he envisions himself as one of the London Worthies exalted in moralistic chronicle plays such as Thomas Heywood's *Edward IV* and *If You Know Not Me, You Know Nobody*. In advocating his grand projects of urban renewal, Mammon repeatedly mouths "the citizen-hero code of social conduct" that had become a conventional heroic signature in Elizabethan drama.[15] Mammon speaks in texts the way possessed souls speak in tongues. His mind is like an editor's nightmare: the texts are garbled, and legible only as a series of overlapping palimpsests. Mammon is approximately six characters in search of a single authentic identity. Surly tells him that, if he can indeed eliminate the plague, "the players shall sing your praises then, / Without their poets" (2.1.71–72), but Mammon is himself a player who has forgotten his author.

When Mammon tries to prove to Surly that his grand visions

are realistic, he constantly resorts to literary models which he carelessly assumes are historical. His carelessness about that distinction reveals not only his determination to believe in the stories that would make him heroic, but also the mode of misreading by which that belief primarily sustains itself:

> I'll show you a book where Moses, and his sister,
> And Solomon have written of the art;
> Ay, and a treatise penned by Adam.
> . . . . .
>        I have a piece of Jason's fleece too,
> Which was no other than a book of alchemy,
> Writ in large sheepskin, a good fat ram-vellum.
> Such was Pythagoras' thigh, Pandora's tub;
> And all that fable of Medea's charms
> The manner of our work:
> . . . . .
> Both this, th' Hesperian garden, Cadmus' story,
> Jove's shower, the boon of Midas, Argus' eyes,
> Boccacé his Demogorgon, thousands more,
> All abstract riddles of our stone.      (2.1.81–104)

The fantasy Mammon has drawn from his readings now shapes all his readings to itself; there is a warning here for critics who heap up instances without examining the validity of their grand unifying theses. He seems to be as much compelled to believe by the glorious heritage his belief provides him, as he is allowed to believe by the existence of such vague precedents.

In the next scene Mammon announces his intention "To have a list of wives and concubines / Equal with Solomon," and to satisfy them by improving his body "With the elixir" until it is "as tough / As Hercules' " (2.2.34–40). Again he is confusing the pursuit of personal physical desires with the pursuit of experiences and identities transmitted by literature.[16] Mammon manages to become enthralled by the voluptuous roles he plays for Surly and Dol, as well as by the contrastingly pietistic role he plays for Subtle; he deludes himself, as he had thought to delude others, with the false glamour the allusions lend to his appetites. The self-alienation of Mammon's self-regard, the fact that he is admiring himself in poses rather than participating directly in the experience of desiring, is further evinced by his narcissistic plan to have his bedroom mirrors "Cut in more subtle angles, to disperse / And multiply the figures as I walk / Naked between my succubae" (2.2.46–48). Even more than Volpone, he lets literature mediate between himself and the most wanton indulgences of his senses: the notes in both the Gifford edition and the Herford, Simpson, and Simpson edition dissect Mammon's visions of pleasure into a string of allusions to Seneca, Suetonius, Aristophanes, Lampridius, Juvenal, Pliny, and Apicius Caelius. The multiple visual refractions of his self-regard correspond to multiple literary ones.

Mammon recurs several times to the comparison between his alchemical triumphs and "Jove's shower." That persistent comparison again reveals the confused grandeur of Mammon's self-conception. His magnificent gilding of the world becomes, through puns on "heighten" and "stone" as well as the overall allusion, a transparent cover for his sexual vanity:

> Now, Epicure,
> Heighten thyself, talk to her all in gold;
> Rain her as many showers as Jove did drops
> Unto his Danaë; show the god a miser
> Compared with Mammon. What! the stone will do't.
> She shall feel gold, taste gold . . .          (4.1.24–29)

A hundred lines later, the same allusion is clearly lurking in his mind, transforming his promise to fulfill Dol's wishes into a Rabelaisian display of sexual megalomania:

> Think, therefore, thy first wish now; let me hear it,
> And it shall rain into thy lap, no shower
> But floods of gold, whole cataracts, a deluge,
> To get a nation on thee.          (4.1.125–128)

The role of gold-maker is conflated, by the mythic allusion, with the role of superhuman lover; and that confusion is precisely what the conspirators use to make Mammon actually apologize to them for the disappearance of his own money and hopes in the laboratory "explosion." Mammon strikes the poses of Neoplatonic, Petrarchan, and Metaphysical love-poet, telling Dol that she "sparkles a divinity beyond / An earthly beauty!" and that he desires only "To burn i' this sweet flame: / The phoenix never knew a nobler death." "O, you play the courtier," is her chiding reply (4.1.64–69), but Mammon can no longer distinguish himself and his sentiments from his various ennobling literary roles. He becomes a gathering of seductive clichés. His arguments against the propriety of virginity for a beautiful woman had been literary commonplaces for centuries, and that derivativeness (as with the similar arguments of Milton's Comus) is part of Jonson's point. The hyperbolic sensual inducements with which Mammon bolsters his rational arguments are (like the ones Volpone offers Celia) commonplaces in the Renaissance catalogue of exotic and exalting pleasures (4.1.96–107, 155–169). Their love affair is to be the living fulfillment of countless old love stories—"we but showing our love, / Nero's Poppaea may be lost in story!" (4.1.144–145)—but that ambition risks converting the affair itself into little more than a literary artifact.

The disaster that befalls this courtship, like the disaster that consequently befalls his pursuit of the philosophers' stone, is a poetically just punishment for the narcissistic use of literary allusions. At some point Mammon's bookish promises inadvertently echo a forbidden book, Broughton's *Concent of Scripture,* by promising to erect her "a fifth monarchy" (4.5.34), and Dol spits back at him her own mad concoction of that and other literature, as if she were Spenser's Dragon of Error vomiting theological tracts on a similarly erroneous knight. It is also fitting that Mammon understands this disaster as poetic justice, but of the sort found in the most conventional moral tale rather than in Jonson's satiric comedy. He interprets as a divine judgment against his lust what is actually a fraudulent exploitation of his literary infatuation (4.5.82–86). The same bookishly self-important sensibility that led him into the alchemical fraud now leads him back out of it without the least sense that he has been cheated. Face finally convinces him to flee empty-handed for fear that to stay "may breed a tragedy" (4.5.91). Even after he learns exactly how he has been gulled, his instinctive reaction is not to renounce all theatricalism, but rather (like Sordido in *Every Man Out of His Humor*) merely to seize a new kind of role on a new kind of stage: "I will go mount a turnip-cart and preach / The end o' the world, within these two months" (5.5.81–82).

Mammon's companion Surly appears to be his opposite, as gruff as Mammon is grandiloquent, as skeptical as Mammon is gullible, and (despite his knowledge of bawdy-houses) almost as anhedonic as Mammon is epicurean. The irony is that Surly is nearly as enamored of his own laconic cynicism as Mammon is of his encompassing visions, and may therefore be gulled through his pride in refusing to be gulled. He resembles Edmund Wilson's image of Jonson in his anal-retentive concern with control, but Jonson's devotion to varied and vivid language contrasts sharply with Surly's monotonous speech, which suggests an overly repressive spirit.[17] Surly resorts again and again to his blunt phrase of resistance to Mammon's sort of letting go. "I would not willingly be gulled," he says (2.1.78); he tells Subtle that he "would not be gulled" (2.3.27), swears he will not "gull myself" (2.3.124), says he is "loath to be gulled" (2.3.263), and urges Mammon to "Be not gulled" (2.3.246) and not "To gull himself" (2.3.282). This is a provocation to both the conspirators and the audience to gull the poor man, much as the wits in *Bartholomew Fair* are provoked to rob Wasp by his nagging censures of Cokes's carelessness. Subtle afterward echoes Surly's phrase (and, in performance, probably his voice also) in gleefully speculating on ways to fool this "Monsieur Caution, that will not be gulled" (2.4.15; cf. 2.3.236); the artist in Subtle knows that "to ha' gulled him / Had been a mast'ry" (3.3.7–8).

Surly perceives that Lovewit's house has become a sort of exploitative theater, with the conspirators' baseness hidden under the grandest disguises. He properly identifies Dol as simply a whore, whereas Mammon has characteristically identified her as "a Bradamante" (2.3.225), a woman knight from Ariosto's *Orlando Furioso*. Face comments that Mammon experiences "A kind of modern happiness, to have / Dol Common for a great lady" (4.1.23–24). It is also a kind of theatrical happiness—to have a boy in secondhand garments for Cleopatra, for example—and Surly is deeply unwilling to suspend his disbelief. He comes to sound less like an incisive critic of this play, however, than like its moralistic chorus:

> Heart! can it be
> That a grave sir, a rich, that has no need,
> A wise sir, too, at other times, should thus
> With his own oaths and arguments make hard means
> To gull himself?
> . . . . .
> I'll have gold before you,

And with less danger of the quicksilver,
Or the hot sulphur. (2.3.278–288)

The closing suggestion that Mammon's trust in this house exposes him to both alchemical frauds and venereal disease[18] has been phrased in such a way that it also resembles the warning of an old-fashioned dramatic chorus, aptly like that of *Doctor Faustus*, about the danger of hellfire.

Surly's response to the false drama he has largely penetrated is to begin writing a moralistic drama of his own. His observations that "The hay is a-pitching" in Subtle's delaying jargon, and that Mammon is "bolted" when he assents to the workings of this "ferret," reveal Surly's fixation on the conventional rabbit-hunting metaphor of coney-catching stories (2.3.71–88). He then begins to speak to the audience in sly asides, like the outcast protagonists of Elizabethan revenge tragedies. But the fact that the role of Hieronimo from Kyd's *Spanish Tragedy* is mentioned so dismissively throughout Jonson's play augurs very badly for Surly's plan to take the role of a Spaniard and overthrow the villains by constructing his own play-within-Face's-play. Surly promises to meet Face, but tells us it will only be

by attorney, and to a second purpose.
Now I am sure it is a bawdy-house;
I'll swear it, were the marshal here to thank me:
The naming this commander doth confirm it.
Don Face!
. . . . .
Him will I prove, by a third person, to find
The subtleties of this dark labyrinth;
Which if I do discover, dear Sir Mammon,
You'll give your poor friend leave, though no philosopher,
To laugh; for you that are, 't is thought, shall weep.
(2.3.297–311)

He will laugh at how deeply Mammon was enthralled by an aggrandized vision of himself, but the way he envisions that triumph suggests much the same narcissistic error.

Surly returns to Lovewit's house prepared to defeat the conspirators at their own game by seizing a position one level deeper into the dramatic irony than theirs. His Spanish costume and language will serve to penetrate their disguises and outflank their alchemical cant. Subtle and Face's usual tactic of plotting their tricks right in front of the gulls in alchemical allegories backfires because the disguised Surly fully understands the English they suppose is foreign to him. But Surly is nonetheless defeated, and he is defeated because he is out of tune with the intentions of his creator. Most editors have remarked how unabashedly Jonson borrows from Plautus here; my suspicion is that Jonson wants us to recognize the borrowing so that he can use the secondhand-edness of Surly's behavior in an allegorical way. Surly has in effect dutifully memorized a role from the *Poenulus,* the role of Hanno, who rescues a young woman from a thieving procurer after stra-tegically feigning ignorance of his native language and enduring the consequent abuse.[19] But when he tries to perform the trium-phant part of his role, Surly discovers to his humiliation that Jonson has chosen to present a version of a different Plautine comedy, the *Mostellaria,* in which a wily servant (Face's ancestor) escapes with the benefits of his chicanery. Neither Jonson nor his characters are interested in letting Surly recite the victorious lines he has so proudly prepared.

In his conference with Dame Pliant, Surly makes the mistake of supposing that, as a sort of morality-play Good Counsel figure to this jeopardized female soul, he can and simply should bring the exploitative play to an end. A Jacobean audience would also have expected such a virtuous reversal at about this point in the play, like the one Wittipol provides at a similar juncture in *The Devil Is an Ass,* rescuing the good woman from both gulls and gullers without preying on her himself.[20] Once he is alone with Dame Pliant, Surly is too obsessed with the notion of his glorious reversal of the plot to act with any spontaneous self-interest or to consider that this distressed damsel might be just a silly girl in-capable of sustaining her part in the noble scene he had envi-sioned.[21] The fact that Lovewit cleverly seduces her away from Surly both completes and represents the triumph of Jonson's more modern and satiric type of plot.

Like Dapper earlier, Surly fully expects the standard reward of a reformed gamester in Jacobean drama—a wealthy widow—to be bestowed on him in a grand scenario of just deserts:

> I am a gentleman, come here disguised,
> Only to find the knaveries of this citadel,

> And where I might have wronged your honor, and have not,
> I claim some interest in your love. You are,
> They say, a widow, rich; and I am a bachelor,
> Worth nought. Your fortunes may make me a man,
> As mine ha' preserved you a woman. Think upon it,
> And whether I have deserved you or no.
> *Dame Pliant*                              I will, sir.
> *Surly*   And for these household-rogues, let me alone
> To treat with them.                                   (4.6.8–17)

This sententiousness is so far removed from Surly's normal identity as to suggest the self-exalting, self-dramatizing impulse Jonson usually felt obliged to punish; in this sense, my view corresponds to the theory that Surly loses because (as a gamester) he is not moral enough for Jonson to permit him the victory.[22] As Lovewit suggests later, Surly was foolish to play such an elaborate and calculated role in courtship and then not follow it through immediately into a profitable marriage (5.5.50–55). When Surly triumphantly throws off his disguise—"I am the Spanish Don that should be cozened"—he is too enthralled with his heroic revelations to notice the accused Face slipping away under cover of the melodramatic rhetoric. Surly is another character who disastrously forgets that his is not the only plot, not the only play, evolving on this particular stage.

Face is wiser in the ways of combining multiple plots. While Surly is complacently casting himself as the hero of the moral comedy playing in his mind, Face concentrates instead on casting Surly as the villain of the formulaic dramas playing in the minds of various other characters. Since Kastril sees himself as a roaring-boy hero who defends his family's honor against intriguers, Face tells him that Surly is the enemy for whom his quarreling skills have been developed, a dishonorable seducer of his sister (4.7.1–3). The fact that Kastril then calls Surly "an Amadis de Gaul, or a Don Quixote" (4.7.40) indicates how successful Face has been in making Kastril perceive Surly as merely a representative foreign opponent for the sort of duel exalted in Renaissance romances. Face similarly convinces Drugger that "This cheater would ha' cozened thee o' the widow" (4.7.29), enlisting Drugger's hackneyed dreams of marrying up into a higher class to cast Surly again in the role of discovered villain—the more so because Surly now appears to be the well-born wastrel who always opposes Drugger's industrious social climber in Elizabethan popular literature. Then the Puritan Ananias arrives, and (after some confusion of language that parallels the confusion of plots) Subtle convinces Ananias that Kastril's motive is

> Zeal in the young gentleman,
> Against his Spanish slops—
> *Ananias* They are profane,
> Lewd, superstitious, and idolatrous breeches.
> *Surly* New rascals!
> *Kastril* Will you be gone, sir?
> *Ananias* Avoid, Sathan,
> Thou art not of the light. That ruff of pride
> About thy neck betrays thee, and is the same
> With that which the unclean birds, in seventy-seven,
> Were seen to prank it with on divers coasts.
> Thou look'st like Antichrist in that lewd hat.
> *Surly* I must give way. (4.7.47–56)

He must give way, not because they are "new rascals," but because they are parts of other old plays. His choice of a dandified Spanish costume is unfortunate, because it encourages Drugger to interpret him as a rival for Dame Pliant, Kastril to interpret him as a quarreling enemy, and Ananias to interpret him as a Catholic and therefore as the Satanic enemy against whom Puritans directed their internal melodramas. Surly had planned to call an end to all their plays by injecting truth and common sense into Lovewit's house, but (like Overdo and Busy in *Bartholomew Fair*) he finds himself absorbed into their plays instead. Face's satiric awareness of humanity's self-dramatizing impulses thus triumphs over Surly's conventional ethical impulse, and that victory asserts symbolically the victory of Jonson's strategic satire over more naively moralistic comedy.[23]

What would serve as the conclusion of many more ordinary didactic plays—Surly's detection of the abuses and his gallant rescue of the maiden—thus becomes merely another plot put into suspension, an interruption that serves to emphasize Jonson's special insight into human nature. Surly's failure forces him to recognize that people would rather be told grand ridiculous lies about their own splendor than plain moral truths about their own folly.

He may therefore again represent the pertinacious and surly artist of social reform that Jonson felt compelled to abandon in himself.[24] The defeat of Surly may be read as a surrender in Jonson's campaign against the evils of Renaissance society, even while representing a new front in Jonson's campaign against the complacency of Renaissance drama. In Jonson's earlier humors comedies a debunking reformer such as Surly might have been the ultimate victor, but here Jonson seems to be playing off his own conventions. Surly's case of the self-dramatizing disease involves a new, mutant strain: he becomes fatally enraptured with his role as Jonson's vindicated skeptic. Perhaps Surly's overconfidence comes from *mistaking* himself for the author's surrogate.

Jonson's characteristic *catastasis,* where the plot pauses near a false resolution, thus subserves a critical argument. In his Preface to the Quarto edition of *The Alchemist* (and in a virtually identical passage in his *Discoveries*), Jonson vividly asserts his superiority over his competitors and their admirers: "For they commend writers as they do fencers or wrestlers, who, if they come in robustiously and put for it with a great deal of violence, are received for the braver fellows; when many times their own rudeness is the cause of their disgrace, and a little touch of their adversary gives all that boisterous force the foil."[25] The scene in which Surly's counterplot brings Face's scheme momentarily to a halt serves as a kind of slow-motion replay of this subtle touch, a touch that (like a judo-throw) uses the headlong enthusiasm of naive melodrama against itself. The moment between Surly's triumphant revelations and his ultimate defeat serves to crystallize our expectations so that Jonson may crush them all the more effectively. He is marking a division that parallels the distinction between conventional comedies and his own.

The false crisis in Jonson's plot has obliged the conspirators to bring all of their plots into collision, instead of keeping them carefully apart as before. The question is what plot will remain running at the end of this literary demolition derby. Drugger, who has had enough theatrical experience to "play the Fool," is dispatched to borrow "Hieronimo's old cloak, ruff, and hat" from the players so that he may properly court Dame Pliant (4.7.64–71). Face evidently has plans to steal this role (4.7.99–100), and it is probably significant that Jonson himself had been mocked in Dekker's *Satiro-mastix* for having borrowed such a costume when he played Hieronimo.[26] Face and Jonson now seem poised to work together, using popular dramatic conventions against the former's gulls and the latter's literary rivals.

But this last flurry of dramatic artifice is interrupted by the return of the real master to this house-turned-theater and is later exploited by him for his own financial and sexual benefit. To meet him, Face must return to an original identity that seems to have become essentially another costumed role: "I'll into mine old shape again, and meet him, / Of Jeremy the butler" (4.7.120–121). There is an intriguing suggestion here of an actor removing part of his mask to deliver an apologetic epilogue to an audience, and the fifth act may indeed be taken as a subversive afterword to the complete moral comedy Surly attempted to conclude. Lovewit is the audience for this afterword, and Jonson invites the gentleman-wits of the Blackfriars audience to identify with Lovewit in order to enlist their support in the overthrow of naive playwrights such as Surly.[27] Face achieves the usual purpose of an epilogue by bestowing his praise and his profits on Lovewit, as a reward for Lovewit's forgiving the cynical plot in which Face usurped his house and humiliatingly plundered the gulls: the audience, to earn an analogous reward, must forgive the analogous usurpation of their playhouse by Jonson's satiric comedy, with its thieving humiliation of conventional playwrights.

The fifth act opens with Lovewit's neighbors playing the parts of dim-witted reviewers, milling around just outside the house with vague and shifting reports about the strange events and personages that had filled it in his absence. Face almost succeeds in ending the show there and denying any misbehavior, except that Dapper has been left in the middle of his fairy tale, which he now pathetically pleads to finish. Face tries to lure Lovewit into unwittingly reenacting the scene from Plautus' *Mostellaria* in which the wily servant Tranio diverts his suddenly returned master from entering the house that has been converted to immoral purposes in his absence. The echo of earlier literature may again be read as an adaptation by a character rather than by the author. Face's remark about his "guilty conscience" (5.2.47) makes sense only as an excerpt from that role, not as an expression of his own character. His insistence that Surly must have the wrong house is directly out of Plautus, as is his boast that he has diverted Lovewit by warning him that "the house is haunted."[28]

But where Theopropides temporarily accepts Tranio's warning that the house is haunted, Lovewit immediately dismisses Face's typically melodramatic suggestion that Dapper's cry proves the house has been visited by "some spirit o' the air" as well as by the plague. In place of this old tale, Lovewit demands "The truth, the shortest way" (5.3.66–74). To prevent Surly's conventional conclusion from triumphing by revealing the blunt facts to everyone, or the play from ending with none of the plots satisfyingly resolved, Face must ask permission to extend the fiction a short while longer and to cast Lovewit as yet another performer assigned to the role of the wooing Spanish count (5.3.87).

Lovewit evidently decides that his servant's plot is good enough to merit his playing a part in it. He answers the furious attack on his doors much as Face had answered it three scenes earlier, when Lovewit himself had been the assailant: "Hold, gentlemen, what means this violence?" (5.5.10). Several of the gulls have returned to demand a proper conclusion to the plots that had lured them to this house in Blackfriars. They behave like the spectators at early performances of Ibsen's *A Doll's House,* who refused to believe that the play was really over at the final curtain, since Nora had not yet returned penitently to her family as convention dictated. Jonson's onstage spectators at least want an opportunity to hiss the company for its expensive and unsatisfying performance of their preconceived scripts, but they cannot even agree on the cast of characters:

> *Mammon*   Where is this collier?
> *Surly*                           And my Captain Face?
> *Mammon*   These day-owls.
> *Surly*                           That are birding in men's purses.
> *Mammon*   Madam Suppository.
> *Kastril*                      Doxy, my suster.
> *Ananias*                                   Locusts
>   Of the foul pit.
> *Tribulation*          Profane as Bel and the Dragon.
>                                                    (5.5.11–14)

Lovewit sees the advantage he can derive from the plots Face has multiplied and driven into conflict and simply asks,

>                             Whom do you seek?
> *Mammon*   The chemical cozener.

| | |
|---|---|
| *Surly* | And the captain pander. |
| *Kastril*   The nun my suster. | |
| *Mammon* | Madam Rabbi. |
| *Ananias* | Scorpions, |
| And caterpillars. | (5.5.18–21) |

This is a sort of Globe of Babel, a chaotic mixture of generic vocabularies. The officers would have to arrest the tiring-house to satisfy these accusations, and even then the evidence would be hard to find, since the costumes are finally provided as much by the desiring imaginations of the gulls as by the shreds of disguise used by the conspirators.

Jonson's audience is left with an easy choice between identifying with these fools in demanding a conventional resolution of the plot, or identifying instead with the aptly named Lovewit and endorsing Jonson's satirical structure that gives innovative wit precedence over standard morality. All the vestigial plots have degenerated into self-parodies, and Lovewit provides Jonson's own sort of conclusion, forgiving the witty for the sake of their wit and punishing the fools with their own folly. He wraps up the loose ends, not only by playing the courting Spaniard with more alacrity and effect than Drugger or Surly, but also by out-quarreling Kastril, by shamelessly seizing all the wealth that Mammon (now ashamed of his greed) had greedily brought to the house, and by cozening Dol and Subtle out of the profits that cozenage had gathered there. As one critic notes, Lovewit "acts like a roguish parody of a romantic protagonist,"[29] and he triumphs over the others because he is fully aware that he is performing a parody rather than a heroic role. He earns our intimacy largely by keeping his satiric distance from the grandiose temptations of his position up on stage.[30]

This theatrical self-consciousness gives Lovewit an obvious advantage over the gulls. What is less obvious, but no less crucial, is the advantage it gives him over the conspirators. Subtle and Dol suffer from a milder form of the self-aggrandizing, self-dramatizing disease that they exploit in their victims, and it leads to their downfall; even Face may not be entirely immune. The disasters that eventually befall the conspiracy at the hands of Surly and Lovewit demonstrate that even such expert plotters sometimes overlook the possibility of another, ultimate plot beyond their own: the conspirators, like their victims, are in headlong pursuit of financial profits and sexual pleasures that may disappear "in fume" with the collapse of the alchemical-theatrical artifice.

Through four acts the conspirators are masters of the stage, and their plots evince a Jonsonian talent for subsuming more conventional plots. In the final act they are still busy sorting the pelf they gained by playing to the melodramatic appetites of a seemingly unlimited supply of gulls: a jewel from a waiting-maid who wanted to know "if she should have precedence of her mistress," a whistle from a woman who wanted to know whether her husband was at sea with the great pirate Ward, and so on (5.4.110–116). (It is worth noting that at least one melodrama on the subject of Ward's adventures, Daborne's *A Christian Turn'd Turk*, had appeared on London's stages shortly before *The Alchemist* was written.)[31] Subtle and Dol even try to convert Lovewit's return into a convenient development in their plot to cheat the cheater Face. But when the master returns to his house in Blackfriars and retrieves it from the realm of conventional theater, those who converted others into actors are revealed as mere actors themselves. A number of critics have suggested that the conspirators must finally be replaced by Lovewit because their immorality is incompatible with the moral purpose of Jonsonian drama.[32] My analysis suggests something rather different: Lovewit replaces the conspirators not because he is more socially ethical but because he is more theatrically self-conscious.

The disguised Surly had nearly overthrown them all in the previous act by enlisting them in his play when they smugly assumed they had trapped him in theirs; Face's failure in the role of Tranio is another indication of the problem. A character who becomes too complacent about his role—even the role of comic manipulator—is at risk in Jonsonian comedy.[33] Plot devices very much like theirs succeed in earlier Renaissance plays such as Aretino's *Cortigiana*, where the wits give one gull a lowly woman pretending she is a noble match (as Dol was given to Surly) and rob and torture another gull pretending to prepare him for a promotion into glory (as Drugger and Dapper are robbed and tortured). The conspirators gloat over their conventional roles as diabolically clever fishers of men (2.4.1–4),[34] and Captain Face seems to assume some correspondence between his role and that of his nominal counterpart in Skelton's *Magnyfycence*, Counterfet Countenance, who brags of his ability to manufacture "counterfet captaynes," and to "Counterfet eyrnest by way of playes." Those plays resemble the stagecraft to which Face gives countenance in Lovewit's house:

A knave wyll counterfet nowe a knyght,
A lurdayne lyke a lorde to syght,
A mynstrell lyke a man of myght,
A tappster lyke a lady bryght:
Thus make I them wyth thryft to fyght.

In the next few lines this character refers to the "Counterfet kyndnesse," "Counterfet langage," and "counterfet coynes" he uses on his victims.[35]

Whether or not Jonson intended any direct allusion to Skelton, it seems clear that Jeremy conceives his role as Captain Face along the lines of a traditional stage Vice. Lois Potter has demonstrated that Vice characters in early English drama often appeared in groups of three, and that the term "Vice" may have referred not to sin, but rather to the "vizard" such characters present to the world.[36] This suggests a parallel to the "venter tripartite" of *The Alchemist*, and to the pseudonym "Face" chosen by its instigator. Face, as a petty schemer in a low farce, is in constant danger of mistaking himself for the grand diabolical tempter of a morality play. Even the stage action of Face's battle with Dame Pliant for control of Kastril during the Surly crisis would have been "reminiscent of the morality conflict of a vice and a virtue over a fateful decision to be made by mankind."[37]

There are hints from the very first lines of the play that the conspirators confuse drama with reality in self-aggrandizing ways. As John Mebane has suggested, the conflict arises because the conspirators are each willing to remind the others, but not to be reminded themselves, that "By assuming theatrical costumes and adopting an inflated jargon they have undergone illusory transformations to higher states of being."[38] The struggle over who will control the "venter tripartite" is actually a struggle over who will be allowed to assert that his pose is his real identity, and the effort to preserve the alliance is actually an effort to preserve their chief asset, which is a lively awareness of the distinction between role and reality. The conspirators vacillate constantly between playfully ironic role-playing and dangerously proud self-dramatizations. Several editors have observed that the opening exchange of insults between Face and Subtle closely resembles an exchange in the *Plutus* of Aristophanes.[39] Dol mollifies them with a literate allegory that makes her the republic (with a pun on *res publica*)[40] in which they play the roles of Sovereign and General. They will soon reward her, not with a cash bonus, but instead with a noble role from *The Mirror of Knighthood*: they tell her she has "Spoken like Claridiana, and thyself!" (1.1.87–88, 110, 175). A similar transaction occurs halfway through the play, when Dol greets Face by quoting an inquiry from *The Spanish Tragedy*, and he replies by calling her "My Dousabel," a typical name for a romance heroine (3.3.33, 41).

The implicit agreement to indulge each other's vain fantasies is necessarily a dangerous one in the context of this play. It holds the conspiracy together, but only by compromising its operating principle of superior realism. The "venter tripartite" finally falls into its own net. Dol aptly asks her partners in crime,

> Ha' you together cozened all this while,
> And all the world, and shall it now be said
> You've made most courteous shift to cozen yourselves?
>
> (1.1.122–124)

By the end of the play, Subtle and Dol will have done very much that: their vision of a triumphant escape is really only a degraded version of Mammon's dreams of unbounded voyages, riches, and sensual indulgences (5.4.74–91), and it is easily exploited by the superior plotters. Jeremy is fortunate that his master is Lovewit, and that his creator is a lover of classical New Comedy, which provides a successful role for a wily servant. He survives, but only by knowing when to stop playing and resume serving, only by surrendering his proud authority along with his Face.

*The Alchemist* ends with a brief Epilogue in which both Lovewit and Face, without moving completely out of character, apologize for any breaches of the conventional rules of drama. It is appropriately unclear, at the end of a play about the confusion of drama with life, whether they are apologizing as actors or as characters, and it would be risky, in a play so carefully positioned against the audience's mindless assertion of dramatic conventions, to accept such apologies at Face value. The only loose end left hanging in

this play of failed plots is a baited hook dangled in front of the
audience by the surviving plotter, Face. He coyly confesses to the
audience that

> My part a little fell in this last scene,
> Yet 'twas decorum. And though I am clean
> Got off from Subtle, Surly, Mammon, Dol,
> Hot Ananias, Dapper, Drugger, all
> With whom I traded; yet I put myself
> On you, that are my country; and this pelf
> Which I have got, if you do quit me, rests,
> To feast you often, and invite new guests.          (5.5.158–165)

It would be a bold audience indeed that dared to criticize Face's
creation, having seen the fate of all those who tried to out-plot
him. He offers to shape any number of new plays from these
various old plots, and the audience would be well advised to stand
aside as his benevolent patron until he invites them into the action,
never letting go of either their wallets or their intellectual alertness,
lest they suddenly discover they have become the complacent gulls
at whom they had been laughing. The only way to avoid being
a gullible guest at future sittings is to make league with the exploitative host. There is still an alchemist at work in the house in
Blackfriars, and he mocks the naive Londoners who gather there,
even while he transforms the base dramas they bring to him into
his own satiric gold.

# CHAPTER SIX

# Bartholomew Fair

## THE THEATER OF FORGIVENESS
## AND THE FORGIVENESS OF THEATER

The critical consensus on *Bartholomew Fair* (1614) is that it represents a radical departure for Jonson in its sheer generosity. What is new is not the wealth of material objects; they are present, at least in verbal form, in *Volpone* and *The Alchemist*. But Jonson has never before been as willing to admit that he enjoys those objects, and to allow us to enjoy them too without falling prey to his satire.[1] By depicting a carnival world that victimizes authority figures, *Bartholomew Fair* enables Jonson to subvert his own authoritarian attitudes toward literature and to relax his hierarchical constriction of the dramatic canon. The ending of the play is an endorsement, rather than a repression, of plays and playfulness. In terms of the parodic strategy described in this book, *Bartholomew Fair* both constitutes and chronicles Jonson's effort to abstain from his characteristic trumping of the dramatic cards of other playwrights. The parodic techniques do not disappear; instead, they themselves become one of the dramatic formulas the play accepts in a limited form. Several standard and specific precedents are suggested by, and humiliated in, characters onstage, and the way each act builds a complicated plot toward an anticlimax rather than a climax[2] recalls the pattern of allusion and decentering by which Jonson's earlier comedies attack their rivals. But at the moment when Jonson usually makes his satiric coup, his triumph of generic imperialism, he instead forgives all but the most censorious plots, and urges that even the silliest and most grotesquely conventional of plays be continued and enjoyed. Only those who would forbid

Jonson the privilege of writing his sort of play are forbidden to complete their own.

There are of course many ways to interpret this change. Perhaps Jonson had a genial change of heart; most of the fools in *Bartholomew Fair* are simply more likeable than those in the earlier comedies, and even the robberies and the physical violence seem more playful than cruel. Perhaps, after the triumphs of *Volpone* and *The Alchemist,* Jonson believed that his artistry and his new artistic mode no longer needed such fierce protection against their competitors. The most intriguing possibility, however, is that social circumstances compelled Jonson to turn his parodic strategy away from his dramatic rivals, and toward the censorious forces that were threatening to close down all the theaters. He may have found himself uncomfortably close to supporting those Puritan attacks, because his parodic strategy depended on portraying, in a grotesquely literal form, the same tendency that was the basis of a standard complaint against the popular theater: the tendency of spectators to imitate the less than ideal behavior they witness on stage.[3] In this way, Jonson had become of the Puritans' party without knowing it, an unwitting witness for the prosecution.

This disturbing alliance would help to explain why Jonson shifts the emphasis in *Bartholomew Fair* away from the specific absurdities perpetrated by his fellow playwrights, and onto the fact "that since theatricality is everywhere it is pointless to object to the stage as if it presented a unique moral threat."[4] Such unmistakably virtuous books as Elizabethan prodigal son narratives, Cicero's *Orations,* Whetstone's *Mirror for Magistrates of Cities* (1584), and even the Bible, prove capable of corrupting such men as Wasp, Overdo, and Busy; the fault is not in men's plays, but in themselves, if they are fools. Theater is not in itself a cause or a version of idolatry, as the Puritans charged;[5] the only danger, and one for which satiric city-comedy certainly cannot be blamed, is the tendency of human beings to seek out fantastic structures that indulge their desire to idolize themselves. Jonson repeatedly insists that the stage, as he employs it, is an entertainer, a teacher, and a mirror of life; it cannot be held exclusively responsible, if responsible at all, for the unhealthy attitudes described by its enemies. By making his most intelligent and successful characters neither the great idolators of the Fair (like Cokes and Littlewit) nor its great condemners (like Busy and Overdo),[6] Jonson is announcing metaphorically that, while he cannot wholeheartedly approve of many popular theatrical conventions, he will no longer offer aid and comfort to the hypocritical enemies of the theater, who had begun renewing their attacks with a dangerous zeal. He judges not, that he be not judged.

Through most of his career, Jonson confidently presupposes the binary distinctions between life and art, and between self and role, that were essential to his parodic strategy, but that New Historicist critics such as Greenblatt argue were profoundly problematic in the Renaissance. In *Bartholomew Fair,* however, Jonson retreats from his binary system. Perhaps his recent work on masques, a genre that fundamentally subverts precisely these distinctions, shifted his perspective. Perhaps, as the commissions for those masques made him feel that his public role was becoming commensurate with his essential worth, his psychological reliance on such distinctions diminished. Or perhaps a change was necessary to enable an answer to the antitheatrical arguments put forward by the Puritans. In any case, Bartholomew Fair was an appropriate locale for staging the change, since it was a place where business and ritual, sensation and law, and history and religion, all conspicuously collided and commingled.[7]

The title page of *Bartholomew Fair* features a quotation from Jonson's literary idol Horace:

> If Democritus were still in the land of the living, he would laugh himself silly, for he would pay far more attention to the audience than to the play, since the audience offers the more interesting spectacle. But as for the authors of the plays—he would conclude that they were telling their tales to a deaf donkey.[8]

*Bartholomew Fair* may be Jonson's way of keeping an eye on his audience and enjoying an amiable laugh at their expense, while still offering that deaf donkey the sorts of entertainment it is capable of enjoying. In accepting that life and plays are inextricably bound up in each other, both propelled by mindless desire and conflict, Jonson (like Busy at the puppet show) tacitly declares that "the cause hath failed me . . . Let it go on. For I am changed, and will become a beholder with you!" (5.5.101–105). Jonson's indictment of popular melodrama and its clientele is still audible— many characters, as in the earlier comedies, humiliate themselves by confusing life with art, and by imagining themselves central characters in melodramatic literature that runs against the realistic grain of Jonson's dramaturgy—but *Bartholomew Fair* no longer displays a prosecutorial obsession with proving those accusations. What Jonson here represents is not his triumph over other playwrights so much as his victory over his own destructive tendencies as a literary imperialist. By creating only foolish and futile advocates of censorship, Jonson parodically reduces his own determination to discipline the crude but lively spirit of the popular theater, and thereby breaks free of his inadvertent alliance with the Puritan determination to suppress that spirit entirely. Authorship, which is the essential form of authority in the earlier comedies, here distances itself from authoritarianism.

From the very start of *Bartholomew Fair* characters struggle for positions of authorship and positions of authority. As in several of his other comedies, Jonson uses an Induction to subvert the audience's comfortable distance from the stage. Beginning in the Induction, we meet a succession of candidates for the role of Jonson's spokesman, each stealing authority from the previous one, in much the way that a succession of robberies passes control of the marriage license from Cokes to Wasp to Edgworth to Winwife in the third act, and that a succession of interruptions passes authority at the puppet show from Littlewit to Leatherhead to Busy to Dionysius to Overdo to Quarlous. Both the contest for control of the marriage license and the contest for control of the puppet show, in fact, are plausible metaphors for the crucial contest for control of the play as a whole. A comedy is essentially a marriage license: the competition in comedy, as with the license in *Bartholomew Fair*, is over which character will be allowed to fill in the names on that license in the final scene (Jonson's *A Tale of a Tub* nicely exemplifies this point). The puppet show is a more straightforward metaphor for the play that contains it. The battle among Jonson's characters is therefore, as in the earlier comedies, a battle over which sort of a plot will be allowed to rule the stage.

The first character to enter in the Induction is the Stage-keeper, a dramatic character who thinks he is a critic rather than a part of Jonson's play.[9] Jonson often assigns an inferior choral figure, such as Mitis in *Every Man Out of His Humor,* to defend the works of Jonson's competitors, because such defenses inevitably reduce those works to formulas vulnerable to Jonson's parodic strategy. This

Stage-keeper is a fine builder of straw men, because he insists on the value of having conventional types, situations, and bits of business in plays, and cannot distinguish between those drawn from life and those drawn from art. He has seen so many fairs, and so many plays, that they have run together in his mind. He complains that Jonson

> has ne'er a sword-and-buckler man in his Fair, nor a little Davy to take toll o' the bawds there, as in my time, nor a Kindheart, if anybody's teeth should chance to ache in his play. Nor a juggler with a well-educated ape . . . Nor has he the canvas-cut i' the night for a hobbyhorse-man to creep in to his she-neighbor and take his leap there! (Induction, 12–20)

Later there should have been "a substantial watch to ha' stol'n in upon 'em, and taken 'em away with mistaking words, as the fashion is in the stage-practice." He is bitter that Jonson has dared to reject such advice from a man who "kept the stage in Master Tarlton's time, I thank my stars" (32–39). A whole range of popular plays suffer guilt by association with the Stage-keeper's naiveté and confusion.

The Stage-keeper is suddenly interrupted by the Book-holder, who supposes that he has the real authority over the stage. He is Jonsonian enough to anticipate the conventional responses of those who will "swear *Jeronimo* or *Andronicus* are the best plays yet" (95–96), and has been authorized to negotiate with the spectators for their approval. However, given the mistrust the play eventually shows for such written contracts, the Book-holder's negotiation becomes in retrospect a gentle parody of Jonson's own efforts to control his audience's responses by his characteristic system of implicit rewards and punishments. The notion that spectators will have to pay to express their dislike of *Bartholomew Fair* (76–86) recalls the way gulls in earlier plays lose their money by failing to appreciate the new mode of comedy they inhabit. Similarly, the notion that spectators who misunderstand Jonson's new mode of satire will "be left discovered to the mercy of the author, as a forfeiture to the stage and your laughter aforesaid" (120–131) recalls the humiliation in earlier plays of gulls who egotistically project themselves onto the stage and thereby enmesh themselves in a satiric mechanism they cannot comprehend.

The play proper begins with John Littlewit, whose authority is directly based on authorship. Toward the end of works such as *Every Man In His Humor, Epicoene,* and *The Alchemist,* a clever playwright-figure appears on stage to seize sovereignty on Jonson's behalf. *Bartholomew Fair* seems to offer a parodic inversion of that pattern by opening with a foolish playwright-figure whose partial plagiarism, appetite for low comedy, and enslavement to his own worthless literary conceits undermines his claim to any such sovereignty of wit. The witty authorial role, it seems, can itself be a derivative, self-aggrandizing, and finally degrading pose. In fact, much of the absurdity of Littlewit's puppet show may be taken as the logical extension of Jonson's own dramatic practice, which involves translating classical plots into Jacobean London. Leatherhead has induced Littlewit to reduce the story of Hero and Leander "to a more familiar strain for our people," leading to the substitution of the Thames for the Hellespont, "a dyer's son about Puddle Wharf" for Leander, "a wench o' the Bankside" for Hero, and a drawer whose sherry encourages the courtship for Cupid and his arrows. The silly rhyme of "Cupid" with "stupid" (5.4.178–179) that typifies Littlewit's doggerel actually appears in Jonson's own "Celebration of Charis" (2, ll. 5–6), and the crude failures of love and friendship in the plot of the puppet show make it arguably a parody of *Bartholomew Fair* itself.[10]

Of course Jonson is not saying that his dramaturgy is as bad as Littlewit's. The very fact that the author-surrogate has become enough of a stock figure to be parodied suggests that Jonson has succeeded in establishing his particular kind of comedy as a Jacobean commonplace. But Littlewit does call attention to Jonson's potential faults—including his overreaching theatrical imperialism—by embodying them in an extreme form. In *Bartholomew Fair* Jonson seems to be offering himself the same sort of warning that his superior surrogate, Tom Quarlous, offers to Littlewit, namely, that his "ambitious wit" may finally betray him (1.5.66). The play begins to resemble an internal dialogue; it becomes a representation of Jonson's debate with himself about the merits of his severe literary ethic, and of his parodic strategy for enforcing that ethic.

Although he is a figure of the author, Littlewit has no immunity to the self-dramatizing disease. His brain is a beehive buzzing with literary conceits as worthless as the trinkets that dance in the brain of Bartholomew Cokes, and he tries to fit everyone he meets, not merely the puppets, into his quibbling sort of text. In his first speech, in what seems to be a parody of Jonson's own obsession with significant naming of characters, Littlewit plays on his own name and on the names of Cokes and Win. Later in the same speech Littlewit gives Win a costume and stage directions to convince himself that she can be "as fine as the players" (1.1.1–37). Before the first act ends, he will write her a new scene to play, in which she will "play the hypocrite" and feign sickness in order to win permission for a trip to the fair (1.5.139–146).

The people of the fair allow Jonson to explore further the tendency of life to imitate art. Nightingale is himself the thief his song describes: his warning against cutpurses is designed to distract fools such as Cokes so that Edgworth can cut their purses. Perhaps Jonson is conceding that his own art, while it claims to be morally edifying, may finally amount to little more than an exploitation of human faults for his own profit; such a concession would be consonant with the spirit of the play as a whole. Perhaps, less radically, Jonson is criticizing the moralistic authors of sensationalistic coney-catching pamphlets who made a similar profit from the naive. Nightingale certainly thinks of his entire enterprise as a coney-catching fiction: "Be this sport called 'Dorring the Dottrel' " (4.2.18–19). In any case, the ironies of Nightingale's practice focus our attention on the ironic interplay of art and life. Ursula, lashing out at whatever comes within her burly reach, may be another character following out the theatrical implications of the name Jonson has given her; she acts as if she were the baited bear who would probably have held the same central place at the Hope theater (where *Bartholomew Fair* was performed) that Ursula and her booth held on other nights.[11] Even Whit "recites some doggerel in which he self-consciously relates himself to the rufflers of the St George plays" (3.2.117–119).[12]

The gallants of the play who, like the fair people, might in earlier plays have been the manipulators of dramatic illusion rather than its dupes, also occasionally have trouble distinguishing the workings of reality from the workings of theater. Winwife—like Nightingale, Edgworth, and Ursula—seems to believe that naming is destiny, setting out as if *Bartholomew Fair* were a typical Middleton comedy concerning what Quarlous dismisses as "thy exercise of widow-hunting . . . this drawing after an old reverend smock by the splay-foot!" (1.3.58–60). It may be objected here that it is normal practice for a playwright to give a character a name that suits the character's role, and that to draw any inference from the fact that Winwife is seeking to win a wife is an over-ingenious misreading of an ordinary literary situation. Such normal practice does not, however, explain why Jonson introduces a man with that name to a pretty young woman named Win, misleading both the audience and Winwife himself—who promptly begins courting her, despite the presence of her husband—into supposing that she is the wife he should win. This little trick, which demonstrates how defenseless both the audience and Winwife are against the authority of the author, is evidence that Jonson is exploiting ironically the ordinary practice of naming, not simply practicing it himself.[13]

When Winwife and Quarlous must choose code names in a lottery for Grace's hand in marriage, they each choose the name of a literary exemplar of love and friendship, Argalus "out of the *Arcadia,*" and Palamon "out of the play" (4.3.64–65). The tendency to view their own roles in aggrandizing literary terms infects even these cleverest of the play's characters. They succeed no better at playing the roles of noble friendship suggested by these pseudonyms than Damon and Pythias do in the puppet show. But Quarlous knows when to stop playing the romantic game of courtship and the romantic role of Argalus. As soon as he finds out that he is the defeated suitor, rather than the victorious one as Argalus was, he adapts his plot to reality, rather than vice versa as Jonson's fools do; if anything, Quarlous reverts to a role like that of Argalus's evil rival Demagoras.[14] Instead of pining for Grace, he promptly connives a profitable marriage; he drops the role of devout, self-sacrificing lover once there is nothing to be gained by it, and turns his attentions instead to the rich widow Dame Purecraft. The contrast between the actual behavior of Winwife, Quarlous, and Grace on the one hand, and the noble roles with which they identify themselves on the other, may partly serve to degrade these characters.[15] But their ability to recognize and adapt to those shortcomings is, in the world of Jonsonian comedy, the essential virtue of an active wit.

Grace Wellborn's situation could easily provoke her to see herself as a standard heroine of romantic literature. Like the noble Eleanor Cobham in Chettle and Day's highly popular *The Blind*

*Beggar of Bednal-Green* (1600), Grace is a damsel in distress who
needs to be rescued from the tyrannical authority that will marry
her to an unworthy Cokes (3.5.252–258).[16] She is too coolly intelligent, however, to follow that script through to a conventional
conclusion: she forbids Winwife and Quarlous to fight an actual
duel for her love (4.3.1–4), as (to choose the example Winwife
seems to have in mind) Palamon and Arcite fought. Instead she
arranges a test which calls on neither poetic destiny nor even her
nominal Grace to redeem her, but instead leaves the essentially
irrational choice of a mate in the appropriate hands of the madman
Trouble-All.

Dame Purecraft knows that she is sometimes merely playing a
role, but (like the disguised Justice Overdo) she does not realize
quite how often. Eventually she reveals that she is consciously a
poser, playing the Puritan zealot "only to draw feasts and gifts
from my entangled suitors" (5.2.50–51). She thus becomes a more
positive character by a double negative, by being hypocritical about
her "hypocrisy," her Puritanism. But she still pursues sincerely
the other cheaply melodramatic role, which her daughter reports
was offered her by "the cunning men in Cow-lane" who "do
ensure her she shall never have happy hour, unless she marry
within this sen'night, and when it is, it must be a madman, they
say" (1.2.42–46). We may suspect that these fortune-tellers were
the operators of *The Alchemist,* since this prophecy is as silly,
humiliating, and easily exploited as the promise that Dapper would
be adopted by the Queen of Fairy. Dame Purecraft's urgent pursuit
of such a suitor would easily suffice for the plot of a lesser Jacobean
farce, and Jonson makes it seem even sillier simply by decentering it, by making it so peripheral to his story that it seems to
be a misguided quirk rather than a magical imperative. Her effort to fulfill this plot, like the self-dramatizing pursuits of other
Jonsonian gulls, only makes her more susceptible to exploitation by the wittier and more cynical plots of Winwife and Quarlous.

This susceptibility in her character finally shapes her destiny.
She loves Trouble-All because "The world is mad in error, but
he is mad in truth" (4.6.157–158); in other words, in a world of
bad actors, she craves someone whose bizarre behavior at least
reflects his true self rather than a dramatic role, whose antic dis-
position is genuine madness rather than merely another perfor-

mance. The irony is that her own effort to act out her melodramatic destiny causes her to marry Quarlous, who is indeed merely playing a madman and can only promise to continue the performance (5.6.85–86). Like Overdo, who also goes wrong by assuming that madness cannot be feigned (4.1.58), she cannot distinguish reality from theater in herself or in others, and that failure eventually deprives them both of control over their lives.

Bartholomew Cokes, with his unabashed and acquisitive good will, imagines himself the central figure of Bartholomew Fair, if not directly of *Bartholomew Fair*; he too supposes that the world is arranged around his egoistic fantasy. This literary self-infatuation is visible in him (as in Littlewit and Overdo) when he indulges in a grand self-apostrophe (3.5.41). He is also another character who believes in the efficacy of his own name, insisting that the fair somehow belongs to him. His surname Cokes (meaning a fool) proves more prophetic than his Christian name Bartholomew, though he almost makes the fair literally his own by his prodigal spending. He will see himself in almost any role except his true native one, as a gull. When his first purse disappears, Cokes promises Nightingale's crowd "a good jest . . . a delicate fine trap to catch the cutpurse nibbling" (2.6.118–120), but he again proves himself a helpless victim rather than a moral practitioner of such trickery. When the fair proves unresponsive to his fantasy that *Bartholomew Fair* is a happy comedy about young Bartholomew's adventures at the fair, he simply reinterprets his defeats as part of a miracle play, with himself as the saintly victim: "an' ever any Barthol'mew had that luck in't that I have had, I'll be martyred for him, and in Smithfield too" (4.2.65–66). L. A. Beaurline asserts that Cokes has here "been flayed like St. Bartholomew" in losing his cloak, and that "Jonson calls the audience's attention to the parallel with the martyr."[17] It seems to me that such a comparison could survive only in Cokes's self-dramatizing, self-exalting imagination, and that it is Cokes, more than Jonson, who asks us to notice it.

Humphrey Wasp, Cokes's guardian at the fair, has a very different but no less conventional understanding of his role in the play. He supposes himself the wise and long-suffering protector of prodigal youth, a figure that appears in many honored guises throughout medieval and Renaissance drama.[18] He tells Littlewit that "the whole care of his [Cokes's] well-doing is now mine," and he fears what may befall Cokes during his interval "under a woman's government" (1.4.64–78)—a standard fear about prodigals. But Wasp's determination to live up to his name, as a stinging little pest, precludes his sustaining any grand role as youth's patient guide. Even before his direct humiliation, Wasp dissipates the dignity and benevolence of this paternalistic role into a bitter farce. The forbidden fruit his prodigal boy pursues is merely fruit, and this prodigal is likelier to lose a testicle than a soul:

> Pray heaven I bring him off with one stone! And then
> he is such a ravener after fruit! You will not believe what
> a coil I had t'other day to compound a business between
> a Cather'ne-pear-woman and him about snatching!
> (1.5.108–112)

Neither the petty scale nor the sexual undertones of these concerns can sustain Wasp's pose, however great a fool and wastrel Cokes may be.

When Wasp complains that Cokes "has a head full of bees" (1.4.74), he may be alluding not only to his own name, but also to the morality play *Respublica,* in which the brain of Avarice swarms with bees.[19] The problem for Wasp is that the childishly likeable Cokes does not really seem in danger from any mortal sins. Cokes constantly undermines Wasp's pose as the prodigal's father by becoming himself a parody of the prodigal son, buying up whole worthless worlds—such as the gingerbread basket and the puppet show—for the sake of "a masque" (3.4.144), losing everything, including his fiancée and the cloak from his back, and being no less happy and no more repentant as a result. When Quarlous tauntingly inquires whether Wasp is "almost tired in your protectorship? Overparted? Overparted?" we may detect a suggestion that Wasp has proved inadequate to his chosen "part" as the prodigal's protector.[20] It is the same pun that appeared twenty years earlier, in Shakespeare's *Love's Labor's Lost,* when Nathaniel cannot sustain the role of Alexander the Great because he is "o'erparted" (5.2.584).

Wasp also envisions himself as a moral version of the wily servant of the classical New Comedy, whose job is to protect his young master's interests, financial and amorous, against the sophisticated swindlers and seducers of the city. It is a moralistic version of the role Brainworm assumed so successfully in *Every*

*Man In His Humor.* But Wasp is "overparted" in this role as well: young Cokes loses not only the rest of his material possessions, but also his prospective bride, through Wasp's intemperate mismanagement. Wasp's patronizing tone toward Cokes concerning the wedding license—"a man must give way to him a little in trifles, gentlemen: these are errors, diseases of youth, which he will mend when he comes to judgment and knowledge of matters" (1.5.40–43)—provokes Winwife and Quarlous into superseding Wasp's sententious plot with their own satiric one. They blackmail Edgworth into stealing the license from Wasp as he stole the purse from Cokes, thereby converting Wasp from the role of wily protector to the role of careless prodigal and hapless innocent. That conversion necessarily robs Wasp of his "authority," in the sense of authorship as well as sovereignty: "Nay, then the date of my authority is out; I must think no longer to reign, my government is at an end. He that will correct another must want fault in himself" (5.4.97–99). Like Surly in *The Alchemist,* he has tried to play the moral hero of a traditional sort of story, only to discover that the play he actually inhabits has no interest in traditional moralism. Both men's roles as the upstanding exposers of coney-catchers are overruled by comedies that exult in the gulling of coneys, including upstanding ones.

Wasp's humiliation, like that of Surly, partly represents Jonson's repression of his own censorious tendencies. This authority-figure's resignation from government is suggestively parallel to the author's decision to surrender his satiric absolutism at the end of *his* play; Jonson thus suggests that he may at times have been more a literary Wasp than a literary lion. Certainly it is suggestive that, shortly before he wrote *Bartholomew Fair,* Jonson was humiliated in his Wasp-like role as tutor and guardian to a wayward son of Sir Walter Raleigh when he became so drunk that the boy was able to display him through the streets of Paris in a cart.[21] In portraying the end of Wasp's authority in the stocks, Jonson may be offering a gently self-mocking autobiographical metaphor for a turning point in his critical attitudes.

The defeat and conversion of Zeal-of-the-Land Busy at the puppet show, like Wasp's humiliation there, may reflect Jonson's own reconciliation to the corruptions of the popular theater.[22] The failures of the various authority-figures to stop the puppet show all demonstrate that the role of magisterial censor can be as hackneyed and hollow as any of the popular stage roles such censors attack. In the case of Busy, as in the cases of Wasp and Overdo, the suggestions of an authorial role undermine authority, rather than supporting it as they did in such playwright-figures as Brainworm, Macilente, and Face. The authoritarian characters' attempts to re-write *Bartholomew Fair* serve only to reveal the self-dramatizing tendencies—the vain, naive, conventional turns of mind—that prevent them from controlling either the stage or the society that they inhabit. In fact, Busy perfectly exemplifies the paradox Jonson described in his Epigram 75:

> I cannot think there's that antipathy
> 'Twixt Puritans and players as some cry;
> Though Lippe, at Paul's, ran from his text away
> To inveigh 'gainst plays, what did he then but play?

Busy gains his power by projecting a self-glorifying scenario onto a world that he deems entirely "subject to construction" (1.6.63–64), but though he is more alert than many Jonsonian role-players to the vagaries of interpretation, he too finally fails by misreading the play in which he dwells.

The play itself reminds us that the word "hypocrisy" became a common dismissive synonym for Puritanism in the seventeenth century, in addition to its etymological meaning of stage-playing and its modern meaning of false piety (5.5.43–44).[23] This pun is crucial to the characterization of Busy, as well as of Dame Pure-craft. Jonson emphasizes Busy's hypocrisy, in all senses of the word, by having him manipulate doctrine to suit his own and his group's desire to visit the fair and eat the pig they claim to despise. Busy's willingness to misread in self-serving ways extends into a boastful misreading of the fair itself, as an allegorical trial rather than a real physical situation. Though he is not so sincere in this misreading as Ananias is in *The Alchemist,* Busy still seems to enthrall himself with his literary romanticization of his visit to the fair.[24] The journey through the stalls becomes his Pilgrim's Prog-ress, the passage of a Puritan soul through the torments and temp-tations of the physical world. Critics who see Bartholomew Fair as Jonson's symbolic embodiment of the entire material world, and its actions as an allegorical Day of Judgment, must be wary of reading Busy's play rather than Jonson's.[25]

Given their premise—that Win's desire to see the fair and eat its food "is the Tempter, the wicked Tempter; you may know it by the fleshly motion of pig" (1.6.13–14)—it is almost inevitable that the Puritan group will be forced further and further into an overblown allegory to sustain their understanding of themselves and their surroundings. Busy's first speech is a wonderful example of the phenomenon Jonson warns against in his *Discoveries:* the danger of losing one's own voice by assuming someone else's.[26] Critics have praised Jonson for capturing so perfectly the absurdly architectonic structure of Puritan rhetoric in this and subsequent speeches,[27] but perhaps Jonson incorporates the standard rhetorical devices in such a stark and extreme form because he wants us to see Busy himself as a mimic. As the rhetoric staggers upward toward cosmic significance, Busy aggrandizes himself, but no more convincingly than he aggrandizes roast pig:

> Verily, for the disease of longing, it is a disease, a carnal disease, or appetite, incident to woman; and as it is carnal, and incident, it is natural, very natural. Now pig, it is a meat, and a meat that is nourishing, and may be longed for, and so consequently eaten; it may be eaten; very exceeding well eaten. But in the Fair, and as a Barthol'mew-pig, it cannot be eaten, for the very calling it a Barthol'mew-pig, and to eat it so, is a spice of idolatry, and you make the Fair no better than one of the high places. This, I take it, is the state of the question. A high place.                          (1.6.45–53)

To escape this authoritative-sounding conclusion, which runs against the authority of appetite that dominates this play-world, Busy must reshape the proposed visit into a spiritual adventure. The "foul face" of the idolatrous fair "may have a veil put over it, and be shadowed, as it were" (1.6.65–66). Once the face is veiled, it may be conveniently mistaken, given dimensions of grandeur that a more direct inspection would not sustain.

The outward landscape may now be reinterpreted on the basis of inward qualities, as in conventional pilgrimage allegories:

> The place is not much, not very much; we may be religious in midst of the profane, so it be eaten with a reformed mouth, with sobriety, and humbleness; not gorged in with gluttony or greediness; there's the fear:

> for, should she go there, as taking pride in the place, or
> delight in the unclean dressing, to feed the vanity of the
> eye or the lust of the palate, it were not well, it were
> not fit, it were abominable, and not good.     (1.6.67–74)

This rhetorical imperative obliges the group to find its way to the
pig-booth led only by the nose and not the eyes or ears. Like so
many self-dramatizing postures in Jonsonian comedy, this project
becomes as absurd in its actual execution as it was ennobling in
its preconception, and Jonson's parodic technique thrives on such
discrepancies. To make the vanity, absurdity, and literary derivation of Busy's role at the head of this procession even more
obvious, Jonson gives him lines which suggest that at moments
he envisions himself as Odysseus leading his crew past the Sirens
and away from Circe.[28] The ease with which Busy blends this
pagan strain into his Christian piety proves that his behavior has
more to do with grand literary fantasies than with Christian devotion.

Perhaps spurred by his own characterization of the threat as
"vanity" through which he must walk a straight and narrow path
(3.2.27–29), Busy develops increasingly elaborate schemes for
chronicling Bartholomew Fair as Vanity Fair, searching out objects
to allegorize in ways that will aggrandize his journey:

> The wares are the wares of devils; and the whole Fair
> is the shop of Satan! They are hooks and baits, very
> baits, that are hung out on every side to catch you, and
> to hold you as it were, by the gills and by the nostrils,
> as the fisher doth.     (3.2.37–40)

Busy settles in to feast in the midst of these "vanities" (3.2.84),
letting go of neither his hearty meal nor his grand conception of
the fair as a vale of soul-making:

> And bottle-ale is a drink of Satan's, a diet-drink of Sa-
> tan's, devised to puff us up and make us swell in this
> latter age of vanity, as the smoke of tobacco to keep us
> in mist and error; but the fleshy woman, which you call
> Urs'la, is above all to be avoided, having the marks upon
> her of the three enemies of man: the world, as being in
> the Fair; the devil, as being in the fire; and the flesh, as
> being herself.     (3.6.29–35)

Leatherhead, selling his musical trinkets, becomes "the proud Nebuchadnezzar of the Fair," his drum becomes "the broken belly of the Beast, and thy bellows there are his lungs, and these pipes are his throat, those feathers are of his tail, and thy rattles the gnashing of his teeth" (3.6.54–65).

If Don Quixote had read *The Pilgrim's Progress* instead of *Amadis of Gaul,* he might have treated his degraded world in much this manner. Both Quixote and Busy are projecting onto the degraded modern marketplace a kind of meaning that cannot survive either the emergent capitalism that characterized much of the Renaissance world, or the subversive realism that characterized much Renaissance literature. Both men—Quixote romantically, Busy hypocritically—conjure up an ethically and culturally fraught context that would allow them to establish their moral worth, their villainy or heroism, by their struggles against it.[29] Neither man is willing to acknowledge the discrepancy between the world he has read about so fervently, and the world he encounters as physical reality. What the knight of La Mancha attempted to transport into his own era, authorized by the literary artifacts of romance, the hypocrite of Banbury attempts to impose on his own situation, authorized by a religious movement that often read the world as a harsh allegory.

Busy does finally earn himself a minor martyrdom by interpreting Joan Trash's gingerbread as the devil's provender and a "basket of popery," and therefore feeling compelled to smash it to the ground. Perhaps he envisions himself as a self-sacrificing Samson (a Puritan hero) as he zealously pulls this little world of idolatry down on himself; or perhaps he thinks he is Christ attacking the merchants in the temple. In any case, it is a grand role he has taken from his books and tried to enforce on his world.[30] Even in the stocks, Busy (like Overdo) strikes a self-dramatizing pose that is badly compromised by his awkward physical posture: "I am glad to be thus separated from the heathen of the land, and put apart in the stocks for the holy cause" (4.6.75–77). Naturally the imprisoned authority-figures see themselves as martyred rather than humiliated when they are placed in the stocks, because there was a great theatrical tradition, in such plays as *Youth, Hickscorner,* and Lindsay's *Satyre of the Thrie Estaitis,* that encourages them to interpret their imprisonment as an allegorical trial and a temporary stage in their grand moral projects.[31]

The audience, however, is in a position to view the incarceration of these authorities differently, as punishments for trying to censor the *theatrum mundi* while engaging in the most indulgent sorts of self-dramatizations. However nobly they may narrate their own situations, we still see them in an ungainly and demeaning position in front of us. Busy tries to fit his release into his self-serving allegory—"We are delivered by miracle; fellow in fetters, let us not refuse the means; this madness was of the spirit. The malice of the enemy hath mocked itself" (4.6.154–56)—but this is obviously a distortion. The play allows these censors to escape, not through some moral right or divine intervention, but instead through Wasp's coney-catcher's trick and the crude brawl between Bristle and Trouble-All. They escape, in other words, through precisely the sorts of amoral energy that they had condemned and that fuel both Bartholomew Fair and *Bartholomew Fair*.

The final humiliation of Busy, who prides himself on his contentious and sententious improvisations on standard Puritan themes, occurs when he is out-improvised by a set of absurdly contentious and sententious puppets. Busy, like Cokes, perceives the puppets as if they were really alive, a symptom of both men's failure to recognize when their own lives become comically puppetlike.[32] As Grace comments, "I know no fitter match than a puppet to commit with an hypocrite" (5.5.43–44). Busy's furious interruption of the puppet show typifies his misconception of the entire play in which he finds himself. He seems to imagine that he will end the plot with his glorious overthrow of this little stage, as the Puritans hoped to close down the theaters of London. But what he supposes to be his moment of triumph over the perfect emblems of idolatry is mocked by Jonson's technique of decentering. Busy assumes that his speech is eloquent and important, but spectators who are focused on the puppet show or on *Bartholomew Fair* as a whole instead of on Busy's imaginary drama will necessarily perceive the interruption as merely a lot of silly noise, no better than the interruptions of Cokes. That discrepancy generates some cruel laughter at Busy's expense. His play, in which he is a progressing pilgrim or an avenging Samson, recovering from the moral weakness and self-induced blindness into which he was seduced by Win and Dame Purecraft, is here heckled back off the stage, and the other play goes on, subsuming his as simply another false and self-serving misinterpretation.

No sooner has Busy surrendered his own idea of the play, and agreed to "become a beholder with you," than Adam Overdo steps in front of the puppet booth with what he too supposes will be the true, triumphant intervention. He confronts the group as if he were Hercule Poirot in "Murder on the Orient Express,"[33] only to discover he is more like Jacques Clouseau in "A Shot in the Dark":

> Now to my enormities: look upon me, o London! and see me, o Smithfield! the example of justice and mirror of magistrates, the true top of formality and scourge of enormity. Hearken unto my labors and but observe my discoveries, and compare Hercules with me, if thou dar'st, of old; or Columbus, Magellan, or our countryman Drake of later times. (5.6.33–38)

Amid the teeming human chaos of *Bartholomew Fair,* and amid the chaotic puppet show that mirrors it, Overdo's accusations of enormities fail him as badly as Busy's accusations of abominations, and his grand play is similarly shouted down at its grandest dramatic moment. No one much cares what he has so cleverly discovered; they prefer to let the undisciplined energy of the puppet show (and, by analogy, of the play as a whole) continue instead. Overdo becomes just one more character who is made to sit down in the pig-booth, where all basic human appetites are crudely satisfied, and accept *Bartholomew Fair* itself. He will be no different from all the others who there yield their own egoistic projects (as moral arbiter, disguised ruler, fortune hunter, or coney-catcher) and accept the Jonsonian project that both outflanks and outlasts theirs. Both Littlewit's reductive puppet show and Jonson's expansive comedy finally manage to contain and overrule all the contradictory plots the various characters have generated. Unlike Jonson's earlier masterplots, however, the play that triumphs at the end of *Bartholomew Fair* does not brag of its originality or its satiric discernment; its proudest claim is that it will be nothing other or better than the rich chaos of ordinary life, augmented only by the inherent pleasure of the theatrical experience (Induction, 101–146).

Overdo had clearly imagined himself part of a very different, and very conventional, sort of play. *Bartholomew Fair* draws heavily on a long tradition of hidden-magistrate plots, but it would be wrong to think of Overdo as simply another, lesser example of a disguised authority-figure. Jonson is not merely creating low comedy by deflating Overdo's pretensions to wisdom and control; he is also attacking the dramatic convention by showing how foolish Overdo appears when he tries to live out such a convention within the world of satiric city-comedy. A character such as Overdo who willingly suspends disbelief concerning his own heroic poses can be easily exploited and mortified in Jonsonian comedy by a disbelieving audience such as Quarlous, or even Wasp, just as a spectator who suspends disbelief at the first hint of romantic melodrama risks exploitation and mortification by a satiric playwright. The shock to Overdo's glorious fantasy constitutes yet another warning to the spectators about their own dangerously trite expectations.

The basic idea of an authority-figure evaluating people from behind a disguise appears often in folktales as well as in serious literature; the gods in classical mythology and archangels in the Bible perform similar visitations. The most famous example of that tactic in Renaissance drama is Duke Vincentio in Shakespeare's *Measure for Measure,* but versions can be found in works such as the anonymous *A Knack to Know a Knave,* Whetstone's *Promos and Cassandra,* Middleton's *The Phoenix,* Day's *Law Tricks,* and Marston's *The Malcontent* and *The Fawn.*[34] Jonson is not exactly denying that this is an honorable tradition; on the contrary, he is showing that the role is so venerated that people are tempted to prefer it to their real identities. In the disguised-magistrate plot Jonson found an excellent opportunity to explore the workings and the dangers of heroic literary mythologies. He has Overdo specifically refer to his conduct as a "mirror of magistrates" (5.6.34), which calls our attention to the fact that Whetstone's *Mirror for Magistrates of Cities* had converted the literary tradition into a recommendation that rulers actually undertake such a disguise to discover misconduct.[35] Furthermore, London's Lord Mayor actually attempted this very stratagem at the time Jonson was writing *Bartholomew Fair,* a fact to which Overdo also alludes (2.1.11–24).[36] Here, then, was a perfect occasion for Jonson to show how literature gradually became confused with reality, until people actually attempted to live out a literary fantasy. The way Overdo humiliates himself is very much the way that many of Jonson's other self-dramatizing fools humiliate themselves, but this time

Jonson could point out that a real and prominent person had proved susceptible to the same confusion. The cycle takes yet another turn nearly twenty years later, when the justice of the peace in Brome's *Covent-Garden Weeded* announces that he is copying Overdo's stratagem.[37]

Overdo intends to conceal himself by pretending to be "a certain middling thing between a fool and a madman" (2.2.137), but he will not be King Lear presiding over a mock trial with the Fool and Mad Tom as his fellow justices. The disguise, like the disasters it generates, indicates that there is something inherently foolish and deranged about Overdo's project. His stratagem will finally reveal more about his own "enormities" than about any at the fair, and more about literature than about commerce. Naturally it never occurs to Overdo that the disguise he intends as part of his hidden-magistrate plot might be subsumed by his creator into a satirical play in which people reveal their own follies by the conventional dramatic poses they choose to strike.

Overdo's shock when he discovers that his accusatory interruption of the puppet show is not the triumphant last word in *Bartholomew Fair* is revealing but not surprising. In other literary works of the period "the conventional justicer is universally and almost miraculously successful."[38] If this were the end of Middleton's *Your Five Gallants,* for example, Overdo would be Fitzgrave, on his way to a handsome victory.[39] If the play were something like Chettle and Day's *Blind Beggar of Bednal-Green,* he could rightly anticipate a glorious redemption like that achieved by Lord Momford after a strikingly similar series of misadventures.[40] If the play were simply a dramatization of Whetstone's *Mirror for Magistrates of Cities,* as it sometimes seems to be, Overdo would be the ideal Roman senator, obeying his emperor's command to "root out iniquitie"; if it were the moral diatribe *Looke on me London,* a pamphlet from which Overdo seems to have taken some of his wording (for example, 5.6.33),[41] he would be the controlling author and the ethical authority.

But the play stubbornly refuses to become any of those things. Shakespeare took a step in this direction when he showed the Duke in *Measure for Measure* unpleasantly surprised when Angelo's utter depravity forestalls the standard happy ending the Duke had envisioned for his disguised-ruler plot (4.2.73–127). *Bartholomew Fair* may be Jonson's way of suggesting that Shakespeare did not go far enough—that, in providing the Duke with a solution in the form of the dead pirate Ragozine, Shakespeare drew back from his recognition that a disguised ruler would not accomplish much in a realistically uncooperative world. Overdo's enterprise is trapped in a world of satiric farce. Barton describes him as "a refugee from another kind of contemporary comedy, one in which the disguised hero acts as a surrogate for the dramatist himself, guiding the action cunningly towards a last scene in which confusion will be reduced to order, vices punished, goodness rewarded, and society left purged and regenerate."[42] That description reminds me of Jonson's own earlier comedies, as much as of the works of any of his contemporaries. Perhaps Justice Overdo is less a refugee than a stubborn holdout, refusing exile from his native territory, where once he might have been the Justice Clement of *Every Man In His Humor,* just as Wasp might have been the Brainworm.[43]

As in the earlier comedies, what may appear to be Jonson's sources are more precisely the sources from which a character derives his own proud posture. Brian Gibbons sees *Bartholomew Fair* as an attempt to "dramatize Coney-Catching pamphlet material, and Jonson deliberately imitates the moralistic, naive tone of Robert Greene in poor Overdo, who like Greene has a 'black book' in which these 'enormities' are to be recorded."[44] This may be so, but *Bartholomew Fair* also represents Overdo's attempt to dramatize the same material, with himself as the author-hero: he seeks out and writes down standard coney-catching tricks (including several that he merely hallucinates), and strikes the grand moral pose he could have admired in Greene's little books. Jonson's effort to dramatize the material and mimic the tone of these pamphlets subserves a parodic strategy that portrays Overdo, rather than Jonson, as the imitative dramatist. It is ironic that Overdo condemns actors and playwrights in the moralistic terms of a Gosson (5.3.65–67), since he is himself a bad actor and a bad playwright; the actual collapse of his disguised-magistrate plot merely confirms those well-established failings. The only sort of poetry Overdo approves is strictly didactic verse (3.5.106)—precisely the kind that lures him into the most mischief, and precisely the kind Jonson has chosen to eschew in *Bartholomew Fair.*

Overdo's peculiarities all point to this same misguided dependence on unassimilated literary antecedents, this tendency to base identity on reading rather than reality. Barish notes that Overdo's main stylistic flaw is that his rhetorical figures "shape Overdo's view of the world instead of being shaped by it."[45] Barton suggests that Overdo fails when he imitates "ways of behaving recommended by the great writers of the past" because of his "lack of any sense of proportion."[46] My impression, conversely, is that he lacks that sense because he has mistaken himself for a classical literary figure: the essential mistake is assuming that life can successfully imitate literature, no matter how great. Jonson mistrusted his own tendency to assume grand roles that his mortal frailties forbade him to sustain, and Overdo becomes the target of that projected mistrust. Overdo invites us to "Hearken unto my labors . . . and compare Hercules with me, if thou dar'st" (5.6.35–37), the same comparison with which Jonson mocks himself in the "Celebration of Charis" sequence (2, l. 32). At the end of *Bartholomew Fair* Adam Overdo is embarrassingly reminded that he is "but Adam, flesh and blood . . . forget your other name of Overdo" (5.6.95–96); Jonson, at the end of poems such as "My Picture Left in Scotland" and "Why I Write Not of Love," abashedly recalls that he is only Ben, flesh and blood—especially flesh—and that he has been overdoing his identifications with great mythological figures.

It will be difficult for Adam Overdo humbly to forget his name, however, because he has been savoring it and its potentially noble associations for so long. Characters with melodramatic self-conceptions tend to apostrophize themselves in impressed tones, as if their mere natural selves were addressing alter egos exalted on a stage. Littlewit's first speech is typical: "Well, go thy ways, John Littlewit, Proctor John Littlewit—one o' the pretty wits o' Paul's, the 'Little-wit of London' (so thou art called) and something beside" (1.1.9–12). As this example suggests, such self-infatuated characters notice only the exalting aspects of their names, allowing us to focus on the degrading aspects: Bartholomew Cokes confirms that he is a cokes, John Littlewit that his wit is little, by the fact that they boast of these compromising names. Adam Overdo falls into the same pattern, until Quarlous reminds him in the final scene that his name may refer to the fallen Adam, rather than to any surpassing enforcement of justice (5.6.95–96).

The obsession with great names, and the grand allusive self-apostrophe, in Overdo's first lines demonstrate his faults all too clearly:

> Well, in justice' name, and the King's, and for the com-
> monwealth! defy all the world, Adam Overdo, for a
> disguise, and all story; for thou hast fitted thyself, I
> swear. Fain would I meet the Lynceus now, that eagle's
> eye, that piercing Epidaurian serpent (as my Quintus
> Horace calls him), that could discover a justice of peace
> (and lately of the quorum) under this covering. They
> may have seen many a fool in the habit of a justice; but
> never till now a justice in the habit of a fool.     (2.1.1–8)

As good as this may sound (to Overdo, anyway), it is fraught
with contradictions that ruin his effort to act as the heroic reformer
of Bartholomew Fair, or to write himself in as the reforming hero
of *Bartholomew Fair*. Horace did use the "piercing Epidaurian serpent" as a symbol of sharp-sightedness, but only in describing the
tendency to scrutinize the faults of others while overlooking one's
own.[47] Furthermore, Overdo no sooner finishes claiming that his
stratagem is novel, and all the more effective because of its novelty,
than he boasts that "thus hath the wise magistrate done in all ages"
(2.1.9–10). This contradiction creates another one. Overdo praises
this tactic because it overcomes a judge's reliance on vicarious
perception: "what can we know? We hear with other men's ears;
we see with other men's eyes. A foolish constable or a sleepy
watchman is all our information" (2.1.25–28). And, indeed, we
have such standard comic failures at law enforcement in Haggis,
Bristle, and Poacher. The irony is, however, that Overdo finally
misinforms himself, primarily because he is neither hearing
with his own ears nor seeing with his own eyes so long as he has
a set notion of what a disguised magistrate should hear and
see—confessions, crimes, and an innocent to be rescued from their
midst.

Overdo is thus an idolator of the theater in a Baconian sense,
because he is one in a literal sense. His perceived "enormities" and
his misguided protection of Edgworth are part of a play he has
unknowingly produced, or more precisely, reproduced, on the
stage of his own mind. When he first sentimentalizes the cutpurse,
he seems to do so as a way of sentimentalizing his own role into
that of a kindly paternal protector (2.4.30–33, 63–66); so Jonson,
in debunking Edgworth's pose as an innocent, can reveal also the
nature and the causes of Overdo's false posture. Like Old Knowell

in *Every Man In His Humor,* Overdo cannot sustain his conventional paternal pose because Jonson refuses to provide him with the right sort of conventional son. Leggatt's study of citizen-comedy argues that "Overdo's role recalls the disguised, moralizing fathers of standard prodigal plays; Wasp suggests the honest servant who tries to keep his master out of trouble; but both are too foolishly self-important to carry any real moral weight, and are reduced to ineffectual grumbling."[48] But this is a factor of context as much as character: they seem self-important and ineffectual only because Jonson declines to write a standard prodigal play or New Comedy. What Leggatt rightly calls "grumbling" clearly sounds to Wasp and Overdo like spell-binding moral oratory. The tone of Overdo's paternalistic speeches rings entirely false, not only because they are saturated with clichés and self-infatuation, but also because they are hopelessly alien to the situation in which Jonson has trapped them:

> If I can, with this day's travail, and all my policy, but
> rescue this youth here out of the hands of the lewd man
> and the strange woman, I will sit down at night and say
> with my friend Ovid, *Iamque opus exegi, quod nec Iovis
> ira, nec ignis, etc.*                                    (2.4.63–6)

Overdo thus not only claims an epic scale for his achievement, but also accounts himself intimate with Ovid as well as Horace. Characteristically, he confuses literary familiarity with personal familiarity and regularly delights to find moments when his own thoughts and feelings can speak through the words of literary classics. His compulsion to cry *"O tempora! O mores!"* (2.2.107) at the first revelations of "enormity" seems to arise as much from a desire to cast himself as Cicero (perhaps as he saw him in Jonson's own *Catiline,* at 4.1.190) as from any spontaneous sense of moral outrage.[49] Barton acquits Overdo of "trying to show off" with his classical quotations on the grounds that "most of these citations occur in moments of solitary self-communion."[50] I would call them instead moments of self-admiration, moments when Overdo is putting Overdo on stage, even though he is his own entire audience.

Jonson makes us so painfully aware that Overdo's behavior is really a collection of old plots and quotations that when Overdo begins to play Mad Arthur of Bradley a few scenes later, the role of madman may strike us as no more a pose than the role of wise man. Overdo's roaring to Ursula is hardly more affected than his Ciceronian soliloquy that leads into it (2.2.107–115). Addressing the supposedly endangered youth Edgworth, Overdo is aware that he is mimicking another man's speech, but we are ironically aware that he has actually been doing so all along; only the pretentious and self-righteous tone that permeates both the role of justice and the role of madman is really his own. The incongruities of this mad warning to Edgworth are merely heightened versions of the incongruities of his earlier speeches:

> These are the fruits of bottle-ale and tobacco! the foam of the one and the fumes of the other! Stay, young man, and despise not the wisdom of these few hairs that are grown grey in care of thee . . . Thirst not after that frothy liquor, ale; for who knows, when he openeth the stopple, what may be in the bottle? Hath not a snail, a spider, yea, a newt been found there? Thirst not after it youth; thirst not after it.                    (2.6.1–13)

This is the rhetoric of a zealous Busy brought to bear on the subject of a junior high school hygiene class. The absurdity of the speech, and the similar absurdities in the seventy lines that follow, are generated by Overdo's failure to determine whether to strike the pose of worrying parent or admonishing preacher, and his failure to understand that his protective role is as much a pose as his prophetic one.

In Overdo's prophetic fulminations, as in those of Busy, the comedy arises from the tension between the exalted syntax and the degraded material it carries. This stylistic technique contributes to the analogous functions of the parodic strategy as a whole, which sets exalted roles against the degraded characters who aspire to fulfill them. Overdo's warnings are marred by classic errors of decorum, and like most such errors, literary as well as social, they arise from a misapprehension of role or precedent. Like Busy, Overdo has a version of Don Quixote's problem here: Jonson has moved the play to a modern English town, as Cervantes moved his story to modern La Mancha, and the inherited literary pose is rendered ridiculous by the sheer mediocrity of setting and action into which it has been displaced:

> Hark, o you sons and daughters of Smithfield! and hear
> what malady it doth the mind: it causeth swearing, it
> causeth swaggering, it causeth snuffling, and snarling,
> and now and then a hurt.                    (2.6.63–66)

Cassandra herself would sound silly if she had only such dangers
to warn about. Indeed, she *does* sound silly to the Trojans, because
she alone is aware that their story is a tragedy. Overdo, conversely,
mistakes *Bartholomew Fair* for a serious and dangerous story.

The grand result of this admonitory speech-making is Quixotic
indeed: Overdo is beaten as a suspected conspirator in some of
the same malfeasances he was warning against. Why he does not
forestall the battery by revealing his identity is unclear. He may
simply be determined to protract his role, or to conceal his folly,
but as John Potter suggests, Overdo may also be following the
example of Dionysius in Aristophanes' *The Frogs,* who barely
resists revealing that he is a god when he is beaten.[51] It would be
like Overdo to endure some bruises and humiliation in order to
sustain what he understands as a quasi-divine role from classical
literature. Recovering, Overdo vows to "make no more orations
shall draw on these tragical conclusions," but from anyone else's
point of view, the deflating poetic justice of the beating (his speeches
were indeed designed to protect a man who is actually a cutpurse)
is much more comic than tragic. Equally comic, in Henri Berg-
son's sense, is the mechanical way Overdo reverts to the grandiloquent pose he has just forsworn:

> I had thought once, at one special blow he ga' me, to
> have revealed myself; but then (I thank thee, fortitude)
> I remembered that a wise man (and who is ever so great
> a part o' the commonwealth in himself) for no particular
> disaster ought to abandon a public good design. The
> husbandman ought not, for one unthankful year, to for-
> sake the plough; the shepherd ought not, for one scabbed
> sheep, to throw by his tar-box; the pilot ought not, for
> one leak i' the poop, to quit the helm; nor the alderman
> ought not, for one custard more at a meal, to give up
> his cloak.                                (3.3.19–28)

This ridiculous bluster (which extends into a misquotation of Virgil) reinforces the impression that Overdo's rhetorical pose as Mad

Arthur was not far from his self-enamored pose as judge; what he thinks of as his natural voice here sounds very much like his mimicry of a madman.

Jonson then shifts the focus suddenly away from this vortex of delighted self-involvement, by having the bystander Winwife comment, "What does he talk to himself, and act so seriously? Poor fool!" (3.3.38–39). To Winwife this furious soliloquy seems entirely compatible with the self-serious madman; and the very shift of focus is a powerful reminder of how unimpressive and unimportant we may look to others at the moments when we see ourselves, in quiet soliloquy, as tragic heroes. Tom Stoppard betrays Hamlet's soliloquies much this way in *Rosencrantz and Guildenstern Are Dead*; it is a matter of perspective, and that is controlled by the dramatist. The most painful blow to such poses—a blow smartingly delivered to most of Jonson's gulls—is the discovery that the play has been satirically recast: their efforts to play the heroes of melodramas have made them the fools of satiric comedies. When Overdo is again accused of complicity in the "pernicious enormity" of pocket-picking, he finds "Mine own words turned upon me like swords" (3.5.192–193); this is one manifestation of the fact that his own play has been turned upon him.

When circumstances press Overdo to recognize that his self-dramatizing tendencies have caused his disasters, he evades the lesson by resorting to yet another pose, as a classical Stoic.[52] That pose helps conceal the problem, because the literature of Stoicism often characterized human beings as essentially actors and defined virtue as the uncomplaining playing out of whatever part has been dictated by the cosmic drama. Overdo, however, fails as a Stoic because he plays his part primarily for the praise of a human audience:

> The world will have a pretty taste by this, how I can bear adversity; and it will beget a kind of reverence toward me hereafter, even from mine enemies, when they shall see I carry my calamity nobly, and that it doth neither break me nor bend me. (4.1.27–30)

And in fact the whole context of Smithfield's mismanaged stocks is so noisy and degrading, and Overdo's physical position is so ungainly, that we do not perceive a man maintaining dignity in adversity. Instead, we perceive a man proudly striking an indefensible classical pose, a man unwittingly parodying his own pride by a form of mock epic: "In the midst of this tumult I will yet be the author of mine own rest, and, not minding their fury, sit in the stocks in that calm as shall be able to trouble a triumph" (4.1.39–41). The classical "author" of his own fate is precisely what Overdo attempts to be, and precisely what the insistently modern and realistic world of this comedy forbids him to be.

When we return to Overdo in the stocks, he is still consoling himself by quoting Horace and Persius as his personal friends: "I do not feel it, I do not think of it, it is a thing without me. Adam, thou art above these batt'ries, these contumelies. *In te manca ruit fortuna.*"[53] Quarlous again is given the right of reply: "What's here? A stoic i' the stocks? The fool is turned philosopher" (4.6.85–92). For those of us who know that Overdo is not really Mad Arthur, the reciprocal conclusion is elicited: the philosophy has been rendered foolishness, perhaps even madness. Repenting the fact that he caused Trouble-All's madness by overplaying his role as a judge, Overdo gives his blank warrant to the disguised Quarlous, and thereby inadvertently subordinates his role as judge to his role as madman. This confirms the earlier impression that Overdo's role as Mad Arthur was no worse a case of miscasting and overacting than his role as disguised magistrate. In signing over his blank warrant, the great justicer has in effect written himself out of the play; his failures of authorship and of authority reinforce each other.

Of course Overdo does not realize that this is what he is doing; he has a much grander idea of the reparation he has made: "Adam hath offered satisfaction! The sting is removed from hence" (5.2.117–118). Adam Overdo evidently believes he has indeed become the second Adam, surrendering his own godlike power to atone for one man's fall, to cure the serpent's sting. This is the veiled precedent that gives special parodic force to the moment at the end of the play when Quarlous reminds Overdo that he is merely the old Adam, "but Adam, flesh and blood" (5.6.95). Overdo's disguises finally allow him to discover, not the sins of others, but rather his own not-so-original sinfulness. His wife echoes his grand and literary interpretation of their experience at the fair. Seeking consolation after her fall into temptation in Ursula's pig-booth, she reacts to her husband's suggestive name by portraying herself as Eve in a dramatic story that was frequently staged from the earliest mummers up through Milton's versions: "Will not my Adam come at me? Shall I see him no more then?" (5.6.71–72). She will, of course, because he has fallen too.

At moments this erring Adam seems to mistake himself for the greatest hidden judge of them all, the Jehovah of the Old Testament. Jackson I. Cope has noted the "near-blasphemous self-references" by which Overdo writes himself into that book: "Clearly Justice Overdo formulates his mission of raining judgment upon Bartholomew Fair in the imagery of Jehovah's judgments."[54] The official opening performance of *Bartholomew Fair* at court on the night of November 1, 1614, would probably have been preceded by the All Saints' Day Evensong, and it seems to me conceivable that Jonson wanted his court audience to perceive Overdo as trying to perform the specific script provided by the liturgical readings, as if Overdo had been in church with the rest of the audience and had become overexcited by what he heard there.[55] Since these passages as a whole "emphasized the reassertion or resurrection of God-given authority after its apparent demise during the chaotic explosion of disorder,"[56] it is not surprising that Overdo casts himself as a figure with a divine right to restore order at the end of the fair. Enduring constant abuse in his disguise as Mad Arthur, Overdo confidently awaits the vindication described in the Evening Prayer reading from *Wisdom of Solomon,* 5: "Then shall the righteous man stand in great boldness before the face of such as have afflicted him . . . And they repenting and groaning for anguish of spirit shall say within themselves, This was he whom we had sometimes in derision, and a proverb of reproach: We fools accounted his life madness . . ." The evening's other lesson, from *Apocalypse,* 19, is a vision of an avenging judge, in a bizarre costume, whose words are compared to swords, the same comparison Overdo offers for his own judging words (3.5.193). The invitation to the joyous marriage supper of the Lamb in the same reading clearly anticipates the ending of *Bartholomew Fair.* The fact that Shakespeare seems to refer to these same readings in *The Tempest,* written for a court production three years earlier to the day, lends credence to the notion that Jonson might attempt such a specific reference, and contributes to a pattern of hints that Prospero is another hidden avenger Overdo foolishly attempts to imitate.[57] When Overdo announces, "Neither is the hour of my severity yet come, to reveal myself, wherein, cloud-like, I will break out in

rain and hail, lightning and thunder, upon the head of enormity"
(5.2.3–6), it is hard to imagine what he could be thinking *except*
that he is Prospero, or God, or both. But, like Prospero, he is
finally obliged to give up his black book of enormities, and with
it his authority, and his glorious scenario of retribution.

As all the conventional figures of authority forfeit their power,
an unconventional figure of the author takes control of events.
Tom Quarlous, already established as a skillful exploiter of dramatic illusions, seizes the opportunity represented by the blank
page of Overdo's warrant. With his own authorial skills, Quarlous
assumes the power surrendered by Overdo's mismanaged authority and fulfills his own plot by converting that warrant to his
own purposes. Quarlous thus becomes the nearest thing in *Bartholomew Fair* to Jonson's surrogates in the earlier comedies, the
playwright-figures who satirically subsume the plots of lesser wits.
Critics have raised a variety of objections, ethical and structural,
to the idea that Quarlous fulfills such a role,[58] and in fact it is
appropriate that a play so resistant to the controls of moral pre-
cisianism would have no precisely moral controlling figure. It is
nonetheless clear that Quarlous is the only character who consistently manipulates the mechanisms of theater to his own profit,
even if it is a more reckless and inclusive sort of drama than we
have come to expect from Jonson's discerning surrogates. Quarlous is a cynical but not ill-willed character who, like the fools,
perceives the fair as a sort of five-act play, but unlike them, is
willing to accept the role of bemused audience rather than that of
romantic hero. He accepts such distance because he recognizes that
the fair is merely a satiric city-comedy depicting the failings of
humanity rather than a romantic melodrama about human glory:
"We had wonderful ill luck to miss this prologue o' the purse,
but the best is we shall have five acts of him [Cokes] ere night.
He'll be spectacle enough! I'll answer for't" (3.2.1–3). Like the
fools, Quarlous imposes a grand allegory on the petty reality of
the fair, but he does so with a playful, ironic detachment, calling
Leatherhead amid his puppets "Orpheus among the beasts," and
Joan Trash offering her gingerbread figures "Ceres selling her
daughter's picture in gingerwork!" (2.5.7–11). He satirizes such
grandiose translations, rather than inflating and infatuating himself
with them.

Quarlous first imitates, then outstrips, the poses and projects of each of the other characters; he takes their inward melodramas and rewrites or recasts them to his own advantage. He castigates Winwife for pursuing wealthy widows (1.3.58)—a dramatically conventional employment for a cynical gallant—but eventually steals Dame Purecraft for himself. This successful bit of widow hunting in disguise makes Quarlous a clear parallel to Fitzgrave, the triumphant hero of Middleton's *Your Five Gallants,* the same role Overdo tried to seize for himself in his final accusatory harangue. When he reveals that the woman who was about to lose her honesty is Overdo's wife, Quarlous not only displaces Overdo from his conventional role as a disguised judge, he also drives Overdo into another type of conventional plot—in which a disguised husband witnesses a test of his wife's fidelity—at a moment when neither Overdo nor his wife are in a position to sustain their roles with any dignity.[59]

Quarlous subverts the performances of Wasp and Overdo as protective fathers by arranging for Wasp to squander his license and Overdo to squander his authority. In place of Wasp's prodigal-son and New Comedy plots, Quarlous reenacts a famous jest played by the hero in the anonymous Elizabethan play *Sir Thomas More.*[60] On Overdo's blank warrant, Quarlous can write whatever script he wishes, and the world will be obliged to act in it; authorship and authority again work in tandem. Like Clement and Lovewit in earlier plays, he out-mads the madmen, outdrinks the drunkards, out-vapors the roarers, all to his own advantage and pleasure, thereby converting the entire play into his own superior version of Littlewit's puppet show.

Quarlous costumes himself as Trouble-All with an awareness of both the power and the limitations of theatricality—"I have made myself as like him as his gown and cap will give me leave" (5.2.13–14)—and afterward concedes that he has been "mad but from the gown outward" (5.6.63–64). That has been enough, however, to win him both wife and warrant, precisely what Over-do lost by playing the same role less skillfully. Quarlous' theatrical adaptability, like the puppet show, promises to survive past the ending of *Bartholomew Fair:* he consoles Dame Purecraft with the assurance that he "can be mad, sweetheart, when I please, still; never fear me" (5.6.63–86). Like all the other characters on their way to the feast of forgiveness, she has really been freed rather than trapped by the superior playwright, and she too can have the rest of the play at home.

Characters and audience alike gain this sort of theatrical liberty, precisely because the representatives of restraint have all been imprisoned in the course of, and by the course of, *Bartholomew Fair*. All three figures of censorious authority—Wasp, Busy, and Overdo—end up in the stocks. This way of humiliating the foolish authorities corresponds to the way Jonson humiliates foolish authors in *Bartholomew Fair:* not by chasing them away from center stage, as in his earlier comedies, but instead by obliging them to continue their romantic fantasies and moralistic judgments in an embarrassingly unromantic context where they themselves are actively judged. As Barish observes, in many of Jonson's early plays "those with a passion for setting others right are themselves right, and end by making their standards prevail," but the censorious figures in *Bartholomew Fair* wait in vain for any such vindication.[61] Whether or not Jonson is employing his parodic strategy specifically against his own earlier works, it is clear that the stocking of these repressive figures, like *Bartholomew Fair* as a whole, reflects a rejection of Jonson's own repressive attitudes: those who would suppress the slovenly pleasures of popular entertainments are now themselves the unwitting creators, and the unwilling victims, of low comedy. The authority-figures of religion (Busy), law (Overdo), and education (Wasp) are all defeated, not merely because they fail to understand the workings of satiric city-comedy in general, but also because they fail to participate in the forgiving spirit that distinguishes this instance of satiric city-comedy from its predecessors.

The fact that Jonson systematically exposes and humiliates these authoritarian figures, while making somewhat more gentle fun of Cokes, suggests the orientation of this play in Jonson's overall campaign for the health of drama. For all its generosity, *Bartholomew Fair* continues the practice of Jonson's earlier comedies, deploying the parodic strategy against the indulgences of romantic melodrama. But here that strategy is aimed most forcefully against representations of the censorious impulses that partly generated those earlier comedies, and thereby against the repressions of Puritan censorship. To combat the harsh new judges of theater, who share with the earlier Jonson a mistrust of the human tendency to idolize and imitate what one sees on stage, Jonson establishes a sort of *tu quoque* defense. He suggests that, in a world of players, the worst hypocrites are those who would forbid anyone but themselves to play, who insist on subjugating all the activities of the world to their own pompously moralistic scripts, who would have theater taking place everywhere *except* in theaters. The Puritan enemies of the stage could see the theatergoing mote in their neighbors' eyes, but not the universally theatricalizing beam in their own. In their bombastic and allegorical misreading of life, as well as in their notion that theater was inherently immoral, Busy's brethren were perfect adversaries of Jonson's artistic mission. *Bartholomew Fair* therefore vigorously subdues them to the spirit of theater and life that promises to fill Overdo's house when the play itself is over. That celebration is a world of play over which, merely by ending *Bartholomew Fair* where he does, Jonson has surrendered his own restrictive authority. Each spectator, heading off from the Hope theater to his own real-life supper, may "ha' the rest o' the play at home."

# CHAPTER SEVEN

# *The Devil Is an Ass*

## FROM MORALITY PLAY
## TO SENTIMENTAL COMEDY

If Jonson's *The Devil Is an Ass* (1616) no longer seems alive as a play, it is nonetheless a valuable fossil, a sort of artifact through which we can trace the evolution of Renaissance drama. The schemes that are outwitted and superseded in the play resemble plots that were conventional on the Elizabethan stage: the ones that outwit and supersede them look ahead to Restoration and eighteenth-century theater. In this regard, the play resembles *Epicoene,* though the effort to encompass and influence dramatic history creates more obvious structural and stylistic problems in this later version. Jonson first offers us a moralistic devil-story, with Pug as the Presenter-Commentator;[1] that story is marked for failure from the beginning. Intriguingly, though, the plot that Jonson brings into a mutually destructive collision with the devil plot is not another hackneyed Elizabethan formula, but a version of satiric city-comedy itself, with Merecraft as the clever manipulator of self-dramatizing gulls such as Fitzdotterel. *The Devil Is an Ass* proves to be neither a didactic story of absolute evil, nor a satiric chronicle of ordinary human frailties. Through the figures of Wittipol and Manly, Jonson strikes a more sentimental and sentencious note than he has in the past, perhaps in an attempt to reserve a place for himself in the next wave of dramatic practice.

The conventional drama most ostentatiously defeated in *The Devil Is an Ass* is Pug's attempted morality play, in which he would arise from hell to lure an Everyman into temptation, and thence into damnation. Jonson inverts that conventional expectation by trapping Pug in a world where he becomes, in effect, an Every-devil, taken beyond his depth in depravity by the self-serving plots of all the human beings around him.[2] Like a Humanum Genus figure, Pug is tested, found wanting, condemned, and carried off to hell. Interwoven with this ironic reversal of Pug's mission is the fate of his new master, Fitzdotterel, whose various theatrical-ized visions of himself—as necromancer, nobleman, and cuck-old—all prove equally ineffectual. Again Jonson invites his spectators to mistake the expectations of these gulls for his own generic signals, and then modernizes their notion of theater by the way he corrects that error. Despite the prominence of devils, mercantile schemes, and potential adulterers early in the play, Jonson rejects the conventional patterns of morality play, social-climbing chron-icle, and fabliau. Instead, he builds these false expectations into something very much like the comedies that were soon to dom-inate the English stage, sentimental enactments of the values of the gentry.[3]

The play's Prologue is an appeal for physical space that develops into an appeal for generic space. The warning that "This tract / Will ne'er admit our vice, because of yours" (8–9) means primarily that there may be no physical space for characters such as the Vice because of the audience's bad habit of crowding onto the stage. It also suggests the ethical message of the play as a whole—namely, that the vices of a modern London audience are so great that an old morality-style Vice is now useless as a moral admonishment. In the context of Jonson's parodic strategy, these two meanings combine into a third: the tendency of spectators to put themselves metaphorically as well as literally onto the stage has compelled Jonson to replace conventional ethical drama with a parodic drama that exposes their vice of self-dramatization. The Prologue then adds a further request:

> If you'll come
> To see new plays, pray you afford us room,
> And show this but the same face you have done
> Your dear delight, "The Devil of Edmonton." (19–22)

This reference to the anonymous popular play of eight years earlier is soon followed by an allusion to Dekker's more recent *If This Be Not a Good Play, the Devil Is In It:* Jonson says that, given a generous trial, "If this play do not like, the devil is in't." After such a Prologue it would be surprising if the play were not concerned with establishing priority over its stage rivals.

Jonson's initial target is the long tradition of morality drama, with its bogeyman devils, its hokey hellmouths, and its ponderous didactic allegories. He positions himself brilliantly against the unrealistic and morally simplistic qualities of this tradition, qualities that probably provided much of its appeal. By showing the greedy fool Fitzdotterel and the greedy schemer Merecraft simulating demonic possession, Jonson takes a spectacle that enlivened many late morality plays and reveals it as merely a set of cheap and dishonest stage tricks. Jonson may also have recognized here another opportunity to combine synergistically his attack on vulgar theatrical conventions, on art that does not imitate life, with a warning about the dangerous tendency of life to imitate such art. As with the Londoners who, like Dapper, were swindled into believing they could live out a fairy tale, as with the London mayor who, like Overdo, tried to live out a disguised-magistrate plot, real people mimicked the theatrical conventions of possession and exorcism, and in the case of simulated possession the resulting disasters were not limited to embarrassment for those who believed their own self-aggrandizing scripts. Because they could not prove that the performances of their supposed victims were merely a play, many innocent women were executed as witches in Jacobean England, and many more would probably have suffered similarly had not King James himself intervened to expose the theatrical tricks of the "possessed."

Stephen Greenblatt is particularly interested in the way imposing the "stage-taint" on these phenomena served the polemical purposes of the Reformation, since it discredited an important affirmation of Catholic theology and an important display of Catholicism's saving power.[4] It discredited these things, furthermore, in precisely the terms in which Protestants so often attacked Catholicism: as a delusive and even dangerous ritual performance. Jonson may, as Greenblatt suggests, have been participating in this Reformation tactic on behalf of the Jacobean ideology. Another, narrower explanation is also possible, however. Like Reformation culture as a whole, Jonson casts the stage-taint on demonic possession for the purpose of disempowering his rivals, but his immediate rivals were other playwrights; he uses the stage-taint paradoxically against the stage itself, against dramaturgy that tried to pass off theatrical conventions as an image of reality. From this perspective, the mere theatricality of exorcism in *Volpone* and *The Devil Is an Ass* is not a special case in Jonsonian drama demanding ideological explication, but primarily another way of discrediting his competition, through the instance of devil plays. As in the cases of Dapper and Overdo, the fact that such phenomena had been exposed as fraud, folly, or worse in real life gave Jonson the opportunity to remind his audiences, with extra impact and conviction, that what other playwrights had been giving them was demonstrably—and dangerously—not the *imago veritatis* he felt drama ought to be.

More broadly, by absorbing the devil play into his own comedy of manners, Jonson characteristically implies that the evils people try to distance into foreign lands and supernatural melodramas are present in less magnificent but no less harmful forms in the daily life of London. The city's sophisticated gallants would no longer feel themselves implicated and threatened by the mistakes of an Everyman spouting fourteeners; for drama to regain the socially corrective function Jonson attributes to it, it must move onto a satiric level that reminds people that they have devils within them, even if they are not spitting fire and speaking in tongues.

There were also more sophisticated rivals against whom Jonson had to position himself, however. Plays such as *The Merry Devil of Edmonton,* which Jonson mentions in the Prologue, and Haughton's *Grim the Collier of Croydon,* which Jonson seems to have known, had already made satiric use of the devil-play tradition. As the titles imply, they were modernized and localized stories, and they both showed devils bewilderingly trapped in a world that outdid them in evil. Jonson's refinement was to use this inviting satiric situation to construct a critique of theater as well as of society. Jonson's parodic strategy, by stressing the theatrical derivation of his characters' self-images and self-infatuations, allows him to undertake those two critiques in a synergistic way: London's literary and social follies reinforce each other. The threat of demonic possession becomes Jonson's way of talking about the misshapen monsters and bizarre tongues that often possessed the stages of London, and about the unhealthily melodramatic behaviors Londoners allowed to possess them in place of their true identities. His attack on the morality play is, in this sense, merely a vehicle for an attack on a range of dramatic conventions, including those of satiric city-comedy, which had forgotten their purpose or lost their effectiveness as social correctives. In *The Devil Is an Ass* Jonson is forging a new kind of ethical drama that points toward the earnest comedies of the decades to follow, a drama directed against cynically exploitative as well as naively vulnerable poseurs.

Pug is a version of the motivating spirit of many old morality plays, and as such he is too naive about the development of Jacobean drama to be an effective invader of Jonson's theatricalized London. Even if he were familiar with recent drama, Pug would still be vulnerable in Jonson's comic world, because his tendency to confuse drama with life matches the fatal flaw of many of Jonson's gulls. When he envisions himself aided by a "playfellow" such as "Fraud; / Or Covetousness; or Lady Vanity" (1.1.37–42), he is listing the diabolical agents in some of the best-known moralities of the previous half-century. This outdated catalogue typifies Pug's failure to reckon with the greater sophistication of Jacobean evildoers and theatergoers.

Pug's master, Satan, faces his own problem of belatedness. He has been represented on the stage so often that he can hardly behave like himself without seeming to us like a piece of theatrical imitation. His roaring entrance reenacts the standard diabolic entrance in morality plays.[5] But Satan is aware that what plays eternally in hell might be laughed off the Jacobean stage as archaic, and he warns Pug that the times have changed since the days when an old-fashioned devil could be sinfully effective in London, just as they have changed since the days when such a devil could be theatrically effective there. When Pug requests the assistance of Iniquity, who played the Vice in *The Nice Wanton* and *King Darius* over fifty years earlier,[6] and who can speak only of outdated strategies in outdated meters, Satan says Pug must be a "dotard" to

> choose
> This, for a Vice, to advance the cause of Hell,
> Now? As vice stands this present year? Remember,
> What number it is. Six hundred and sixteen.
> Had it but been five hundred, though some sixty
> Above; that's fifty years agone and six,
> (When every great man had his Vice stand by him,

In his long coat, shaking his wooden dagger)
I could consent.                                     (1.1.78–86)

Satan predicts that Pug's own "plot" will consist merely of the petty antics of country elves, no better than those of Faustus' clownish underlings (1.1.12–23). Though Pug claims to have higher aims, he is easily enthralled by the more urban but no more urbane pranks suggested by Iniquity; he has no notion of what is involved in a modern plot.

Satan is much more of an up-to-date playwright. In a sense, he is Jonson's collaborator, authoring the initial action of the plot by authorizing Pug to undertake his doomed mission. He agrees to let Pug attempt to invade London, but only after stipulating some revisions in Pug's plot that bring it into line with principles of dramatic unity and verisimilitude:

I am content, assuming of a body,
You go to earth, and visit men, a day.
But you must take a body ready-made, Pug,
I can create you none: nor shall you form
Yourself an airy one, but become subject
To all impression of the flesh you take
So far as human frailty.                             (1.1.133–139)

This can be seen as a rivalrous parody of God's dramaturgy in the Incarnation, but it also echoes Jonson's characteristic insistence that evils be presented in realistic terms rather than grand abstract ones, and that they be understood in the context of the human body's frailties. Jonson's own intention to keep his play within some bounds of dramatic unity may partly have dictated these rules, but they are set up so as to suggest that Satan himself is such a careful playwright: Jonson's play, after all, accepts neither earth as its unitary place nor Pug as its unitary hero. Satan functions as a didactic satirist for the population of his own world, as Jonson does for his. In fact, as I suggest at the end of this chapter, Satan's explicit warning to his diabolical underling seems to express Jonson's own implicit warning to lesser playwrights. The plot Satan sets in motion, furthermore, is one of Jonson's favorite classical inheritances, the wily-servant plot derived from New Comedy: "Only, thus more I bind you / To serve the first man that you meet" for the course of a single day (1.1.151–156).

In revising this collaborator's work, however, Jonson establishes dominion over it; he subsumes the diabolical plot in a way that announces the superiority of his own artistry. Satan could write something like *The Merry Devil of Edmonton* or *Grim the Collier of Croydon,* but only a sophisticated seventeeth-century court author could write *The Devil Is an Ass.* If Jonson's comedy is any kind of morality play, then it is one in which two rival playwrights, Jonson and Satan, struggle for the soul of an Everyplay that at each of its crises could either collapse into a nasty low comedy or be redeemed (as it is each time) into a suave display of virtue. The conversions of Wittipol away from adultery and Fitzdotterel away from his diabolism and perjury may be as unconvincingly abrupt as critics have suggested. But that very abruptness draws our attention to Jonson, the playwright *ex machina,* reclaiming his play from the patterns that shape his source works, diabolical patterns that Satan had hoped to renew.

Even after Pug has learned that to bring a Vice into London is as superfluous as to "transport / Fresh oranges into Spain" (2.2.3–6), he is still at least one step short of Jonson's recognition that to bring an ordinary play into London society is equally superfluous. *Totus mundus agit histrionem,* all the world plays the actor, according to the commonplace that was supposedly the motto of the Globe theater, and the better men are the ones who understand that concept well enough to choose and revise their parts carefully and ingeniously. In *The Devil Is an Ass,* as in so many of Jonson's comedies, there is a hierarchy of increasingly self-conscious wits who take control of the play they inhabit, and Pug is near the bottom of that hierarchy. He recognizes the self-dramatizing impulse in Fitzdotterel well enough to exploit it occasionally, but not well enough to realize when he is falling into the same trap. When he tries to concoct an "act" that will exalt him into the role of the perfect devil, the result is a disaster, because his plot demands that Fitzdotterel's considerably more intelligent spouse play along:

> My first act, now,
> Shall be to make this master of mine cuckold:
> The primitive work of darkness I will practise! (2.2.12–14)

The idea that the guard will cuckold the overjealous husband is only too conventional—a famous example would occur a few years later in the subplot of *The Changeling*—but Pug is badly mistaken in assuming that Jonson will indulge such a standard low-comic subplot within the main morality plot. Since the notion that the morality play is itself being satirized is naturally beyond Pug's comprehension, he gamely struggles to play out the diabolic role. He even tells Mrs. Fitzdotterel that he is "Your little worm that loves you" (2.2.127), which may be an effort (conscious or not) to pose as the fawning serpent, inhabited by a devil, who seduced Eve.[7]

Pug's reliance on old-fashioned literary precedents is largely responsible for his downfall. Where Wittipol impresses Mrs. Fitzdotterel by courting her in the sharp new manner of Donne, Pug merely amuses her, because he is appropriately trapped in the style of courtly poetry from the days of the late morality play:

> *Pug*                          let me assure
>   The excellence of mistresses, I am,
>   Although my master's man, my mistress' slave,
>   The servant of her secrets, and sweet turns,
>   And know what fitly will conduce to either.
> *Mrs. Fitzdotterel*
>   What's this? I pray you come to yourself and think
>   What your part is: to make an answer. Tell,
>   Who is it at the door?                          (2.2.34–41)

He is relegated to this far less glorious "part" because his outdated mode of courtship makes him seem so hollowly theatrical; he is suspected, for the same reason, of merely playing the role of wooer at Fitzdotterel's instigation, to test Mrs. Fitzdotterel's fidelity (2.2.46–51). She calls in her husband "from your watch, to applaud your squire" (2.2.132), but Fitzdotterel applauds this performance only with his cudgel, because unlike his wife, he finds this enactment of the cuckolding plot only too convincing. The discrepancy is instructive: Fitzdotterel and his wife interpret Pug's formulaic performance so differently precisely because they assimilate it into the different conventional plots that were already playing in their minds. Pug is caught playing a part both in the scene Fitzdotterel envisions, in which a wife is cunningly seduced, and in the scene Mrs. Fitzdotterel envisions, in which a hidden husband witnesses a vindication of his wife's virtue.[8] Indeed, both scenes appeared in *Grim the Collier of Croydon,* which Jonson evidently had in mind while writing *The Devil Is an Ass.* Pug expects Mrs. Fitzdotterel to behave like Haughton's Mariana, who cuckolds her unworthy husband, but she chooses instead to emulate Honorea, who remains faithful despite the greatest provocation; Mrs. Fitzdotterel's mistaken assumption that her husband is spying on her display of fidelity, as Honorea's husband is on hers, suggests that she has this sort of stock scene in mind. Pug's reflexive obedience to a literary tradition is thus fittingly punished by the similar errors of his master and mistress. From the audience's perspective, subservience to hackneyed roles, as much as lechery, is the deadly sin that earns Pug his cudgeling.

Clearly Pug's theatrical disguises do him more harm than good. He could perhaps have avoided this beating by revealing his true identity, but like Justice Overdo in *Bartholomew Fair,* he is apparently too enthralled with the idea of himself as a master plotter to do so. Fitzdotterel is unafraid to beat Pug, because Pug has hidden his true identity as fiend and hellhound behind his role as courtly seducer. While beating Pug, Fitzdotterel does call him "You fiend apparent you! You declared hellhound . . . Now, I do find you parcel-devil, indeed" (2.3.13–15); but he thinks he is merely punning cleverly on his servant's name. Pug has lost control of his role: although he came to play the mischievous incubus of devil stories, he is forced to experience all the humiliations conventionally visited on a country gull in Jacobean comedy.[9]

Pug's initial pose as a noble outcast—a conventional one among disguised characters seeking a vantage point for their own spiteful or redemptive projects on the Elizabethan stage—is far from necessary to insinuate himself with Fitzdotterel. The truth, as Pug discovers too late, would work better on this fool:

> Sir, your good pardon, that I thus presume
> Upon your privacy. I am born a gentleman,
> A younger brother; but, in some disgrace,
> Now, with my friends: and want some little means,
> To keep me upright, while things be reconciled.
> Please you to let my service be of use to you, sir.
> *Fitzdotterel*   [*Aside.*]
> Service? 'Fore Hell, my heart was at my mouth,

Till I had viewed his shoes well: for those roses
Were big enough to hide a cloven foot.
No, friend, my number's full.                            (1.3.1–10)

The tactics of the morality-play tempters are out of place in a world where a man's folly and vanity make him actively seek the devil's company.

Pug therefore compromises by claiming his family name is Devil, and Fitzdotterel then decides to "entertain him for the name sake" (1.3.36), while the women decorously emend it to the more continental "DeVille" so he will fit into their cosmopolitan vision of their own society.[10] Their chief concern is that the cast of characters which constitutes their world sound elegant; the hard realities of good and evil have disappeared behind the masks, and the women are determined to keep it that way. When Pug tries to drop his pose as the cunning servant DeVille and announces triumphantly that the old morality plays have invaded the reality of the Jacobean world, no one seems interested, let alone terrified (5.5.13–32).[11] His earlier efforts to behave diabolically had been described as "acting of the incubus" (2.3.26), merely a naughty imitation of true evil. Now Merecraft asserts that a contemporary audience will be more convinced by the usual acting tricks of devil plays than they would be by any true devil: "Why, if he were the Devil, we sha' not need him" (5.5.38). In fact, the tricks are much the same as the ones performed by Corvino in *Volpone,* and, as in *Volpone,* they are merely a stratagem within a courtship-and-inheritance plot more typical of the eighteenth century than the sixteenth. A new mode of theater has cynically subsumed an old one.

Fitzdotterel dismisses Pug's revelation of his true diabolical nature as an effort to "gull me with your Aesop's Fables" (5.5.30), and in a sense he is right; the morality play has become merely one more antique and inadequate moral fiction. Like Surly throwing off his disguise in Lovewit's house in *The Alchemist* and Overdo throwing off his disguise at the puppet show in *Bartholomew Fair,* Pug finds that his best scene has been stolen from him by a playwright skeptical of stock dramatic effects. Instead of being allowed to carry his erring Everyman into hell when he casts away his pose as a mere mortal, Pug is himself carried off to prison, and thence defeatedly back to his infernal home. Satan had plans for

Pug to stage one last show of evil on the cart, as in medieval cycle plays, complete with appropriate makeup, costume, and lines. Iniquity says that Pug's "triumphal egression" was to take place

> in a car,
> The chariot of triumph, which most of them are.
> And in the meantime, to be greasy, and boozy,
> And nasty, and filthy, and ragged, and lousy,
> With damn me, renounce me, and all the fine phrases;
> That bring, unto Tyburn, the plentiful gazes.          (5.6.22–28)

But the humiliating failure of Pug's plots is transmitted to Satan himself, who authorized them—in the hierarchy of plotters, Satan is behind Merecraft as well as Wittipol and Jonson (5.6.56–62)—and Satan decides that the show must not go on. Instead, it is retracted in a classic black-magical manner: Satan has the standard ending of the morality play performed backward. Where "the Devil was wont to carry away the evil," Iniquity now carries off the hapless Pug (5.6.74–77). Jonson has redeemed his play from his Satanic rival-playwright, who has been forced to unwrite his favorite plot.

This rescue fulfills the yearning Pug expresses throughout the play, a yearning as much for the world of an old play as for the environs of hell itself. He begs to be removed from these cosmopolitan plots and returned to a world of standard witchcraft and hellfire, concluding his plea with the observation that "There is no hell / To a lady of fashion" (5.2.1–15). That observation perfectly evokes the historical situation of Jonson's play, with a figure from the Tudor morality play bewildered in the nascent world of Restoration drama. Nothing in Pug's role, to twist a line of Shakespeare's, becomes him like the leaving it; only in his violent return to hell does Pug manage to impress Fitzdotterel and convince him that the morality he is flouting is important. By the same token, the essential cautionary focus of the morality play is revived here only by the defeat of such a play: Jonson is able to warn against the moral disease of self-dramatization only by exposing the morality play as an ass.

Fitzdotterel confuses art and life even more seriously than Pug does. He is uncertain, from his first few lines onward, whether he is most eager to "see the Devil" (1.2.10) or to see " 'The Devil' " (3.5.38), the real creature or his theatrical simulation.

Fitzdotterel's concern about getting to the theater in time to see the very play he inhabits is further evidence of his confusion. He recovers his senses only when he learns with terror that a real devil has indeed visited his life, that his reality has become a sort of morality play; he instantly senses that this is very different from his unrealistic flirtations with the devil through necromancy and theater. He understands, in retrospect, that the devil had indeed entered within him, not because he started spitting fire and speaking in tongues, but on the contrary precisely because his pride and greed had led him to fake these symptoms of possession. His determination early in the play to behave theatrically and honor the fiend becomes at the end a determination to "tell truth / And shame the fiend" (5.8.142–143), but only after his misinterpretation of his world as a traditional stage leads to a series of devastating miscalculations.

Fitzdotterel is hopelessly "in love with his own favour," as Merecraft says (4.6.49), but what he actually gazes at so adoringly is not his true face, but rather the theatrical masks with which he has unconsciously replaced that face. His wife's reply to his longest social-climbing rhapsody is apt: "You ha' strange fantasies" (2.3.61). They are strange because they are a hodgepodge of popular theatrical stories; what makes Fitzdotterel behave so oddly is not so much greed or vanity or a satanic nature, as an all-consuming desire to expunge the line separating his life from the plays he loves to attend. It is revealing that his acquaintances cannot agree on Fitzdotterel's true motivations. Wittipol believes that Fitzdotterel seeks diabolic contact only

> For hidden treasure
> He hopes to find: and has proposed himself
> So infinite a mass as to recover
> He cares not what he parts with, of the present,
> To his men of art. (1.5.17–21)

This diagnosis is partly confirmed when Fitzdotterel so easily shifts his foolish obsession to Merecraft's grand capitalistic schemes. But if Fitzdotterel's devil worship arises from a Mammon-like pursuit of gilded fantasies, the romance of satanism seems at times to supersede the greed. His first soliloquy offers to sacrifice anything merely to encounter a devil, even without the opportunity to exploit that devil for profit. Most people, furthermore, would

probably seize on some less storybook way of using evil to gain
wealth than searching for buried treasure. The explanation that
lends the most consistency to Fitzdotterel's character is that he has
an insatiable and irrational appetite, not for money, devils, clothes,
or rank, but rather for melodramatic fantasies of himself in which
those things are simply the conventional props. He is dangerously
susceptible to the temptations of self-dramatization, a primal social
evil which Jonson saw possessing many Londoners, ousting their
true identities, and making them speak in bizarre tongues. Fitzdotterel remarks that devils supposedly appear only to those who
are rash and corrupt enough actually to invite them (1.2.27–30);
similarly, characters can be lured into the exploitative plots of the
superior playwright-figures only because they already have foolish
plays running through their heads. The danger for gulls in Jonsonian comedy, as for conjurers in devil plays, lies in starting
something one cannot control to the finish.

As in his earlier comedies, Jonson ridicules his fool by distorting
and decentering the conventional stories in which that fool has
cast himself. Fitzdotterel remains quite visible, but the morality
play, the cuckolding plot, and the social-climbing story occur only
on the stage of his mind (and perhaps on the stages of other London
theaters). His bold project of avenging his supposed cuckolding
and robbery does not survive even as farce, as the duels among
cowards do in *Twelfth Night* and *Epicoene*; it simply drops out of
sight. Fitzdotterel's warnings that Wittipol "shall hear from me"
toward a duel over his wife are swallowed up by Wittipol's more
subtle plot. Instead of seeing Fitzdotterel always at center stage,
bravely attired and fiercely disputing, we are told about him from
another viewpoint. As when Macilente reveals the truth behind
Brisk's pose as a court lover in *Every Man Out of His Humor*
(4.2.25–30), the cool detachment of the new perspective inevitably
ridicules a character's self-infatuation. Wittipol tells us that Fitzdotterel

> would conclude him ruined should he scape
> One public meeting, out of the belief
> He has of his own great and catholic strengths,
> In arguing and discourse.                    (1.4.33–36)

Such an introduction could make even a Demosthenes sound
pompous and foolish, and to the extent we recognize that fact,

we must recognize the power of the dramatist, who can impose satiric distance as well as tragic or comic intimacy.

In taking the opportunity to criticize the gallants who attend plays only to display themselves, Jonson gives us a clue to Fitzdotterel's self-dramatizing nature:

> Today, I go to the Blackfriars Playhouse,
> Sit i' the view, salute all my acquaintance,
> Rise up between the acts, let fall my cloak,
> Publish a handsome man, and a rich suit
> (As that's a special end, why we go thither,
> All that pretend, to stand for't o' the stage).          (1.6.31–36)

The man who costumes himself lavishly and outlandishly for the theater, who expects to be the center of attention there and thinks he cannot possibly afford to miss a single performance, has mistaken his role in the audience for a role in the play.[12] Wittipol, speaking for Mrs. Fitzdotterel, observes that "no fear, no, nor authority, / Scarcely the King's command, sir, will restrain him, / Now you have fitted him with a stage-garment"—a fittingly ambiguous term for the garish cloak that is essential to Fitzdotterel's performance at Blackfriars (1.6.184–186). The Prologue's demand that such gallants dispense with the fashion of sitting on the stage thus has a symbolic, critical purpose as well as a practical one. Again the error Jonson especially ridicules is the failure to recognize the distinction between a play and real life. Wittipol's remark that Fitzdotterel "dares not miss a new play, or a feast, / What rate soever clothes be at; and thinks / Himself still new, in other men's old" (1.4.23–25) can be generalized into a Jonsonian commentary about our theatricalized lives, in which we think ourselves to be most unique and alive at the moments when we have cast and costumed ourselves in the oldest dramatic roles.

In fact, in this world's normal social intercourse, the line between living and acting is very thin. Fitzdotterel seems unaware that, in directing Pug's performance as emissary to the Spanish lady, he is making life no less theatrical than the play which will occur simultaneously at Blackfriars. Jonson virtually insists, however, that the audience take note of this irony:

*Fitzdotterel*
Remember kissing of your hand, and answering

With the French-time, in flexure of your body.
I could now, so instruct him—and for his words—
*Merecraft*    I'll put them in his mouth.
*Fitzdotterel*                          Oh, but I have 'em
O' the very academies.
*Merecraft*           Sir, you'll have use for 'em,
Anon, yourself, I warrant you: after dinner,
When you are called.
*Fitzdotterel*            'Slight, that'll be just play-time.
It cannot be, I must not lose the play!                (3.5.29–36)

He needn't worry: like the characters at the end of *Bartholomew Fair,* he will "have the rest of the play at home," because he never really stops acting for the theater of the world. For people like Fitzdotterel, social moments are always "play-time."

Fitzdotterel thus announces himself as a character in the play he fears to miss; that play, ironically, is built around his failure to understand what sort of a play it is. Perhaps the clearest indication that Fitzdotterel is an inadvertent role-player is the fact that he worries constantly about missing a play called *The Devil Is an Ass,* while in fact his misadventures in missing it are themselves that play. This parodic drama can play itself out in his life because he lives that life as if it were a conventional drama; the play humiliates Fitzdotterel, instead of exalting him as he had hoped, because Jonsonian city-comedy attacks the very confusion of life and art in which it traps him.

At moments it seems as if Fitzdotterel has seats in the most distant gallery at an enactment of his own story and can make out his own character only as a man with points on his head. Unable to recognize them as the ears of an ass, he spends most of his time trying to decide whether the headgear is (as he hopes) the coronet of a duke, or perhaps (as he excitedly surmises) the horns of a diabolical recruit, or (as he fears) the horns of a cuckold. In his unhappy moments he chronically conflates the roles of cuckold, ass, and devil.[13] All three concerns are prominent in Fitzdotterel's first speech, which describes his obsession with conjuring the devil out of artifice and into reality, his fear of a cuckolding plot, and his craving for confirmation of his sense of nobility:

> I would give
> A hundred o' these pictures, so to see him [the devil]
> Once out of picture. May I prove a cuckold,
> (And that's the one main mortal thing I fear)
> If I begin not, now, to think the painters
> Have only made him. 'Slight, he would be seen
> One time or other else. He would not let
> An ancient gentleman, of a good house
> As most are now in England, the Fitzdotterels,
> Run wild, and call upon him thus in vain,
> As I ha' done this twelvemonth.          (1.2.10–20)

He would be so honored by such a visitor that he would gladly serve instead of command that devil, serve him even with the wife whose fidelity he had claimed to desire above all mortal things:

> If he had a mind to her, too, I should grant him,
> To make our friendship perfect. So I would not
> To every man. If he but hear me, now?
> And should come to me in a brave young shape,
> And take me at my word? Ha! Who is this?       (1.2.49–53)

And pat he comes, like the fiend of the old morality play. It is Pug, precisely the handsome-shaped devil he was concerned about, who undertakes to fulfill this plot quite literal-mindedly, only to discover that Jonson has more complicated plans. He will not let Fitzdotterel win his cuckold's horns, nor will he permit Pug to earn his devil's horns; what they both acquire instead are some rather embarrassing ears. As each tries to make the other merely an actor in his own glorious play, Pug and Fitzdotterel alike succeed only in making themselves asses in Jonson's.

Fitzdotterel, like Pug, most convincingly plays the ass when he is most convinced he is playing the devil. Manly calls him an ass after he fakes diabolical possession (5.8.154), and Pug does so twice (2.2.107–108) before calling the devil one (4.4.243). Indeed, Fitzdotterel and his devil-servant Pug are twice gulled together, once by Mrs. Fitzdotterel's disguised message—after which Pug exclaims that "The devil is an ass!" (2.6.25)—and again by the stolen ring. When Wittipol offers to exchange his cloak for the opportunity to court Fitzdotterel's wife, Fitzdotterel replies as if he were

a morality-play Vice, agreeing to buy a man's eternal jewel in
exchange for some brief, unfulfilling worldly pleasures. (It is of
course characteristic of Fitzdotterel to equate a man's clothing with
his soul.) Where Iniquity's first words are, "What is he calls upon
me, and would seem to lack a Vice?" (1.1.44), Fitzdotterel says,

> Which of you is it is so mere idolater
> To my wife's beauty, and so very prodigal
> Unto my patience, that, for the short parley
> Of one swift hour's quarter, with my wife,
> He will depart with (let me see) this cloak here,
> The price of folly?                                    (1.4.54–59)

The echo suggests that Fitzdotterel unwittingly casts himself in
the role of potential cuckold here because he is so eager to see
himself as a diabolical power. That piece of theatrical mismanagement is a logical extension of the fact that Fitzdotterel's fervent
but futile necromancy is (as Wittipol senses) what comes closest
to costing him his wife's fidelity, by making her lonely and ashamed
of him (1.6.91–99).

Fitzdotterel's quest for a coronet, like his quest for the horns of
a devil, almost provides him with the horns of a cuckold, and
certainly gives him the ears of an ass. In hopes of making his wife
more like a noblewoman, he actually forces her to exchange a ring
and a pledge of service with her wooer Wittipol, who is disguised
as a Spanish lady offering lessons in courtly behavior. Earlier he
had complained bitterly to his wife that she had taken advantage
of his preoccupation with his soggy peerage to flirt with Wittipol
(2.7.28–37). When he mentioned his unhappiness to Merecraft a
few lines later, the projector replied, "Oh, sir! No toys must
trouble your grave head, / Now it is growing to be great" (2.8.3–
4). We may infer that Fitzdotterel's head is growing great with a
cuckold's horns rather than with a duke's coronets, and the accidental conflation of the two sorts of growths underscores the
dangerous ease with which a role-player may slip from a glorious
role to an inglorious one. He cannot escape from the theatricalized
world he has rashly created, and he cannot control what sort of
play it will be if he does not fully understand that he is playing.

His efforts to win the title of Duke of Drowned-land thus only
serve to confirm his family name as Fitzdotterel, a simpleton's
heir. His project of recasting the play he inhabits, his practice of

significant naming, cannot finally overrule the casting and naming imposed by Jonson. Fitzdotterel's obsession with titles, typified by this pursuit of noble new identities for himself and his wife, repeatedly leads him astray. It is a costly and essentially theatrical folly, closely associated with the tendency to view society as a cast of characters rather than as real individuals continuously shaping their identities. His longing to become the Duke of Drowned-land reveals his willingness to admire almost anything, if it is titled. A similar principle evidently underlies his decision to hire this self-proclaimed Mr. Devil (or DeVille) "for the name sake" (1.3.36). Fitzdotterel echoes this remark when he insists on making a spectacle of himself at the theater "For the mere name's sake" (1.6.187). As eager as he is to become a Duke, he is unwilling to become one in Gloucester, because others with that particular title have been unfortunate; this information Fitzdotterel has "from the play-books"—perhaps Shakespeare's 3 *Henry VI* (2.6.106–109)—which he characteristically trusts as "more authentic" than the historical chronicle. For him, the role is everything; not even the role, but the cast list. He would evidently be consoled if it could be shown that his unlucky predecessors in Gloucester had been listed as earls rather than dukes (2.4.4–14).

All of Fitzdotterel's enemies find some way to exploit this mindless preference for names over realities. Merecraft in effect sells Fitzdotterel some swampland by calling it a dukedom, and convinces Fitzdotterel to surrender his entire estate—everything that makes his family name worth having—to save his good name in his feud with Wittipol. The added irony is that Fitzdotterel tries to nominate that same enemy as the heir, and only the legal problems of a false name prevent the disguised Wittipol from accepting Fitzdotterel's final self-humiliation (4.6.43–52). In his effort to seduce Mrs. Fitzdotterel, Pug strategically and sarcastically conflates Fitzdotterel's pursuit of a noble name and his equally mismanaged fear of the name of cuckold into the single category of title-hunting. Why, Pug asks, does she

> defraud the poor gentleman,
> At least delay him in the thing he longs for,
> And makes it his whole study, how to compass
> Only a title. Could but he write cuckold,
> He had his ends.
> . . . . .

                                    If it were not clearly,
His worshipful ambition; and the top of it;
The very forked top too: why should he
Keep you thus mured up in a back room, mistress,
Allow you ne'er a casement to the street,
Fear of engendering by the eyes, with gallants,
Forbid you paper, pen and ink, like ratsbane.
Search your half pint of muscatel, lest a letter
Be sunk i' the pot: and hold your new-laid egg
Against the fire, lest any charm be writ there?        (2.2.81–97)

The point of Pug's sarcasm in this speech is that Fitzdotterel is a sort of Oedipus, whose efforts to avoid acting this scenario are precisely what write him into it. His obsessive fear of being in a cuckolding story is part of most cuckolding stories, and, like Kitely in *Every Man In His Humor,* he characteristically lacks the theatrical sense to recognize that he is casting himself into this humiliating part instead of the ennobling one he craves. He takes many conventional precautions to ensure that, while he is off at the theater, no such conventional story is acted out in his house; but they ensure quite the contrary, because they remake his house in the image of a *commedia dell'arte* theater.

   Jonson establishes a suggestive parallel between Fitzdotterel's listing of all the standard motifs of cuckolding stories[14] and Satan's dismissive listing of all the standard motifs of devil stories in the opening scene. The point is that neither diabolical visitations nor cuckolding schemes in Jacobean London are likely to follow the timeworn formulas of Renaissance drama. Fitzdotterel tells Pug,

                                    let in
No lace-woman; nor bawd, that brings French masks,
And cut-works. See you? nor old crones, with wafers,
To convey letters. Nor no youths, disguised
Like country wives, with cream and marrow-puddings.
Much knavery may be vented in a pudding,
Much bawdy intelligence: they are shrewd ciphers.
Nor turn the key to any neighbour's need;
Be't but to kindle fire, or beg a little,
Put it out, rather: all out, to an ash,
That they may see no smoke.                  (2.1.161–171)

Fitzdotterel is willing to sacrifice clothing, food, and warmth, not to mention neighborly charity, in order to exclude some standard markers of the cuckolding plot. His desperate effort to avoid the trappings of a role thus becomes at least as farcical as his efforts to fulfill other, more aggrandizing roles.

When Fitzdotterel discovers that his various melodramatic undertakings—to conjure the devil, to win a dukedom, and to protect his wife—have only exposed him to cuckolding, he insists he will not "act" to undo the damage. Instead he furiously attempts to reassert himself: "I will be what I am, Fabian Fitzdotterel, / Though all the world say nay to't" (4.7.89–94). The irony is that this poor gull has become so absorbed in dramatizing himself that not even his bold assertion of autonomous identity is really his own. It seems to be derived from bold assertions of the oppressed self that had recently been heard on the Jacobean stage: "This is I, / Hamlet the Dane," "I am Antony yet," "I am Duchess of Malfi still." Fitzdotterel's devotion to the theater, which led to his humiliation, now prevents him from recovering his dignity. He is belittled, not only by the comparisons, but also by his unwitting and symptomatic allusiveness in inviting those comparisons.

Eventually Fitzdotterel is forced to recognize that he can escape from the archetypically inglorious role of cuckold only by deliberately acting the more deeply depraved archetype of fiend, only by a dramatic simulation of demonic possession: "Well, I'll begin to practise; / And scape the imputation of being cuckold, / By mine own act" (5.5.51–53). He thinks he would rather play a fallen Everyman than an embarrassed pantaloon. To end the cuckolding play, he must return to the morality play, with all its morality now subordinated to hypocrisy. Instead of trying to bring life to the devil-figures from old plays, Fitzdotterel will now convert his own life into such an old play, with all the usual low-budget special effects (5.3.1–8; 5.5.47–48). If London's plotters can make the devil into an ass, they can also make this ass into a devil. What Merecraft really teaches him, in rudimentary form, is the Jonsonian art of channeling his allusions into a profitable scheme for deluding the gullible. Clearly Fitzdotterel has harnessed, rather than cured, his reliance on dramatic precedents. When he tries to speak in tongues, he characteristically ends up speaking in plays; his bit of Greek, for example, is stolen from the *Plutus* of Aristóphanes.[15]

In the final scene, the various observers concur in calling Fitz-dotterel's performance theatrical, but they dispute the implications of that finding. The crucial difference is that Wittipol's sarcastic question—"How now, what play ha' we here?" (5.8.38)—implies that the possession is merely simulated, and that the essential per-former, the motivating vice, is human. The less intelligent char-acters, by contrast, suppose that an actual diabolical Vice is performing his real self through a passive human agent:

> Gilthead                How the Devil can act!
> Eitherside   He is the master of players! Master Gilthead,
>     And poets, too! You heard him talk in rhyme!      (5.8.77–79)

The irony is that twenty-five lines earlier Eitherside himself had unconsciously joined in Fitzdotterel's rhymes:

> Fitzdotterel
>     And now, and now, I do not know how, nor where,
>     But she pricks me here, and she pricks me there: oh, oh:
> Eitherside   Woman, forbear.
> Wittipol                         What, sir?
> Eitherside                             A practice foul
>     For one so fair.                              (5.8.51–54)

This rhyming, and the accompanying echo of the weird sisters in *Macbeth,* may be Jonson's way of indicating that Eitherside's mor-alistic stance throughout this scene is as much a self-dramatization, and as far from a moral absolute, as Fitzdotterel's feigned demonic possession. As Greenblatt's argument suggests, to debunk the ex-orcism is to discredit the authorities who believe in it: the stage-taint is in that way contagious. Wittipol's more modern and skep-tical view of Fitzdotterel's "play" carries the authority of Jonson's truth. As in *Volpone,* human greed for a patrimony is vice enough to generate such a frenzy of "possession."[16] While both Voltore and Fitzdotterel think they are simulating some absolute theolog-ical evil, they are actually displaying, unwittingly but graphically, the evils in their society and in their own human nature. The motivating Vice of morality plays, a physically present devil, again yields to the motivating vice of much Restoration and Augustan drama, a thematic presence reflecting the gentry's concerns about pretensions and greed.

The great exploiter of pretensions and greed in *The Devil Is an*

*Ass* is the projector Merecraft, who is also the great exploiter of theater. He plays on the humors of the fools, and serves as both author and director of the feigned demonic possession which Fitz-dotterel must "act" as "an after-game" to Wittipol's dramatic stratagem (4.7.84–90). For some time, in fact, we may mistake Merecraft for Jonson's dramatic stand-in, a master of wit and imagination who exploits the witless imagining of others. Even Merecraft's mistrust of the players as the ideal actors for his Span-ish-lady scheme may reflect Jonson's own growing doubts about the adequacy of his performers for his plots (2.8.56–62). In offering the role to Wittipol, Merecraft again sounds like a playwright, describing the demands of "the place, designed / To be the scene, for this our merry matter" (3.4.38–39). But this correlation may serve only to subordinate Merecraft's stagecraft to that of Jonson. There were doubtless heavy ironies about the confusion of life with art in Merecraft's ruminations about whether Wittipol or the actor Dick Robinson would be better as the Spanish lady, since Dick Robinson was probably the actor playing Wittipol.[17] Cer-tainly Merecraft's fear that someone like Robinson might give his plot away to the playwrights, who would then put it on the stage, reveals both the theatrical nature of his plot and its essential futility in the context of *The Devil Is an Ass*. Merecraft's battle for secrecy and control is one he has automatically lost by the very fact that it occurs within the bounds of Jonson's play.

Merecraft's strategy of dramatic deception is based on the same human tendencies as Jonson's humors comedy, and he does help Jonson expose the play's fools. Engine introduces Merecraft as

> one sir, that projects
> Ways to enrich men, or to make 'em great,
> By suits, by marriages, by undertakings:
> According as he sees they humour it.    (1.7.10–13)

The difference is that Merecraft serves private gain rather than public reform, and he therefore struggles to sustain, rather than deflate, people's self-indulgent fantasies. He is a lesser version of *The Alchemist* conspirators,[18] living on his ability to intuit the sort of scenario to which each victim is susceptible; the projector is a projectionist. At first glance Merecraft's projects may seem close kin to those of Sir Politic Would-Be; the difference is that Sir Pol's grand schemes fool no one but himself, because they are self-aggrandizing, whereas Merecraft's fool almost everyone but himself, because they are designed to exalt the believer. (The distinction resembles that between Volpone's performance as a sergeant, which collapses from its own abusiveness near the end of that play, and Mosca's earlier performance as a wily servant, which holds his audiences by flattering them.)

This technique allows Merecraft to exploit for his own profit, and thereby to expose for ours, Fitzdotterel's image of himself as a man whose worth and enterprise (as in a Dekker play or a Deloney novel) will promote him and his family into nobility. The projector's first words to Fitzdotterel engage that fantasy:

> Sir,
> You are a gentleman of a good presence,
> A handsome man (I have considered you
> As a fit stock to graft honours upon:)
> I have a project to make you a duke, now.    (2.1.22–26)

Once this note proves responsive—and Fitzdotterel promptly raves to his wife that the projector "will make me a duke!" (2.3.34)—Merecraft strikes it repeatedly (2.1.114–126; 3.2.10–11; 3.3.100–102). The terms in which Jonson has Merecraft push this project emphasize that it will be merely a replacement for the devil-populated melodrama already playing on the stage of Fitzdotterel's mind: "Come, get 'The Devil' out of your head, my lord, / (I'll call you so in private still) and take / Your lordship i' your mind" (3.5.49–51). Merecraft entices Fitzdotterel by suggesting that an entire new ducal identity awaits only his willingness to play the role. "Now you are toward the lord, you must put off / The man, sir," Merecraft insists, and speaks of the enormous changes that must follow "When he has put on his lord's face once." This reminds Fitzdotterel of his own schooling where he learned "To make my legs and do my postures," and he wonders aloud whether a similar academy could be found to prepare his wife to play the role of Duchess (2.8.6–22). Fitzdotterel tells his wife that, if she will accept the schooling Merecraft has arranged, she can be "fine, or fair, or great, or proud, / Or what you will, indeed" (4.4.112–113). Stephen Gosson's famous attack on the theater had condemned it as a "School of Abuse." Jonson, engaged in a subtler attack on the stage, conversely portrays Merecraft's school of abuse as a conventional theater, designed (as the titles of Marston's and

Shakespeare's plays announce they are designed) to give its audience "What You Will."

The minor characters in *The Devil Is an Ass* pursue little dramas of their own, dramas that are ridiculed as much by decentering as by direct defeat. Merecraft, significantly, has a major role in subordinating them all to his own plots. The story of Ambler's day would certainly suffice for a low comedy. A friend convinces him that his sexual abstinence has been unseemly and unhealthy, so he finds a whore; fearing for his reputation, he takes her to a secluded spot, but they awaken to find a huge crowd nearby to witness an execution. They fall asleep again as they try to lie still in their hiding place, and reawaken to find that their clothes have been stolen (by the devil Pug), obliging them to make a furtive and uncomfortable trip back home and an elaborate excuse when they arrive there. But neither Merecraft nor the audience is prepared to pay much attention to Ambler's story when it is finally told, because it is peripheral to the story on which the play has focused for four acts. No one except Ambler is much concerned about whether or not Lady Tailbush will excuse his absence:

> *Ambler*   I would beseech your worship stand between
>    Me, and my lady's displeasure, for my absence.
> *Merecraft*   Oh, is that all? I warrant you.
> *Ambler*                              I would tell you, sir,
>    But how it happened.
> *Merecraft*                     Brief, good Master Ambler,
>    Put yourself to your rack: for I have task
>    Of more importance.                                    (5.1.10–15)

So Ambler is obliged to tell his tale "with extraordinary speed," as the stage direction indicates, lest he lose his audience. "Nay, if you fall from your gallop, I am gone sir," Merecraft warns him. Three centuries before Pirandello, here is a character abandoned by an author who finds "task / Of more importance" and leaves the poor creature's perfectly adequate tale largely untold. It is hard to conceive of any condemnation from Lady Tailbush that would be as humiliating as Merecraft's, "Oh, is that all?" When Ambler finally catches up with the man who stole his clothes, he encounters a similar obstacle. Pug evades the accusation, not by some diabolical conjuration like the one by which Marlowe's Faustus rebuffs those he had robbed, but instead by a simple refusal to engage in the interrogation Ambler intends. Pug shatters the attack by strategic misprision, turning it into a dozen conversations of no relevance to Ambler's indignation (5.2.18–40); he dismisses Ambler, in other words, much the same way Jonson does.

Fitzdotterel's persistent and hackneyed fantasy of social promotion recurs in Gilthead's promise to his son "to make you a gentleman," a catchphrase he reiterates four times within twenty-six lines (3.1.1,14,21,26). Gilthead's explanation of how his son came to be called Plutarchus shows that he also shares Fitzdotterel's misconceptions about the significance of names, assuming that they can shape character and destiny as if they were on a list of dramatis personae instead of merely a baptismal roll:

> That year sir
> That I begot him, I bought Plutarch's lives,
> And fell so in love with the book as I called my son
> By his name; in hope he should be like him:
> And write the lives of our great men!    (3.2.21–25)

There is nothing so unusual about this procedure, but by making it so literal-minded in the final line, Jonson alerts us to the absurdly theatrical assumptions underlying the common act of naming children for people we admire. Merecraft then strategically revises the father's vision by adapting Plutarchus' name into another role that is more flattering to the youthful imagination than that of historian.[19] Merecraft's reading offers Plutarchus a soldierly role that comes complete with costumes, sets, and a heroic plot:

> Buy him a captain's place, for shame; and let him
> Into the world, early, and with his plume,
> And scarfs, march through Cheapside, or along Cornhill,
> And by the virtue of those, draw down a wife
> There from a window worth ten thousand pound!
> Get him the posture book, and's leaden men
> To set upon the table 'gainst his mistress
> Chance to come by, that he may draw her in,
> And show her Finsbury battles.
> *Gilthead*                                    I have placed him
> With Justice Eitherside, to get so much law—
> *Merecraft*
> As thou hast conscience. Come, come, thou dost wrong

> Pretty Plutarchus, who had not his name
> For nothing: but was born to train the youth
> Of London, in the military truth—
> That way his genius lies.                    (3.2.33–47)

Plutarchus' reiterated "Good father, do not trust 'em" (repetitiousness, generally a symptom of an obsessive fantasy in Jonsonian comedy, seems to be hereditary) immediately changes to "Father, dear father, trust him if you love me." Nearly every man has his play, as well as his price: Merecraft concocts an alluring script capable of supplanting the equally conventional Middletonian plot that was apparently playing in Plutarchus' mind and making him so wary.[20] Merecraft bolsters this vision of glory by enlisting a motif which pervaded the works (such as Shakespeare's romances) that were popular on the English stage in the years preceding *The Devil Is an Ass*. The motif is a version of what Freud would call "the family romance," a fantasy in which the noble blood of a lost parent mysteriously enables a child to pursue a nobler destiny than the child's visible parentage would justify. Merecraft asks Plutarchus,

> Was not thy mother a gentlewoman?
> *Plutarchus*                                           Yes, sir.
> *Merecraft*
> And went to Court at Christmas, and St George's tide?
> And lent the lords' men, chains?
> *Plutarchus*                              Of gold, and pearl, sir.
> *Merecraft*  I knew thou must take after somebody!
> Thou couldst not be else. This was no shop-look!
> I'll ha' thee Captain Gilthead . . .           (3.3.164–169)

Such is the magic of Merecraft.

Merecraft similarly allows Lady Tailbush to cast a theatrical spell over herself, while he collects admission from her as well as from the others who can be lured to the play under the illusion that it is part of their own. He has sold her a role under the guise of selling her a prospective monopoly on cosmetics, by which she expects "to grow great, and court it with the secret" (3.4.56). She suspends her disbelief so thoroughly that she unflaggingly accepts the thinly disguised Wittipol as a Spanish noblewoman, since that role fits into her play. Once her monopoly is granted, she assures Lady Eitherside,

> Have with 'em for the great caroche, six horses,
> And the two coachmen, with my Ambler, bare,
> And my three women: we will live, i' faith,
> The examples o' the town, and govern it.
> I'll lead the fashion still.                              (4.2.11–15)

Lady Tailbush thus pursues a grand vision of her future self built almost entirely on theatrical devices for self-transformation: the makeup that will create her prestigious role at court,[21] and the "new gown" that will revive its prestige each month (4.2.20). Even if this play were to become reality, the reality of it would still be little more than a play; the fools cannot break out of their theatrical mode of perception, and thus they invite their own cozening.

Merecraft tells Fitzdotterel that Wittipol's trick is "A plot o' your wife's, to get your land"; Merecraft clearly realizes that the way to gain this fool's attention is to depict a standard plot device in which he is the noble victim. He thus lures Fitzdotterel into an array of conventional melodramatic stances—as a bitterly exiled Malvolio, a sorrowful Adam, a nobly disdainful Claudio, a forbearing Frankford—that Merecraft will be able to use to his own advantage:

> *Merecraft*
> But this way, sir, you'll be revenged at height.
> *Everill*   Upon 'em all.
> *Merecraft*                Yes faith, and since your wife
>   Has run the way of woman thus, e'en give her—
> *Fitzdotterel*   Lost by this hand, to me; dead to all joys
>   Of her dear Dotterel, I shall never pity her:
>   That could not pity herself.
> *Merecraft*                Princely resolved sir,
>   And like yourself still, in potentia.            (5.3.22–28)

He can now make Fitzdotterel think he is fulfilling his true noble potential, when Fitzdotterel will in fact be acting like a devil in a play.

Although Merecraft is the author of all these Jonsonian exposures and exploitations of the self-dramatizing instinct, the play affords him very little respect—less, for example, than *Volpone* and *The Alchemist* afford their conspirators. If *The Devil Is an Ass* had been like these earlier works, Merecraft could rightly have expected his successes to overshadow his eventual rebuff in the eyes of the audience. Jonson pulls a nasty trick on this modern schemer, a trick that should probably surprise the audience as well as Merecraft himself. Usually in Jonsonian comedy a playwright-figure is defeated only when he falls into the prime error of his victims, by subscribing to an outdated mode of theater and mistaking it for his real life. Merecraft's scheme collapses for virtually the opposite reason: his puppet Fitzdotterel is frightened out of his modern "possessive" performance because he discovers that his life had truly become an old-fashioned morality play with an actual diabolical tempter. The mode of play that Fitzdotterel was imitating turns out to be his reality after all, and that revelation inevitably disables the sort of Jonsonian schemer who exploits the discrepancy between art and life.

This twist, this intervention of a moral absolute through the revival of an old dramatic mode, allows Wittipol to take control from Merecraft. Wittipol, like Jonson, must finally depend on the resuscitation of an antique plot to undermine what had become a standard sort of plot in Jacobean city-comedy (coney-catching on a grand scale) and to build a radically modern one in its place. This new plot (like that of *Epicoene*) uses such devices as a deed of feoffment, a school of social fashion, and a transvestite disguise to pluck an inheritance from an unworthy heir on behalf of true justice and equality in marriage. In other words, it is the sort of plot that would become typical in the century following *The Devil Is An Ass*.

The only melodramatic poses Jonson fails to undercut are those of reformed rake and witty but sentimental gentleman, poses struck by both Manly and Wittipol in the courtship segments of the plot. Theirs is similarly the only scheme that incorporates Merecraft's instead of being incorporated by his. Admittedly, Manly's courtship of Lady Tailbush—in which he suffers the conventional betrayal by his messenger Everill—does undergo the decentering that humiliates several other failed projects in the play (4.1.18–31). And Wittipol never manages to fulfill the role of adulterous seducer toward which he seems to aspire. But both those failures are finally ennobling rather than degrading, and they subserve the stories of cynicized wooer and the romanticized cynic that would become no less standard in subsequent satiric and sentimental comedies. Manly's conclusion that " 'twill prove a medicine against marriage; / To know their manners" (4.4.5–6; cf. 191–192) certainly sounds familiar to a modern reader, as does Wittipol's discovery of one worthy woman who converts him from artful seducer to sentimental protector. Jonson is here (as in *Epicoene*) pointing toward dramatic conventions that have not yet fully established themselves as conventions; perhaps that is why he fails to employ his parodic strategy against what must certainly strike a twentieth-century reader as a self-aggrandizing posture susceptible to ridicule.

The play's three most conventionally admirable characters—Manly, Wittipol, and Mrs. Fitzdotterel—are gathered into act 4, scene 6, for little apparent purpose other than to allow them to espouse noble sentiments and to assure us that there will be no illicit physical consummation of this marriage of true minds. Wittipol enters proclaiming, "Be not afraid, sweet lady: you are trusted / To love, not violence here; I am no ravisher." She answers that when she had responded to his flirtatious advances,

> my hope was then,
> (Though interrupted, ere it could be uttered)
> That whom I found the master of such language,
> That brain and spirit, for such an enterprise,
> Could not but if those succours were demanded
> To a right use, employ them virtuously! (4.6.1–15)

Manly then steps out from behind a screen with his own piece of sanctimony:

> Oh friend! Forsake not
> The brave occasion virtue offers you
> To keep you innocent: I have feared for both;
> And watched you, to prevent the ill I feared.
> But, since the weaker side hath so assured me,
> Let not the stronger fall by his own vice,
> Or be the less a friend, 'cause virtue needs him.
> *Wittipol* Virtue shall never ask my succours twice;
> Most friend, most man; your counsels are commands:

Lady, I can love goodness in you more
Than I did beauty.                                          (4.6.28–38)

This is hardly consistent with any plausible interpretation of their earlier actions or any plausible degree of foresight, and it comes dangerously close to the pietistic tone of Celia and Bonario in *Volpone*.[22] In the earlier great comedies a sharper (or at least more satirical) wit would have emerged to prey on this self-congratulatory tone. Like Lovewit in *The Alchemist,* of course, Jonson is generally prepared to forgive a great deal if it is cleverly executed; furthermore, Jonson always stops his plots when an honest woman is about to lose her sexual purity. The failure to challenge the heroic stances taken by Manly and Wittipol may serve to confirm that Jonson is less concerned with attacking proud poses per se than he is with attacking poses derived from, or representative of, dramatic traditions prior and alien to his own. But that failure badly weakens the play for any post-Restoration audience.

It is also possible, of course, that these speeches would have seemed as unpleasantly sanctimonious to an audience in 1616 as they do today. Jonson is never at his best with fine romantic sentiments, and his deeper allegiances may still have been with the satiric cynicism from which *The Devil Is an Ass* struggles to extricate itself. Certainly the collision Jonson arranged between the vivid energies of the morality play and those of satiric city-comedy yielded something noticeably less vivid and less energetic than either. If the only compensating virtue was novelty, then it is hardly surprising that *The Devil Is an Ass* eventually slipped from the core of the Jonson canon toward the group of "dotages."[23]

Jonson does not exempt Wittipol's activities entirely from the taint of literary pretension. In courting Mrs. Fitzdotterel, Wittipol often seems as much an anthology of Jacobean love poetry as a sincere and substantial wooer. Jonson's mistrust of this sort of conventional poetic wooing is evident from such works as the "Celebration of Charis"; in fact, during the second interview, Wittipol actually steals several conceits and phrases from that ambiguous sequence, then quotes in full one of its poems.[24] He begins the first interview with a formulaic *occupatio,* telling her he will not praise her magnificent beauty. He then turns to versions of Donne's "The Apparition" concerning her misalliance and her husband's midnight sorcery, and Donne's "The Exstasie" con-

cerning the physical and metaphysical implications of their forbidden attraction, with some highly conventional *carpe diem* material
thrown in:

> That you are the wife
> To so much blasted flesh as scarce hath soul,
> Instead of salt, to keep it sweet, I think
> Will ask no witnesses to prove. The cold
> Sheets that you lie in, with the watching candle,
> . . . . .
> Will confess for you.
>
> Think of it, lady, be your mind as active
> As is your beauty: view your object well.
> Examine both my fashion, and my years.
> Things that are like are soon familiar:
> And Nature joys still in equality.
> Let not the sign o' the husband fright you, lady.
> But ere your spring be gone, enjoy it. Flowers,
> Though fair, are oft but of one morning. Think,
> All beauty does not last until the autumn.
> You grow old while I tell you this.
>
> And but I am,
> By the said contract, thus to take my leave of you
> At this so envious distance, I had taught
> Our lips ere this, to seal the happy mixture
> Made of our souls.                  (1.6.88–198)

Manly is right to call this "the strangest motion I e'er saw" (1.6.230);
Wittipol, like Fitzdotterel, is as unrealistic as a puppet here, a
puppet controlled by a literary script. Even as he begins to fondle
her, his heated narration (2.6.71–78) is suspiciously reminiscent
of Donne's "Elegy: Going to Bed."
    But if Wittipol's infatuation leads him to deceive either Mrs.
Fitzdotterel or himself with his secondhand poeticisms, he is at
least alert enough to know that he is staging a play, and furthermore to know what power such plays can have. And he does win
her love, however chaste. In abandoning Merecraft, Jonson has
by no means abandoned dramatic self-consciousness as a criterion
for success in his plays; authorship still generates authority. When
Wittipol takes a role, such as that of the Spanish lady, he is fully

aware of the scripting and costuming involved, aware that he is merely replacing a professional actor (3.4.2–34). He even jokes ironically about the relationship between that dramatic role and his true self, assuring Fitzdotterel that Manly is no more a friend to Wittipol "than I am, sir!" (4.7.25). He cleverly incorporates the ring that is a prop in Fitzdotterel's and Merecraft's plots into his own courtship of Fitzdotterel's wife (4.4.100–109).

The other side of the "motion" Wittipol stages with Mrs. Fitzdotterel is his projection of her answer. This is itself a device derived from the seducer Zima in Boccaccio's *Decameron,* but Wittipol makes it a device of self-discovery rather than of self-deception.[25] In this situation, as Barton remarks, "Playing shapes reality, not because it is an agent of deceit and imposture, as it was in the hands of performers like Volpone, or Face and Subtle, but because it is a way of uncovering and articulating hidden emotional truths."[26] Wittipol not only avoids the pitfalls of his role as a dramaturge; he also (like Jonson) uses that role in ingenious ways to assure himself of a positive response. He gives Mrs. Fitzdotterel's character in his little drama a reply that ennobles her through her acceptance of his advances; in other words, like the coney-catchers throughout Jonson's drama, Wittipol offers her an appealing part which also serves his interests. She must assume the proffered role as receptive mistress in order to assert not only her intelligence, but even her existence: "I would not have him think he met a statue: / Or spoke to one, not there, though I were silent" (2.2.69–70). Wittipol has arranged his play so that she must respond to him, or else cast herself as "that dull stupid creature / He said" (2.2.28–29). When she has an opportunity to respond in her own words, her terminology is suggestively theatrical. For the benefit of the messenger Pug, she chooses lines that fit the role of a loyal wife, but she trusts Wittipol to read between those lines: "wish him to forbear his acting to me, / At the gentleman's chamber-window in Lincoln's Inn there / That opens to my gallery" (2.2.52–54). The invitation, on both sides, is an invitation to play, in both senses.

A similarly strategic offer is made to the audience in the final lines of the play proper: there is room for us in this virtuous transaction, if we approve of Jonson's play. The alternative, for us as for Mrs. Fitzdotterel, is to declare ourselves dull, stupid statues. Though we have been silent, we can allow Manly to offer

a virtuous response on our behalf, and thereby form a marriage
of true minds with the playwright against the unappreciative fools
around us in the audience, as Mrs. Fitzdotterel does with Wittipol
against her husband. Manly's closing remarks thus make us, like
Mrs. Fitzdotterel, the objects of a verbal seduction that is finally
moral rather than salacious. In this regard, Manly serves a purpose
similar to that served by Clement in *Every Man In His Humor* and
Lovewit in *The Alchemist:* they are all representations of the ideal
audience, positioned so that we will want to identify ourselves
with their remarks at the very moment they implicitly praise Jonson's comic dramaturgy.

After luring us (as well as the fools onstage) into several false
assumptions about the sort of play-world we were visiting, Jonson
obliges us to listen to Manly reproaching his fellow Londoners
for the same sorts of conventionalized misprisions. At the end of
the play the characters on stage think they are seeing what we at
the beginning thought we were seeing, namely, a devil play. The
story we have watched and often mistaken as it developed will
now be told to them in a clarifying and mortifying retrospect, as
we are obliged to review it for ourselves:

> Please you go in, sir, and hear truths, then judge 'em:
> And make amends for your late rashness; when,
> You shall but hear the pains and care was taken,
> To save this fool from ruin . . .
> And how much
> His modest, and too worthy wife hath suffered
> By misconstruction, from him, you will blush,
> First, for your own belief, more for his actions!
> His land is his: and never, by my friend,
> Or by myself, meant to another use,
> But for her succours who hath equal right.
> If any other had worse counsels in't,
> (I know I speak to those can apprehend me)
> Let 'em repent 'em, and be not detected.
> It is not manly to take joy, or pride
> In human errors (we do all ill things,
> They do 'em worst that love 'em, and dwell there,
> Till the plague comes). The few that have the seeds

> Of goodness left will sooner make their way
> To a true life, by shame, than punishment.     (5.8.155–174)

These lines can be taken as directed by the playwright to the audience, as well as by Manly to the other characters. Perhaps we, too, rashly underestimated the virtuous modesty of Mrs. Fitzdotterel, and had worse counsels than the heroes did for what should be done with Fitzdotterel's land. That recognition obliges us to "blush, / First for your own belief, more for his actions"; to complain that we expected and desired a more exploitative solution is to confess our attachment to the cynical conventions of satiric city-comedy. Jonson has entered a new and different phase in his drama, a phase in which he tells us "It is not manly to take joy, or pride / In human errors"; and he is using our desire to be Manly, with or without the capital "M," to compel our approval of this new phase. By altering the usual resolution of his satiric plots, Jonson establishes a higher moral tone for his comedy; and by giving Manly this speech, Jonson defends this altered mode of comedy from criticism.

Certainly the tradition in which Jonson had seemed to be writing pointed toward a different conclusion. Witty gentlemen such as Callimaco in Machiavelli's *La Mandragola* generally finish the job when they set out to seduce the beautiful wife of a fool such as Nicia.[27] The suitor in the Boccaccio tale who, like Wittipol, bribes the husband for the right to address his beloved and speaks for her when she is silent, eventually achieves his adulterous satisfaction. Critics from Dryden onward have complained that, by allowing his heroes to take this unconventional moralistic stance toward the end of *The Devil Is an Ass,* Jonson has imposed an abrupt, awkward, and unconvincing twist on the play which "destroys the aesthetic and moral structure with which he had unified his mature comedies."[28] What I have attempted to demonstrate in this book, however, is that Jonson's major comedies are united by their systematic destruction of any established aesthetic or moral structure that might permit the audience to escape its obligation to sustain an ethical and intellectual alertness.

In this sense, the surprising abandonment of adulterous flirtation and of property fraud by the three admirable characters can be defended as a tactic in Jonson's parodic strategy. If we complain

that we were misled by conventional theatrical cues into anticipating a more exploitative conclusion, if we accuse Jonson of
playing the tempter to our baser appetites that enjoy watching
predatory coney-catching and adulterous seductions, then we really
only equate ourselves with the demonstrated inadequacies—ethical and intellectual—of Merecraft and his play-drunk gulls. Jonson
employs this tactic somewhat less gracefully than in the earlier
great comedies, but again the quirks of Jonsonian plotting serve
to shake our complacency about both the form and the content
of drama.

If Manly's tendentious speech is designed as a rebuff to the less
receptive spectators, the Epilogue that follows it may be designed
as a rebuff to the playwrights those spectators favor. At the start
of the play Satan warns Pug against the old ways of bedeviling,
and the warning sounds suspiciously like a Jonsonian warning to
other authors against the old ways of playwriting, which can no
longer earn drama the respect it deserves from a cosmopolitan
audience:

> Stay i' your place, know your own strengths, and put not
> Beyond the sphere of your activity.
> You are too dull a devil to be trusted
> Forth in those parts, Pug, upon any affair
> That may concern our name, on earth. It is not
> Everyone's work. The state of Hell must care
> Whom it employs, in point of reputation,
> Here about London. You would make, I think,
> An agent to be sent, for Lancashire
> Proper enough; or some parts of Northumberland . . .
>
> (1.1.24–33)

The implication is that lesser playwrights should open out of town
until they acquire a Jonsonian approach to drama, a skeptical,
controlling distance from literary commonplaces. The Epilogue
indicates that Jonson includes Shakespeare in that group of lesser
playwrights. Its opening lines strike me as a clear (and clearly
parodic) allusion to the opening of Shakespeare's great Epilogue
of five years earlier, suggesting a comparison between Shakespeare's theatrical magic and Merecraft's impressive but absurd
scams. Prospero's "Now my charms are all o'erthrown, / And
what strength I have's mine own," becomes, "Thus, the projecter,

here, is overthrown. / But I have now a project of mine own."
Whether we take the *Tempest* Epilogue as Shakespeare's grand farewell to the stage or merely as Prospero's plea for a protraction of
his dramatic identity, it is appropriate that a play satirizing the
tendency to make life into a drama should feel compelled to revise
statements that blur that boundary. Jonson has been advocating a
sort of farewell to the stage through the anti-conventional dramatic
techniques of all his comedies, and has been more concerned with
the realistic problems created by a fantasy of living in a play than
the fantastic problems of a stage character trying to partake of real
life. The playwright, Jonson's Epilogue goes on to argue (ll. 3–6;
cf. 3.5.44–47), will not be either made or annihilated by the audience's approval or disapproval of his work; all that is at stake,
as at the end of *Bartholomew Fair,* is an invitation to supper.

As the playwright heads home to supper with the players, and
the audience home to supper with its fellow actors in the *theatrum
mundi*, Pug has been carried away in defeat, and Satan himself has
retreated in embarrassment from London's streets and Jonson's
stage. Much of the appeal of devil plays had been their willingness
to help people imagine what it would be like if a devil were actually
to enter their world. Jonson demonstrates that if there were a Vice
at work in London, people would hardly notice him in the midst
of their own sharper vices. Old-fashioned allegorical representations of evil therefore give way to a realism in which the evils
arise from the social structure, and in which the true villains are
not the horned visitors from another world, but rather those who
blend in most skillfully, who superficially conform to the refined
conduct of their societies. Shakespeare's "honest" Iago may represent a prototype for the chameleonlike characters who, from
Luke Frugal in Massinger's *The City Madam* (1632) through Charles
Surface in Sheridan's *A School for Scandal* (1777), become a favorite
sort of literary villain. Restoration comedy and eighteenth-century
satire will be more at home at supper than they will around any
melodramatic hellmouth.

But *The Devil Is an Ass* is not merely the sort of light, scoffing
satire that feeds naturally on pretentious poses. It is Jonson's way
of insisting that a satiric perspective on the foolish or wicked role-
players of society can still generate a positive moral viewpoint and
a solid dramatic entity not yet petrified into conventionality. It
can be argued that in *The Devil Is an Ass,* for the first time since

the representations of Queen Elizabeth in *Cynthia's Revels* and the original version of *Every Man Out of His Humor,* Jonson places a truly admirable woman at the focal point of a comedy.[29] If, as I have suggested, those representations of Queen Elizabeth were Jonson's desperate device to locate an ethical object impervious to his satire, then it may be more than a mere coincidence that *The Devil Is an Ass* resumes the earnest quest of those early plays for a healthy and valid mode of comedy. Without such an unassailably ideal woman and the sentiments she arouses in an otherwise satirical playwright-figure, comedy cannot escape the implied cynicism of even avowedly moral plays such as *Volpone* and the self-consuming character of plays shaped by the parodic strategy. The morality-play motif of *The Devil Is an Ass* serves not only to humiliate a popular theatrical tradition, but also to alert the audience to Jonson's new project: the creation of a dramatic mode that neither (like so much earnest Renaissance comedy) abandons its comic quality to make way for moral admonition, nor (like most satiric city-comedy) undercuts its ethical orientation to preserve the comic spirit. Jonson is not saying whether or not devils really exist. What he is saying, to twist a phrase of Voltaire's, is that if the devil does not exist, it will no longer be necessary to invent him on the stage to enable moral drama.

The resolution of the plot of *The Devil Is an Ass* is both puzzling and intriguing. At the trial, Merecraft and Wittipol are truly engaged in a *poetomachia* like the one Jonson had engaged in years earlier, trying to jeer each other's plays off the stage. They subvert each other's *sprezzatura* by revealing the theatrical artfulness behind each other's claims to simple honesty. The decision, surprisingly, comes when Jonson chooses to credit rather than discredit a popular old dramatic motif. Wittipol assumes control of the play from Merecraft only when the morality play becomes as authentic as the satiric city-comedy, only when Pug's devil story is revealed as truth rather than stagecraft, only when reality conforms to conventional art.

The final events of *The Devil Is an Ass* seem to reverse the pattern and the ethos of Jonsonian comedy, because they represent the defeat of Merecraft's plot, which is a version of satiric city-comedy, by the archaic plot of a morality play. This may, however, be Jonson's way of distancing himself from a subgenre that was

by 1616 showing some troubling signs of senescence, and identifying himself with the next stage in the dialectical development
of drama. Merecraft may be a kind of scapegoat for the weakening
vitality of the satiric mode, and Jonson sacrifices him so that he
can invest his literary sovereignty in Wittipol instead. In retrospect,
certainly, the ascendancy of Wittipol's type of comedy seems less
a triumph of a superior Jonsonian wit than a triumph of literary-
historical inevitability. Perhaps Jonson foresaw, as well as provoked, the transition toward sentimental comedy, and tried to
make himself a place in it. Such allegorical and anachronistic speculations must of course remain highly tentative, but they do make
some sense of what is clearly an odd new variation in Jonson's
life-long struggle for artistic *Lebensraum*. The momentary revival
of the morality play, which imposes its own reality on the cynical
playwright Merecraft, may be Jonson's device for restoring morality to the increasingly cynical world of satiric city-comedy. The
new mode will consist of a dialectical synthesis of conservative
morals with satiric wit, a synthesis embodied by Wittipol and
exemplified by *The Devil Is an Ass*.

# CHAPTER EIGHT

# The New Inn

## AN EPILOGUE

The disastrous unpopularity of *The New Inn* (1629) must rank among the great ironies of English literary history, because the play represents a profound and ceremonious concession to the popular tastes Jonson had resisted for so long. The new inn, for the audience as well as the characters, is a place where their long-cherished fantasies are miraculously fulfilled. The location of the inn in a distant London suburb may reflect the location of the play halfway between the satiric world of city-comedy and the romantic world of pastoral. Beaurline suggests that the reputation of suburban inns would have kept the audience wondering "whether the inn can be merry without being debauched";[1] I believe Jonson is raising the same question about comedy in *The New Inn*. He may well have believed he had found a way to please a general audience without rendering himself vulnerable to the sort of intellectual scorn he had formerly visited on his popular rivals; sadly, he failed on both counts. Jonson's righteously indignant "Ode to Himself," and his peevish complaints about the actors and the audience, suggest not only that this rejection infuriated Jonson even more than the failure of *Catiline,* but also that, this time, he was not sure whom or what to blame first. In his "Dedication to the Reader" Jonson says that he prefers to entrust the play "rather to thy rustic candour than all the pomp of their [the original audience's] pride and solemn ignorance" (ll. 14–16); he now resents the ostentatiously sophisticated theatergoers of Caroline London at least as much as he mistrusts the unsophisticated sort of audience against whose nostalgic desires the earlier plays had positioned themselves.

Jonson is not willing to forget all about satiric comedy, but he does the next best thing. He locks it down in the basement, where all the low-life characters pass their time much as the similar swindlers, gulls, and profligates did in the earlier comedies: crudely indulging their greed, lust, anger, and appetite, and toying in very Jonsonian ways with their names and their roles.[2] If, as detractors of the play maintain,[3] these are rather boring versions of Jonson's satiric dramatis personae, it may be because Jonson himself was becoming bored with them. The Epilogue points out that Jonson

> could have haled in
> The drunkards and the noises of the inn
> In his last act; if he had thought it fit
> To vent you vapours in the place of wit:
> But better 'twas that they should sleep or spew
> Than in the scene to offend or him or you.          (13–18)

Because this playwright "meant to please you" (l. 5), he forbade the characters of satiric city-comedy to taint the romantic solutions achieved in the exalted world upstairs, let alone exploit those solutions as they surely would have in the early comedies. Where formerly the romantic fantasies would have been decentered in favor of these below-stairs puns, schemes, and brawls, in *The New Inn* the downstairs folk are gradually forgotten while the play focuses on fulfilling the sentimental hopes of the upstairs characters and of the credulous members of the audience.

Jonson feints at again leaving these romantic stories unfulfilled—both Lovel and the host Goodstock complain about the unsatisfying way their little plays have apparently ended (4.4.247–253; 5.1.24–33)—but then he relents. Even such self-indulgent characters as Beaufort and Lady Frampul are finally led to the wedding altar of comedy rather than to the whipping post of satire. Jonson follows his usual pattern by propelling his audience from romantic expectation to satiric disillusionment, but in this case he then invites us back into the pleasures of romantic illusion. There is something distinctly palinodal, in other words, about *The New Inn*. Jonson is not completely retracting his criticisms of the unrealistic oversights and reunions of romance plots; like Shakespeare in *The Winter's Tale,* he insists repeatedly that we recognize the story as a literary fantasy.[4] But he seems to be acknowledging that such falsehoods have a place in the theater because they can evoke true feelings by corresponding to the true desires of the human heart.

This may be one reason critics have been so radically divided on whether *The New Inn* is a romantic indulgence or a dismissive burlesque of romance.[5] It is the work of a man who could neither submit completely to dramatic illusions nor resist completely their seductive appeal. Jonson plays the literary conventions and improbabilities to their height, but he offers no direct indication, either within the play or in his subsequent defenses of it, that he wants the play to be taken ironically. Indeed, the fact that he places so much blame for its failure on the way it was "negligently play'd" argues against the ironic reading, since awkward performances would damage a delicate romantic fantasy far more than they would a broad burlesque of such fantasies. Furthermore, the virtues advocated, and the feelings aroused, seem quite authentic. By emphasizing the conventionality of his story, without denying the profit and pleasure such a story could bring to its audience as well as its characters, Jonson invites the contradictory responses that have characterized criticism of *The New Inn.* The contradictions can be partly resolved by recognizing that the play offers a running commentary on the struggle between satiric distance and romantic absorption involved in its own composition. *The New Inn* is Jonson's genial reevaluation of his approach to moral drama, and at its center is a reevaluation of his parodic strategy.[6] The irony is that the spirit of parodic satire Jonson had nurtured for so long, a spirit whose natural prey is conventional romantic melodrama, escaped from the cellar of the new inn into the audience at the first performance and (like Frankenstein's monster) attacked its maker.[7] Jonson would have found himself trapped in a bitter role-reversal, chastised by his audience for his own apparent excursion into melodramatic conventionality.

Jonson, of course, had no intention of surrendering unconditionally to the melodramatic delusions he had mocked for so long. My analysis of *The Devil Is an Ass* suggests that Jonson deviated radically from his parodic principles in allowing Mrs. Fitzdotterel to discover her true self through theater, a self which would otherwise have remained submerged. *The New Inn* expands that moment into an entire play. It is the creation for which the accepting spirit of *Bartholomew Fair* and the sentimental twist of *The Devil Is an Ass* had cleared the ground. Jonson still realizes that theatricalism can be self-deception: he invites to the new inn, for the purpose of chasing them out, Nick and Pinnacia Stuff, who use costumes and role-playing to deceive themselves about their own and each other's true identities. But the play indulges, and shares with the audience, the more enlightened kind of role-playing that allows Lady Frampul and Lovel to discover and develop their mutual romantic interest, and allows Prudence to discover and develop the nobility of her inner nature. As long as the characters know that they are playing, and as long as the audience is kept similarly aware that this is only a play, Jonson will permit such indulgences. By acting out their roles in the play-within-the-play, the characters can become what they had long yearned to be. At the same time, by remembering that the play is merely a fiction, Jonson frees himself to fulfill the audience's posited yearning for the sort of romantic conclusion he had formerly refused to tolerate.

The new inn, like Lovewit's house in *The Alchemist* and the bedchamber in *Volpone,* is a metaphorical theater. The comparison is established in the first lines of the Prologue: "You are welcome, welcome all, to the new inn; / Though the old house"—apparently the Blackfriars Theater[8]—where "the same cook / Still, and the fat," will cook them up a play. Although Jonson is as conscious as ever that the line between players and real people can be a shaky one, he no longer seems as uneasy about the ethical costs of that confusion, nor as eager to seize the opportunities it offers him to shape his plot and to outposition his rivals. When Prudence fears that Lady Frampul will be dishonored if some of her clothing ends up adorning actors, the Lady replies that "all are players, and but serve the scene" (2.1.39). It is a platitude, but here it is also a truth; is the *theatrum mundi* commonplace ironized, or is it vindicated, when it is expressed by a character whose world is indeed a play? The tendency of life to imitate art, which Jonson had earlier used in a penetrating critique of both human behavior and dramatic convention, here becomes mostly a subject of whimsically detached observation. Lovel questions Goodstock's decision to run an inn, "It being i'your free-will (as 'twas) to choose / What parts you would sustain" (1.3.108–109), and Goodstock responds that the inn allows him to

> imagine all the world's a play;
> The state and men's affairs all passages
> Of life, to spring new scenes, come in, go out,
> And shift, and vanish; and if I have got
> A seat to sit at ease here i' mine inn,
> To see the comedy; and laugh, and chuck
> At the variety and throng of humours
> And dispositions that come jostling in
> And out still, as they one drove hence another:
> Why, will you envy me my happiness?    (1.3.128–137)

The question is quite relevant to my critique of Jonson, because in his late plays he seems increasingly content to observe the variety of the world's humors and steer them toward a standard happy ending.

Jonson, like the disguised Lord Frampul, is the host of this new inn, and both men are determined to make "the Light Heart" suit its name. Jonson's tenacious dignity in poetry, earthy realism in drama, and general scorn for humors, all melt away in the person of the host:

> *Host*  "Be merry, and drink sherry"; that's my posy!
>   For I shall never joy i'my light heart
>   So long as I conceive a sullen guest,
>   Or any thing that's earthy!
> *Lovel*                 Humorous host.
> *Host*  I care not if I be.    (1.2.29–33)

To emphasize that the host is a version of the jovial playwright, the play brings in the otherwise superfluous information that, before assuming his disguise as this innkeeper, Lord Frampul had worked for some time as a "puppet-master" for "Young Goose, the motion-man" (1.5.61–62). When he finally reveals his true identity at 5.5.91–100, his speech "reads almost like [Jonson's] autobiography, personal and literary."[9] The disguise plots from which Jonson generates his happy ending are also "Supposititious fruits of a host's brain" (5.5.41).

Prudence is another version of the playwright, assigned as "sovereign / Of the day's sports devised i'the inn" (1.6.43–44). She shares with Jonson the responsibility (as efficient cause and first cause, respectively) for introducing the peculiarities for which *The*

*New Inn* has been condemned: the somewhat forced shift into romance, and Lovel's long presentations on love and valor that slow the action. Pru rescues the inn, as Jonson does the theater, from a melancholic, alienated, anatomical spirit—the spirit of satire—and converts it to a joyous spirit of union and reunion, the spirit of romantic comedy. Her main decree compels Lovel (who, we learn at 1.1.24–33, has been conducting scientific anatomies in the new inn) to play the advocate of love for two hours (the standard duration of an Elizabethan play) to Lady Frampul, in her role as a disdainer of such tender sentiments. Since that is precisely what he had long wished he could do, theater becomes a way of achieving authenticity, rather than of compromising it. The characters in Pru's little drama, like those in Jonson's larger one, become more real, more true to themselves, in their roles than they were before they started playing. She herself is able to display her true nobility only because she is given the role of Queen of the Revels, and the result is her transformation into a true noblewoman by marriage to Lord Latimer.[10]

As Lovel's discourse begins to move her heart, Lady Frampul acknowledges the transformation in terms that remind us of the false transformations in *The Alchemist*. Her speech about Lovel could very easily be spoken about Subtle by any of the *Alchemist* gulls:

> How am I changed! By what alchemy
> Of love or language am I thus translated!
> His tongue is tipped with the philosophers' stone,
> And that hath touched me thorough every vein!
> I feel that transmutation o' my blood
> As I were quite become another creature,
> And all he speaks it is projection!
> *Pru*   Well feigned, my lady: now her parts begin!
> *Latimer*   And she will act 'em subtly.          (3.2.169–177)

We are likely to share the mistaken assumption of Pru and Latimer that this is merely another theatrical illusion, but the new inn is a place where such transformations can actually take place, under the guise and even the guidance of theater. Thirty lines later, Prudence again praises as a theatrical performance Lady Frampul's affectionate commendation of Lovel: "Excellent actor! How she hits this passion!" But reality is rapidly catching up to the fiction, as the jealous Latimer senses: "But do you think she plays?"

The answer is, of course, yes and no. Both the context and the content of this courtship are literary, but the literature liberates and reflects genuine sentiments; life engages in a dialogue with art, instead of merely imitating it. Lovel's bookish speech about love generates real love from Lady Frampul, and then, conversely, his real act of valor generates a call from Lady Frampul for a bookish speech about valor. Lovel's speeches and Lady Frampul's reactions display the sort of derivative literary flavoring that, in earlier plays, would have invited humiliation and augured defeat for a character's desires. Lady Frampul praises Lovel's discourse on love as

> the marrow of all lovers' tenets!
> Who hath read Plato, Heliodore, or Tatius,
> Sidney, D'Urfé, or all Love's fathers, like him?
> He is there the master of sentences,
> Their school, their commentary, text, and gloss,
> And breathes the true divinity of Love!          (3.2.202–207)

Evidently Lovel's reading of Sidney did not include the first sonnet in the "Astrophil and Stella" sequence, which warns against the futility of trying to express one's own passion by imitating the high-poetical expressions of earlier lovers. Jonson's earlier plays would surely have admonished an anthologist such as Lovel in much the same way that Sidney's Astrophil is admonished: " 'Fool,' said my Muse to me, 'Look in thy heart and write.' " But in *The New Inn* Lovel finds a more receptive audience in Lady Frampul, who replies by offering to "say some hundred penitential verses, / There, out of Chaucer's 'Troilus and Criseyde' " to atone for her earlier impieties toward love (3.2.217–218). After Lovel scatters the ruffians, she praises him in terms that (as the closing parenthetical remark makes clear) are better suited to an encomium from classical drama than to ordinary conversation:

> I ne'er saw
> A lightning shoot so, as my servant did,
> His rapier was a meteor, and he waved it
> Over 'em like a comet! As they fled him!
> I marked his manhood! Every stoop he made

Was like an eagle's at a flight of cranes!
(As I have read somewhere.)
*Beaufort*       Bravely expressed:
*Latimer* And like a lover!      (4.3.11–18)

Is it necessarily wrong to indulge in the brave poetical expressions that love inspires? Lady Frampul's approach to praising is a little absurd, but Lovel's action *was* essentially heroic, and her reaction comes from her heart as well as from her reading.

As those who interpret the play ironically have stressed, speeches throughout *The New Inn* have this sort of derivative literary flavor, which renders them vulnerable to mockery. That only makes it more striking, however, that Jonson does not mock them, either by offering the commentary of a witty author-surrogate, or by leaving the yearnings they express notably unfulfilled. Self-dramatizing poses are punished so systematically in Jonson's earlier comedies that some critics virtually hallucinate such punishments in *The New Inn*,[11] but Jonson no longer seems determined to challenge the validity of literature as a mediator for human experience. Lovel begins his presentation on love by swearing on a copy of Ovid's *De Arte Amandi* (3.2.40), and his presentation on honor by similarly swearing on a copy of Thomas Usk's *Testament of Love;* but since Lovel truly adores Lady Frampul and truly rescues Pinnacia Stuff, Jonson is not inclined to prosecute him for experimenting with literary fantasies about his own passions and virtues. What is wrong with lovers being dreamers and role-players, if those dreams and roles are ways of expressing and promoting authentic sentiments?

The chief danger to a romance that has been, in effect, jump-started by drama is that the participants themselves may assume that the romance must cease when the play does. After Lady Frampul gives Lovel his second kiss, Lovel pleads for more, but Prudence forbids it:

*Pru* The Court's dissolved, removed, and the play ended.
 No sound, or air of Love more, I decree it.
*Lovel* From what a happiness hath that one word
 Thrown me into the gulf of misery?
 To what a bottomless despair? How like
 A court removing or an ended play
 Shows my abrupt precipitate estate.    (4.4.247–253)

These actors temporarily assume that they cannot carry the reality they discovered within their theatrical roles back into their lives. This, of course, is virtually the opposite of the errors mocked by Jonson's earlier comedies, where the only successful characters were those who knew and respected the moment when playing ended and an entirely different reality replaced it. Lady Frampul is quite prepared to remove the "visor" or "mask" of her role as a scorner of love and to allow Lovel to continue his wooing in a more direct manner. She cannot modestly suggest it herself, however, and Pru, the playwright-figure with the "authority" to compel it, fails to "read" that desire in Lady Frampul's "character" (4.4.283–302). Pru has not realized the potential of theater to shape a better reality, and she therefore deserves to sink from her costumed role as Queen of the Revels back to her original identity as a servant:

> *Pru*   I swear I thought you had dissembled, madam,
>   And doubt you do so yet.
> *Lady Frampul*                Dull, stupid wench!
>   Stay i' thy state of ignorance still, be damned,
>   An idiot chambermaid! Hath all my care,
>   My breeding thee in fashion, thy rich clothes,
>   Honours and titles wrought no brighter effects
>   On thy dark soul than thus?             (4.4.310–316)

The failure properly to integrate drama and life, to read and write them into each other, is now as serious an error as the failure properly to separate them was in the earlier plays.

By the same token, the specific lesson of *Epicoene* about the dangers of mistaking theatrical truth for actual truth is reversed in Laetitia's cross-dressing. In *Epicoene* Jonson plays on the theatrical assumptions of a Jacobean audience to hide the fact that the bride is really—that is, within the reality of the play-world—a boy. Because the audience had adjusted its perceptions to the fact that a girl's part was conventionally played by a boy, it would not have recognized what might otherwise have been an obvious truth, and that failure generated not only a surprise ending, but also a rebuff to the audience's conventional thinking. In *The New Inn* the audience can hardly be expected to "penetrate" Laetitia's longstanding disguise as the boy Frank, because the actor is in fact a boy, and when she is cast and costumed as "Laetitia," she may indeed look more like a transvestite than like a revealed woman. Our hard-wired theatrical reflexes, our willing surrender to dramatic conventions, make us as susceptible as Morose to Epicoene's disguise. But that lesson of Jonson's satiric comedies—to think skeptically about such dramatic illusions—now renders us less perceptive than the shallow Lord Beaufort. Beaufort takes Laetitia's "costume" for a reality, more of a reality than her everyday self as "Frank," and so it proves to be.

The audience might well expect that "Laetitia" would turn out to be a boy, as the actor playing the role was actually a boy; Ferret has compared Frank to a skillful "play-boy" (1.3.5), and act 5, scene 3, is a scene right out of *Epicoene*. This time, however, to the surprise of the clever characters on stage as well as of the audience, the confusion finally resolves into romantic fulfillment rather than into a satiric attack on romantic illusions. Beaufort's marriage turns out to be, not a farce like that of Morose, but a real and happy conclusion. Like a naive spectator at the theater, Beaufort assumes that the boy dressed up as a girl is really a girl, that her costume is a reality that will allow him to live his fantasy; instead of being punished for those assumptions, he is rewarded. What appears to be Laetitia—the name means "joy"—turns out to be Laetitia and joy after all, not merely an alluring fraud set out to entice dreamers into the frank world of satire. The theatrical view, so often humiliated on stage in the earlier plays, here triumphs over what we had assumed was our more realistic perspective. We are forced to suppress our cynical awareness that the actor is nonetheless a boy—in larger terms, that the play is finally just an illusion—if we want to share in the pleasures of a happy ending. Like Busy at the puppet show in *Bartholomew Fair,* we are induced to surrender our censorious attitude and (like Goodstock watching over his own "new inn") become happily passive beholders with the rest.

When the disguised Laetitia is assigned to "play" a girl, Lady Frampul quite accidently gives her her real name. This suggests another area in which *The New Inn* inverts the parodic strategy of the earlier plays. The problem now is not that characters pursue their names too avidly, in search of melodramatic vindications; on the contrary, the problem is often that characters are slow to recognize the melodramatic truths their names reveal. As Harriett Hawkins points out, Frances Frampul speaks more truly than she is aware when she tells young "Frank" that her name is "the same with yours"; they in fact share a last name, just as they appear to share a first. The host's assumed name, Goodstock, is a clue to his noble blood, and also to the fact that "Frank" is actually his lost child, since his wife (disguised as the nurse) describes the boy as "descended of a right good stock, sir" (2.2.23; 2.6.23).[12] When the host of the new inn asks Lovel, "But is your name Love-ill, sir, or Love-well?" he simply replies, "I do not know't myself, / Whether it is. But it is love hath been / The hereditary passion of our house" (1.6.95–98). In earlier plays a character named Lovel would probably have believed that his name established him as a figure of successful love and gone off in some humiliatingly overconfident pursuit of romance. Now, however, Jonson's play and Pru's play both pursue the question on Lovel's behalf, compelling him to show that he loves well, and then making him well in love.

Some characters in *The New Inn* do let themselves be bullied by simplistic readings of their own names, and mock the names of others in equally reductive ways. But this narrowing and degrading reading of names, which Jonson imposed on complacent characters throughout the earlier comedies, is now confined to the below-stairs group, whose relentless literal-minded quibbling over one another's names has often been adduced as evidence of Jonson's dotage.[13] It may be so, but the enlightening exploration of names upstairs suggests that Jonson is deliberately establishing a contrast between the witty but limiting ironies of his former satiric practice and the satisfactions of this new play, which permits self-discovery through theatricality.

Jonson establishes a similarly sharp contrast within *The New Inn* between the healthy role-playing that moves the play into the realm of romance, and the self-dramatizing disease that invites satire. As Barton observes, "In a comedy where play-acting, as exercised in the Court of Love, is charged with such significance, its travesty cannot help but meet with punishment of a singularly harsh and unforgiving kind."[14] Sir Glorious Tipto is a less attractive version of Bobadill from *Every Man In His Humor,* a *miles gloriosus* whose rightful home is satire; since his martial role directly contradicts his true cowardly nature, Jonson explodes Tipto's pretenses early in the fourth act and banishes him from the stage and the story thereafter. The tailor Nick Stuff is a similarly degraded version of Puntarvolo from *Every Man Out of His Humor,* who woos his wife each day in the guise of a visiting knight-errant. Pinnacia Stuff explains,

> When he makes any fine garment will fit me,
> Or any rich thing that he thinks of price,
> Then must I put it on and be his countess,
> Before he carry it home unto the owners.
> A coach is hired and four horse, he runs
> In his velvet jacket thus to Rumford, Croydon,
> Hounslow, or Barnet, the next bawdy road:
> And takes me out, carries me up, and throws me
> Upon a bed.                                    (4.3.66–74)

Stuff errs, not simply by role-playing, but instead by deriving the roles from pornography rather than some higher literary form, and by using them to efface true selves and replace true feelings rather than to evoke them. This is, as Beaufort says, "A fine species / Of fornicating with a man's own wife," not merely because it emphasizes concupiscence, but because it involves a standard literary fantasy of sexual violation, and one in which his wife's personal identity is obliterated by the role her costume implies. Indeed, when Pru finally receives the dress Pinnacia was wearing (which was supposed to be Pru's costume as Queen of the Revels), Lady Frampul assures her that the tailor will ravish her too if she

> com'st unto him
> *In forma pauperis* to crave the aid
> Of his knight errant valour, to the rescue
> Of thy distressed robes! Name but thy gown,
> And he will rise to that!
> *Pru*                          I'll fire the charm first,
> I had rather die in a ditch with Mistress Shore,
> Without a smock, as the pitiful matter has it,
> Than owe my wit to clothes, or ha' it beholden.
> *Host*   Still spirit of Pru!                    (5.2.19–27)

Like Mistress Shore, Pru flirts with a royal identity, but she will not permit the role implied by her costume to override her own desires or efface her own identifying qualities.

A few scenes earlier Pru had similarly threatened to abandon her makeshift costume as Queen of the Revels, to preclude further insults from Lady Frampul. What is interesting about the precedent is that Pru was insulted for failing to understand the way roles can play into reality. She had failed to extrapolate from her own happy transformation that Lady Frampul might want to carry Lovel's courtship from its theatrical context into her real life (4.4.283–316). Lady Frampul therefore compared her to Pinnacia Stuff:

> *Lady Frampul*
> Were not the tailor's wife to be demolished,
> Ruined, uncased, thou shouldst be she, I vow.
> *Pru*   Why, take your spangled properties, your gown
> And scarfs.
> *Lady Frampul*   Pru, Pru, what dost thou mean?
> *Pru*   I will not buy this play-boy's bravery,
> At such a price, to be upbraided for it,
> Thus, every minute.                                    (4.4.317–323)

A play-boy's bravery is exactly what it is; a boy is playing a chambermaid who is playing a queen. But within the context of a theater it is also the costume of a queen, and the new inn is a place where theatrical truths overwhelm realistic ones. By the fifth act Pru has recovered her rightful costume, and resumed her royal role so ably that Lord Latimer will insist on making her a noblewoman in real life. She is no longer merely a pretender, in either sense of the word. Her grace in these grand garments is now ostentatiously contrasted with Pinnacia's ungainliness:

> *Lady Frampul*
> Sweet Pru, aye, now thou art a queen indeed!
> These robes do royally! And thou becom'st 'em!
> So they do thee! Rich garments only fit
> The parties they are made for! They shame others.
> How did they show on goody tailor's back!
> Like a caparison for a sow, God save us!          (5.2.1–6)

Costume and body complement each other here, as role and reality do so often in *The New Inn*. Theatricalism becomes a ritual of discovery, rather than the instrument of deception it had been in so much Jonsonian comedy.

Jonson characteristically ends his fourth acts with a *catastasis* that represents the defeat of a predictable ending, in favor of a more satiric ending that exalts Jonsonian wit. It seems for a while that Goodstock's hopes for a light comic resolution, in which Lovel, would win Lady Frampul, will similarly be the victim of the *catastasis* of *The New Inn*. He expresses the defeated bewilderment experienced by so many gulls in the earlier comedies who waited overconfidently for a conventional happy ending to the story they inhabited:

> I had thought to ha' sacrificed
> To merriment tonight, i' my Light Heart, Fly,
> And like a noble poet to have had
> My last act best: but all fails i' the plot.
> Lovel is gone to bed; the Lady Frampul
> And sovereign Pru fallen out: Tipto and his regiment
> Of mine-men all drunk dumb from his whoop, Barnaby,
> To his hoop, Trundle: they are his two tropics.
> No project to rear laughter on but this,
> The marriage of Lord Beaufort with Laetitia.    (5.1.24–33)

Goodstock is disappointed that the romantic comedy he envisioned has degenerated into a sex farce, and will be surprised again (as I think Jonson expected his audience to be surprised) when the romantic comedy triumphs after all. But he will appreciate that triumph when it comes, and find that he is part of it himself, rescued from the alienation he had hidden for so long under his merry disguise as a comic humorist. The host finally bequeaths the inn to Fly before departing, which offers a highly suggestive contrast with Shakespeare's farewell, in which Prospero sets the Ariel of his imagination free and returns to the grim realistic business of governing the mortal flaws in himself and his city.[15] Eighteen years later, in failing health, Jonson has his surrogate leave a familiar spirit of satire (a nominal kinsman of Mosca) to carry on the admonitory business of city-comedy in his theater if it wishes to do so, but he himself escapes into the fulfillment of an airy romantic dream.

At the end of his hours of theatrical courtship, Lovel goes to bed to "sleep, / And dream away the vapour of Love" (4.4.280–281), but he awakens in the final scene to the news that his play-love Lady Frampul will indeed be his wife, and he asks his host,

Is this a dream now, after my first sleep?
Or are these fantasies made i'the Light Heart?
And sold i' the new inn?
*Host*                              Best go to bed,
And dream it over all.                              (5.5.120–123)

The allegory now rests lightly on the happy reality of the play-
world; Jonson acknowledges, without criticizing, the pleasant fantasy he has sold to his London audience and perhaps to his own
often melancholic heart. The Host's reply takes us beyond the
ending of *Bartholomew Fair,* which invites us to "have the rest of
the play at home," toward something like the ending of Shakespeare's *A Midsummer Night's Dream,* which enchantingly blurs all
boundaries separating fantasy from reality. Real life melts into
theater as wakefulness melts into sleep, and in that sleep of fantasy
the dreams that come are not costly delusions, but instead pleasant
fulfillments which at moments can bring a little of their fantastic
happiness across the now-unguarded border into the lives of the
audience.

The mixed tone that made *The New Inn* so unpopular at its initial
performance, and so unsettling to critics ever since, allows Jonson
to acknowledge a retreat from the harshness that his parodic strategy had created in his plays, without conceding any loss in his
powers of discernment. The many unfulfilled hints of parody in
the play's grandiose and derivative speeches are Jonson's way of
calling his critical strictures before the bar for reexamination. The
combination has not proved a great success; it demands far too
much alertness from the audience to the history and the implications of Jonson's parodic strategy.[16] But it is certainly interesting
for what it attempts. Jonson may have surrendered some of his
most powerful satiric weapons on his way to *The New Inn,* but
he was fully conscious of the genial choice he was making, so
conscious that he explains it metaphorically to the audience in the
course of the play. He was too sharp a satirist not to realize the
trite and sentimental qualities of this late play, but his benevolence
seems all the more touching if we understand that he was fully
aware of its costs. *The New Inn* is an act of generosity toward its
characters, who seem to appreciate that fact, and toward its audience, who evidently did not. It is an act of generosity toward

the natural desires of the human heart and toward theater itself, which Jonson now concedes can sometimes help fulfill those desires without generating either naive self-dramatizations or manipulative cynicism.

Lovel is reluctant to play the role of Lady Frampul's wooer in Pru's play, because he fears that the joy of those two hours will only accentuate his bitter inability to play that role in all the other hours of his life. The Host urges him to participate nonetheless: "take your hours and kisses, they are a fortune" (2.6.197). Jonson seems to be encouraging the audience to accept the two hours of romantic indulgence represented by *The New Inn* in much the same way. Jonson's theater is no longer simply a mirror of manners, as he so often said it should be; it is now an escape from the harsh disappointments of life. At the time he wrote the play Jonson would have been feeling sharply all the sufferings Lovel enumerates as the most fearful: "poverty, restraint, captivity, / Banishment, loss of children, long disease" (4.4.106–107).[17] After struggling from a working-class background and a series of prison terms into power and glory as the leading poet of the royal court, Jonson now found himself crippled and permanently confined to his room by a stroke, banished from royal favor, pleading repeatedly for a more adequate pension, and forever deprived of the children—his daughter Mary and his son Benjamin—for whom he mourns so affectingly in his epitaphs. *The New Inn* is a poignant document in Jonson's personal biography precisely because it is such a clear symbolic palinode in his literary career. It is both striking and suggestive that, after a career devoted to separating the grim truths of life from the pleasant fantasies of popular theater, and extirpating romantic melodrama from that theater, Jonson could suggest so seductively that life can be like theater after all, and could dismiss realism in favor of a conventional happy ending which brings lost children miraculously back to life and a melancholic old intellectual back into the flow of life. The romantic plot of *The New Inn* may have been for him, as it was for Lovel, a fantasy so badly needed that it overrode the guiding principles of a lifetime.

*Notes*
*Index*

# NOTES

## Introduction

1. John Dryden, *An Essay of Dramatick Poesie,* in his *Works* (Berkeley: University of California Press, 1971), XVII, 57. For Jonson's views on imitation, see his *Discoveries,* in Herford, Simpson, and Simpson, *Ben Jonson,* VIII, 638–639, ll. 2466–82. *Discoveries* also provides ample evidence that Jonson understood his writing as a constant and violent battle for precedence over contemporary rivals, for freedom from ancient authorities, and for space within genres; see for example Herford, Simpson, and Simpson, pp. 567, 627 (ll. 129–142, 2095–2100); similar arguments are made in the Induction to *Every Man Out of His Humor,* ll. 226–261.

2. Rosalie Colie, *The Resources of Kind,* ed. Barbara K. Lewalski (Berkeley: University of California Press, 1973), p. 117, describes *Don Quixote* as "a book in which literary myths of reality are faced up against that reality, to show the shallowness of rigid doctrines of *mimesis.*"

3. Various critics have noted aspects of this pattern. W. David Kay, "Ben Jonson and Elizabethan Dramatic Convention," *Modern Philology,* 76 (1978), 18–28, discusses Jonson's strategies for positioning himself against the practices of his theatrical rivals; Jonas Barish, "Jonson and the Loathèd Stage," in *A Celebration of Ben Jonson,* ed. W. Blissett et al. (Toronto: University of Toronto Press, 1973), pp. 27–53, connects Jonson's mistrust of the popular theater with his satires on self-dramatizing characters. Nancy Leonard, "Shakespeare and Jonson Again: The Comic Forms," *Renaissance Drama,* n.s. 10 (1979), 46, notes that satiric comedy can be distinguished from romantic comedy by its tendency to "disconfirm" its characters' beliefs. Gabriele Bernhard Jackson, "Structural Interplay in Ben Jonson's Drama," in *Two Renaissance Mythmakers,* ed. Alvin Kernan (Baltimore: Johns Hopkins University Press, 1977), p. 116, similarly sees the destruction of a character's fantasy as a basic action of Jonsonian comedy, but she focuses on the disillusionment of a single central figure, rather than the many peripheral ones who particularly interest me.

John Gordon Sweeney III, *Jonson and the Psychology of Public Theater* (Princeton, N.J.: Princeton University Press, 1984), describes Jonson as perpetually struggling with the problems of reconciling a naive but judgmental paying audience to the moral and intellectual stringencies of his art. Randolph Parker, "A Rite for Scholars: The Experience of Jonsonian Comedy" (Ph.D. diss., Cornell University, 1975), p. 17 and passim, discusses Jonson's exploitation of the audience's expectations. Horatian satire, the sort with which Jonson associates himself nominally in *Poetaster* and practically throughout his works, generally depends on obliging the reader "to feel complicity in the guilt" of the baser characters; see Ronald Paulson, *The Fictions of Satire* (Baltimore: Johns Hopkins University Press, 1967), p. 30. Paulson (p. 5) also argues that "satire is partly defined by its use of commonly accepted forms, both as a false face for itself and as a cogent demonstration that what we ordinarily think of as good or real may be only a masquerade." Alvin Kernan, *The Plot of Satire* (New Haven: Yale University Press, 1965), p. 221, notes the energizing interpenetration of satire and other genres in Jonson's plays. Muriel Bradbrook, *The Growth and Structure of Elizabethan Comedy* (1955; rpt. London: Chatto & Windus, 1973), pp. 47–48, discusses some moments when "Jonson worked out his theory by parody." Alan Dessen, *Jonson's Moral Comedy* (Evanston, Ill: Northwestern University Press, 1971), p. 106, remarks on "Jonson's characteristic assumption that his audience must be bullied out of their complacency and stupidity into a realization of the truths he is about to offer"; I am suggesting that the complacency is generic as well as moral, and that the truths include dramatic realism as well as moral insight.

4. Thomas Middleton and Thomas Dekker, *The Roaring Girl,* in *The Works of Thomas Middleton,* ed. A. H. Bullen (Boston: Houghton, Mifflin, 1885), IV, 9.

5. The point, of course, is not that these characters are real people who went to plays, but that Jonson, for his own polemical purposes, portrays them as if they were.

6. Herford, Simpson, and Simpson, *Ben Jonson,* VIII, 627; Jonson is here responding to *The Advancement of Learning* rather than to *The New Organon,* but the point is the same.

7. Paul Hernadi, *Beyond Genre* (Ithaca, N.Y.: Cornell University Press, 1972), pp. 5–6, cited in Heather Dubrow, *Genre* (London: Methuen, 1982), p. 36.

8. Gail Garloch, "Role-Playing and the Idea of the Play in Ben Jonson's Comedies" (Ph.D. diss., University of Tennessee, 1975), pp. 212–213, comments on the applicability of Caesar's question to a wide range of Jonson's characters.

9. Jonson could have found rough models for some of these innovations—intertwining social satire with literary parody, performing parody by juxtaposition as well as exaggeration—in the works of Juvenal and Petronius.

10. The epigram appears in *The Poems of the Reverend Charles Fitzgeoffrey,* ed. Alexander B. Grosart (London, 1881), part 2, pp. xv–xvi, with a translation by Grosart on pp. xxi–xxii. On the nature of strong poets, see Harold Bloom, *The Anxiety of Influence* (New York: Oxford University Press, 1973), and *A Map of Misreading* (New York: Oxford University Press, 1975).

11. Quoted in Dubrow, *Genre,* p. 90.

12. Alastair Fowler, *Kinds of Literature* (Cambridge, Mass.: Harvard University Press, 1982), pp. 156, 162–164.

13. Kernan, *Plot,* p. 36.

14. Jonson's characters attempt to make sense of their Dickensian names in this same misguided way. They often seem to be obeying their names, or awaiting the fulfillment of those names, as if (like the woman in Robert Frost's "Maple") they thought baptismal lists were a deterministic dramatis personae. The irony, of course, is that the expectation partly fulfills itself, but rarely in the form the characters anticipate.

15. Stephen Greenblatt, *Renaissance Self-Fashioning* (Chicago: University of Chicago Press, 1980). A similarly mixed critique would appear in France a half-century later. Jonas Barish, *The Antitheatrical Prejudice* (Berkeley: University of California Press, 1981), p. 219, finds La Rochefoucauld's antitheatrical argument particularly searching because "it diagnoses in implicitly antitheatrical terms a social and psychological malady without reference to the theater at all. La Rochefoucauld is not thinking about the stage, but about the stagey quality of life in urban Paris. He is antitheatrical not in objecting to plays or players, but in recoiling from the histrionic falsity—the deceitfulness and covert exhibitionism—of so much ordinary behavior."

Michael Shapiro, "Audience vs. Dramatist," *English Literary Renaissance,* 3 (1973), 400–417, comments on the methods by which Elizabethan and Jacobean playwrights attempted to combat the counter-performances of their spectators and the self-dramatizing tendencies of the Renaissance aristocracy in general. His understanding of those methods, however, is nearly the opposite of mine.

16. Greenblatt, *Self-Fashioning,* p. 227. Greenblatt sees *Othello* as the great document of such exploitative improvisation, but Jonson may have gotten there first (indeed, it is clear that *Othello* is full of things Shakespeare learned from the Jonson of *Every Man In;* see note 21 to Chapter 1, below).

17. Stephen Greenblatt, "Invisible Bullets: Renaissance Authority and Its Subversion," in *Shakespeare's "Rough Magic,"* ed. Peter Erickson and Coppélia Kahn (Newark: University of Delaware Press, 1985), pp. 276–320, discusses Thomas Herriot's exploitative improvisation within the belief-system of the Algonkian Indians. Steven Mullaney, "Strange Things, Gross Terms, Curious Customs: The Rehearsal of Cultures in the Late Renaissance," *Representations,* 3 (1983), 40–67, describes a similar pattern on a smaller scale, with Elizabethan culture symbolically asserting its imperial hegemony by gathering, rehearsing, and licensing bits of other cultures. But while it is intriguing to speculate on the broader history of the culture out of which the comedies arise, I do not think it is indispensable for explaining their imperialistic elements. Few Renaissance writers were as concerned as Jonson with pure professional competition, and this book attempts to show that the parodic strategy can be quite adequately explained as an approach to that competition.

18. Anne Barton, *Ben Jonson, Dramatist* (New York: Cambridge University Press, 1984), p. 2. Jonson's witty reproof of his host Lord Salisbury, of which he boasts in the *Conversations* (I, 141, ll. 317–321), is similarly derived from classical literature.

19. Kernan, *Plot*, p. 24, comments that "satire draws much of its nourishment from . . . false styles, delighting in parodying and inflating them until they burst"; see also p. 36. Gilbert Highet, *The Anatomy of Satire* (Princeton, N.J.: Princeton University Press, 1962), p. 68, remarks that satiric parody, unlike mere playful imitation, "wounds the original."

20. Mikhail Bakhtin, "Epic and Novel," in his *The Dialogic Imagination*, ed. Michael Holquist, trans. Caryl Emerson and Michael Holquist (Austin: University of Texas Press, 1981), pp. 4–5.

In fact, Jonsonian comedy shares with Bakhtin's typical novel not only this omnivorous subsumption of other genres but also the incorporation of a variety of prose styles at various degrees of ironic distance, the combative presence of the author within his represented world, a self-critical mechanism to keep the genre alert, a literary foundation in Menippean satire, a historical foundation in the upheavals of Renaissance society, and a thematic juxtaposition of low contemporary reality with a hollowly aggrandized cultural past, in order to control our tendency to substitute literary fantasies for the realities of life. Compare Bakhtin's notion of the orchestrated heteroglossia with the ideas of Jonas Barish, *Ben Jonson and the Language of Prose Comedy* (Cambridge, Mass.: Harvard University Press, 1960). Compare the way Bakhtin's novelist enters "the field of his represented world" to "polemicize with his literary enemies" (p. 27) with Jonson's practices in his "comicall satyres." On the "ability of the novel to criticize itself" and thereby to remain "an ever-developing genre," see Bakhtin, p. 6. On Menippean satire, see Bakhtin, pp. 21–22, 26–27, and Kernan, *Cankered Muse*, pp. 13, 164, 242. On the threat "that we might substitute for our own life . . . dreams based on novelistic models," as occurs in Dostoyevsky's *White Nights*, Flaubert's *Madame Bovary*, and Cervantes' *Don Quixote*, see Bakhtin, p. 32. On the shared parodic response to that threat, see Bakhtin's discussion, p. 21, of the way "all high genres" are "brought low, represented on a plane equal with contemporary life" in the novel.

Bakhtin envisions a moment in the early Renaissance at which "a lengthy battle for the novelization of the other genres began, a battle to drag them into a zone of contact with reality" (p. 39). Jonson, by this standard, succeeded in this battle with startling speed—or else he created a new genre which was inherently "novelized." It is clear, however, that his project failed, that conventional assumptions still dominate our view of comedy, and that the novel has appropriated the role Jonson sought for comedy: as the multilayered genre that dominates literary consciousness, arbitrates social morality, and reflects contemporary reality (cf. Jonson's favorite definition of comedy, as *"imitatio vitae, speculum consuetudinus, imago veritatis"*; see for example *Every Man Out of His Humor*, 3.6.179).

Two important reservations about these connections need to be expressed here, however. The first is that the traits Bakhtin attributes exclusively to the novel arguably appear in several other genres, as well as in satiric city-comedy. The second is that Jonsonian comedy is not as freely "heteroglot" as the Bakhtinian novel, because in most of the plays Jonson finally insists on a moral hierarchy of languages, or at least on designating some verbal styles as authentic expression and others as mere deception or affectation. In this as in other things,

Jonson seems to be waging an unsuccessful battle against his own authoritarian instincts.

21. Here I am combining several familiar terms in an effort to suggest the range, the precedents, and the inward tensions, of Jonsonian comedy. Jonson himself described some of his early plays as "comicall satyres," and many works by Jonson's contemporaries have been categorized as "city-comedies," a genre largely adapted from classical New Comedy and augmented with sharp portrayals of contemporary social follies. Lee Bliss, *The World's Perspective* (Brighton, Sussex: Harvester Press, 1983), p. 10, mentions "satiric city comedy" in a discussion of Webster's literary milieu, and discusses the nature of city-comedy in general on pp. 2–3, 7–8. Brian Gibbons, *Jacobean City Comedy,* 2nd ed. (London: Methuen, 1980), p. 45, building on O. J. Campbell's theory, argues that the early Jonson "sought to evolve a dramatic mode closely equivalent to non-dramatic classical Roman satire." Fowler, *Kinds of Literature,* p. 223, comments on the successful promotion of satire as a genre in the seventeenth century; see also Harry Levin, "Notes toward a Definition of City Comedy," in *Renaissance Genres,* ed. Barbara K. Lewalski (Harvard English Studies, 14) (Cambridge, Mass.: Harvard University Press, 1986), 126–146.

22. Theodore Leinwand, *The City Staged* (Madison: University of Wisconsin Press, 1986), p. 87.

23. R. A. Foakes, *Shakespeare: The Dark Comedies to the Last Plays* (Charlottesville: University of Virginia Press, 1971), pp. 39–43, elucidates this parodic function in *Antonio and Mellida.* Lionel Abel, *Metatheatre* (New York: Hill and Wang, 1963), p. 47, describes *Hamlet* as a competition among the characters for the role of controlling playwright: Abel's approach contrasts with mine, however, in that he is concerned with characters who "are aware of their own theatricality" (pp. 60–61)—precisely what Jonson's gulls are disastrously unaware of.

24. Barton, *Dramatist,* passim.

25. This is true primarily because Jonson's imitation theory focuses respectfully on inheritances from the great authors of antiquity, rather than on plagiaristic or parodic borrowings from contemporaries. Jonson parodies his rivals by mortifying the fools who imitate them. Only Jonson's warning in *Discoveries* that the classics should be treated as "Guides, not Commanders" (VIII, 567, ll. 138–139) seems directly relevant to these overeager imitators. See also Thomas M. Greene, *The Light in Troy* (New Haven: Yale University Press, 1982), on the radical potential of imitation in the Renaissance.

26. Douglas Duncan, *Ben Jonson and the Lucianic Tradition* (New York: Cambridge University Press, 1979), pp. 6, 232, suggests a reader-response model for understanding Jonson's poetic method, though Duncan's approach is rather different from mine.

27. For a slightly different perspective on this tension, see Thomas M. Greene, "Ben Jonson and the Centered Self," *Studies in English Literature,* 10 (1970), 325–348, which describes a chronic tension between Jonson's ideal of centered identity and the histrionic medium he was using to assert that ideal.

28. To some extent, again, the discrepancy is explicable simply by distinguishing between the respect Jonson recommends toward classical authors from

whom he has learned, and the ridicule he imposes on his contemporaries, whom he professes to teach. But that distinction does not hold up very well in the comedies, and the real explanation may lie in a conflict between Jonson's conservative critical persona and the rambunctious self that slips out in the "carnivalized" world of his comedies.

29. Indeed, the ambiguities of Jonson's situation may reflect the peculiar ambivalence of parody, which to some extent necessarily inscribes the very modalities it is ironizing; parody is, paradoxically, "an authorized transgression"; see Linda Hutcheon, *A Theory of Parody* (New York: Methuen, 1985), pp. 26, 69–83. This phrase, like the metaphor of imperialism, suggests analogies between my essentially formalistic argument and the work of New Historicist critics.

30. David R. Riggs, in his forthcoming biography of Jonson, shows that this peculiar spelling was part of Jonson's deliberate fashioning of an extraordinary new identity.

31. Richard S. Peterson, *Imitation and Praise in the Poems of Ben Jonson* (New Haven: Yale University Press, 1981), examines the ambivalent imitation of the classics in Jonson's poems. Stanley Fish, "Authors-Readers: Jonson's Community of the Same," *Representations,* 7 (1984), 26–58, shows Jonson's poems defending themselves in one of the ways I see the plays defending themselves: by suggesting that only those who already admire Jonson's particular approach to the genre are actually able to see the works at all.

32. T. S. Eliot begins his essay on Jonson in *The Sacred Wood* (1920; rpt. London: Methuen, 1972), p. 104, by observing that Jonson's cruel fate has been "to be damned by the praise that quenches all desire to read the book; to be afflicted by the imputation of the virtues which excite the least pleasure; and to be read only by historians and antiquaries."

33. Barbara K. Lewalski, *Paradise Lost and the Rhetoric of Literary Forms* (Princeton, N.J.: Princeton University Press, 1985), convincingly describes that work as a strategic array of subgenres.

34. Greenblatt, "Invisible Bullets," discusses this exploitation; see n. 17 above.

35. The failure of Jonson's *Pleasure Reconciled to Virtue* (a work that obviously made an impression on Milton) shows how badly this reformist impulse could compromise the accessibility of Jonson's art when he dared to indulge his moralism explicitly, as the early patronage of Charles encouraged him to do.

36. Stanley Fish, *Surprised by Sin* (Berkeley: University of California Press, 1971), demonstrates the workings of this tactic in *Paradise Lost.*

37. Lawrence Danson, "Jonsonian Comedy and the Discovery of the Social Self," *PMLA,* 99 (1984), 186, sees it as paradoxical that "though Jonson despises the social self and affirms his belief in an alternative, repeatedly his most vivid characters are versions of that creature." Jonson's parodic strategy helps to explain why he gives such prominence to these despicable role-players, whether we call them social selves or theatrical selves.

38. As Jonson's comedies reenact his rejection of a number of conventional story lines in favor of a revolutionary dramatic mode, so *Paradise Lost* shows traces of the Arthurian epic Milton had planned to write, then abandoned, apparently when historical events made him keenly aware that the myths sustaining

England's ideology needed subversion rather than affirmation. Obviously Milton is writing in a different key from Jonson's, and with richer counterpoint, but he conducts his intertextual orchestration in a similar way.

## 1. *Every Man In His Humor*

1. I have chosen to use the Folio version of *Every Man In His Humor* (1616), as a more finished statement of Jonson's critical perspective on comedy. It is also, I think, simply the better, and better-known, version of the play. I have been able to find only one brief and obscure precedent for my suggestion that *Every Man In His Humor* offers a kind of key to Jonson's efforts to reform Elizabethan drama: a *Birmingham Post* drama critic, reviewing a 1937 production at Stratford, England, suggests that *Every Man In His Humor* "outlines a scheme by which [Jonson] hoped to give a permanent place to realistic and satiric comedy."

2. See A. Richard Dutton, "The Significance of Jonson's Revision of *Every Man In His Humour*," *Modern Language Review*, 69 (1974), 247; Charles Baskervill, *English Elements in Jonson's Early Comedy* (1911; rpt. New York: Johnson Reprint Corp., 1972), p. 107; William Archer, *The Old Drama and the New* (1923), in *"Every Man in His Humour" and "The Alchemist": A Casebook*, ed. J. V. Holdsworth (London: Macmillan, 1978), p. 75; and Jonas Barish, *Ben Jonson and the Language of Prose Comedy* (Cambridge, Mass.: Harvard University Press, 1960), p. 79. Brian Gibbons, *Jacobean City Comedy*, 2nd ed. (London: Methuen, 1980), p. 51, lodges the same accusation, though he does grant some unifying value to "the collisions in which characters challenge one another's rival solipsistic delusions." J. A. Bryant, Jr., "Jonson's Revision of *Every Man In His Humor*," *Studies in Philology*, 59 (1962), 645–646, comments that in the Quarto version Jonson "required his intrigue to be little more than a correctly constructed showcase designed to hold attention and exhibit the contents. The result is that such meaning as Jonson has put into this play actually works against the intrigue rather than with it and ends up as so much moralizing, just as meaningful out of the showcase as in it." My argument, on the contrary, is that even in the Quarto version the moral derives very much from the apparent disunity of the plot.

3. G. B. Jackson, Introduction to the Yale edition, p. 1.

4. J. W. Lever, in the Introducton to his parallel-text edition of *Every Man In His Humour*, Regents Renaissance Drama Series (Lincoln: University of Nebraska Press, 1971), pp. xiv–xv, sees Jonson's incomplete fulfillment of these conventions as an accidental result of Jonson's effort "to adapt his pagan story to Elizabethan propriety." My suggestion, conversely, is that Jonson wants us to see the characters forcing their ordinary Elizabethan reality into the shape of the pagan stories offered by their literature.

5. Several critics have noted Jonson's neglect of this "central" plot line; see, for example, Holdsworth, Introduction to *"Every Man" and "Alchemist*," p. 21, and Freda L. Townsend, "The Unclassical Design of *Every Man In His Humor*," in Holdsworth, ed., *"Every Man" and "Alchemist*," p. 77.

6. Richard Helgerson, *The Elizabethan Prodigals* (Berkeley: University of California Press, 1976).

7. Martin Seymour-Smith, in his note to this passage in the New Mermaids

edition of the play (London: Ernest Benn, 1966), cites the parallel to the speech of the devoted father Hieronimo at 4.1.71–74 of Kyd's play:

> When I was young I gave my mind
> And plied myself to fruitless poetry:
> Which though it profit the professor naught,
> Yet is it passing pleasing to the world.

8. See, for example, Mary C. Williams, *Sources of Unity in Ben Jonson's Comedy*, Salzburg Studies in English Literature, Jacobean Drama Studies, 22 (Atlantic Highlands, N.J.: Humanities Press, 1972), p. 106.

9. Herford, Simpson, and Simpson, *Ben Jonson*, IX, 351n; see also Seymour-Smith, New Mermaids edition, p. 16n.

10. Holdsworth, ed., *"Every Man" and "Alchemist,"* p. 71. Baskervill, *English Elements*, pp. 140–141, remarks on the extreme conventionality of Knowell's paternal soliloquy.

11. Anne Barton, *Ben Jonson, Dramatist* (New York: Cambridge University Press, 1984), p. 52.

12. Baskervill, *English Elements*, p. 141, comments on the anticipation of Polonius; Herford, Simpson, and Simpson, *Ben Jonson*, IX, 348, point out an echo of Seneca in the same speech.

13. Barton, *Dramatist*, p. 54, argues that "however misapplied in the particular circumstances of his son's visit to town, his anatomy of the decline in contemporary standards of moral education bears the unmistakable stamp of Jonson's approval." From my viewpoint, the misapplication is itself Jonson's point.

14. See for example Herford, Simpson, and Simpson, *Ben Jonson*, IX, 366–367, and Seymour-Smith, New Mermaids edition, pp. 46–48. For analogues in Tudor drama, see Baskervill, *English Elements*, p. 142.

15. Baskervill, *English Elements*, pp. 113–114.

16. Theodore B. Leinwand, *The City Staged* (Madison: University of Wisconsin Press, 1986), p. 87.

17. Jonson was not alone in his resentment. There are parodic allusions to Kyd and Marlowe in Shakespeare's works—*2 Henry IV* and *Hamlet*, for example—as well as in the works of Tourneur and Webster. Matthew also draws on the works of Daniel, whose writing Jonson openly scorned; see 1.5.60–65 and 5.5.23–24, with Seymour-Smith's notes on p. 29 and p. 124 of the New Mermaids edition of the play.

18. Barish, *Ben Jonson*, p. 103. Even Bobadill's praise of tobacco is derivative, echoing the writings of Hakluyt and Davies; see Baskervill, *English Elements*, p. 128.

19. Lever, Regents edition, p. xiv, remarks that "only in his own heated imagination was Kitely identified with the ridiculous cuckolds of the *scenari*"; this strikes me as part of an effort to discredit the stereotype with the audience, rather than (as Lever suggests) an effort to retain it within a modernized and Anglicized context.

20. See, for example, Seymour-Smith, New Mermaids edition, p. 40n. Lever, Regents edition, p. xix, suggests that "Kitely's insecurity originates in

his merchant's fear of seditious elements within his cherished domains." As interesting as such arguments may be, they do not explain why Jonson would link Kitely so strongly with a two-dimensional theatrical stereotype, if he intended to offer a radically three-dimensional psychological diagnosis.

21. See Jackson, Yale edition, pp. 237–239. Lever, Regents edition, pp. xxiv–xxvi, speculates further on the connections, including the historical links between Shakespeare and *Every Man In His Humor,* and the anagrammatical link between Othello and Kitely's name in the Quarto, Thorello.

22. Robert N. Watson, *Shakespeare and the Hazards of Ambition* (Cambridge, Mass.: Harvard University Press, 1984), pp. 240–241.

23. *Romeo and Juliet,* Prologue, l. 12; see, similarly, Shakespeare's *Henry VIII,* Prologue, l. 13, and Jonson's *The Alchemist,* Prologue, l. 1.

24. Herford, Simpson, and Simpson, *Ben Jonson* IX, 371; see, for example, Shakespeare's *The Rape of Lucrece,* ll. 876–924.

25. Baskervill, *English Elements,* pp. 137–138, expands on Gifford's observations.

26. Marvin T. Herrick, *Italian Comedy in the Renaissance* (Urbana: University of Illinois Press, 1960), p. 117.

27. Lever, Regents edition, p. xiv, mentions the partial correspondence between this house and the brothel of the *scenari.* Baskervill, *English Elements,* p. 131, notes extensive parallels between Cob and a water-bearer named Simplicity in *Three Lords and Three Ladies of London,* whose relations with Fraud resemble those of Cob with Bobadill. Baskervill suggests that the similarities may reveal Jonson's effort to reproduce the didacticism of morality plays with more artistic subtlety. Cob strikes me as a weak vessel for such an effort; perhaps Jonson instead wants to reveal Cob's determination to identify with a perfectly virtuous and ultimately victorious guild-mate he had seen on the popular stage.

28. Ian Donaldson, "Jonson and the Moralists," in *Two Renaissance Mythmakers,* Selected Papers from the English Institute, 1975–76, n.s. 1, ed. Alvin Kernan (Baltimore: Johns Hopkins University Press, 1977), p. 158, suggests that Edward's cry of "O manners!" at 4.7.130 signals a Ciceronian pose conventional in Jonson's works. Some of the communications between Edward and Wellbred recall the Horatian "familiar epistle," but Jonson would probably have been very sympathetic toward that genre and may therefore have chosen to leave this instance of "literariness" largely unpunished.

29. As Jackson's note to 4.8.118 in the Yale edition (p. 157) observes, two lines later Bridget compares Wellbred to a "squire," a term which meant "bawd" as well as "knight's apprentice" in Elizabethan parlance.

30. On the importance of Brainworm's theatrical self-consciousness to his success, see Peter Hyland, *Disguise and Role-Playing in Ben Jonson's Drama,* Salzburg Studies in English Literature, Jacobean Drama Studies, 69 (Atlantic Highlands, N.J.: Humanities Press, 1977), p. 42; also Ingeborg Maria Sturmberger, *The Comic Elements in Ben Jonson's Drama,* Salzburg Studies in English Literature, Jacobean Drama Studies, 54 (Atlantic Highlands, N.J.: Humanities Press, 1975), pp. 246–247.

31. Gail Garloch, "Role-Playing and the Idea of the Play in Ben Jonson's Comedies" (Ph.D. diss., University of Tennessee, 1975), pp. 125–126, mentions

"Brainworm's likeness to a poet" and uses passages from Jonson's *Discoveries* to associate Brainworm with poetry itself. See also C. G. Thayer, *Ben Jonson* (Norman: University of Oklahoma Press, 1963), pp. 23–24.

32. Baskervill, *English Elements,* pp. 132–134.

33. Baskervill, *English Elements,* p. 134, suggests the parallels to *The Jests of Peele* and *The Blacke Bookes Messenger.*

34. Jackson's note to 2.4.11–12 in the Yale edition (p. 194) mentions the dual meaning of "motley."

35. James E. Savage, *Ben Jonson's Basic Comic Characters* (Jackson: University Press of Mississippi, 1973), pp. 129–131, identifies Clement with Jonson. Robert Witt, *Mirror within a Mirror,* Salzburg Studies in English Literature, Jacobean Drama Studies, 46 (Atlantic Highlands, N.J.: Humanities Press, 1975), p. 88, views Clement as the play's director.

36. Jackson, Introduction to the Yale edition, p. 19.

37. Williams, *Sources of Unity,* p. 118, approaches this viewpoint when she characterizes Clement as "the comic spirit" which rewards Brainworm as "the imaginative creator of fun and laughter."

## 2. Every Man Out of His Humor

1. Jonson makes this association explicit at l. 21 of the Epilogue he wrote for a performance before Queen Elizabeth, though William W. Main, " 'Insula Fortunata' in Jonson's *Every Man Out of His Humor,*" *Notes and Queries,* 199 (1954), 197–198, perceives an allusion to the birthplace of Folly in Erasmus' *In Praise of Folly.*

2. Anne Barton, "Shakespeare and Jonson," in *Shakespeare, Man of the Theater,* ed. Kenneth Muir et al. (Newark: University of Delaware Press, 1983), p. 160; as Herford, Simpson, and Simpson point out (*Ben Jonson,* IX, 455), it is as plausibly associated with plays like Greene's *Friar Bacon and Friar Bungay.*

3. Two scenes after his description of comedy, Mitis again asserts his expectations of a conventional direction in the plot and his general strictures about the comic genre; Cordatus again answers by citing the precedent of Plautus that antedates any Elizabethan traditions. Mitis yields, and Cordatus issues him a very Jonsonian warning against anticipating the shape the play will take: "never preoccupy your imagination withal. Let your mind keep company with the scene still" (3.8.66–86).

4. Hallett Smith, *Elizabethan Poetry* (1952), discusses this triple embodiment of the satirist. See also the illuminating discussion of these figures in R. A. Foakes, *Shakespeare: The Dark Comedies to the Last Plays* (Charlottesville: University of Virginia Press, 1971), pp. 34–36.

5. Juvenal, i, 30–31, cited by Wilkes in the Oxford edition of the play, I, 285n. Herford, Simpson, and Simpson, *Ben Jonson,* IX, 417, list several other echoes of Juvenal in Asper's opening remarks.

6. Charles Baskervill, *English Elements in Jonson's Early Comedy* (1911; rpt. New York: Johnson Reprint Corp., 1972), p. 148.

7. Frank Kerins, "The Crafty Enchaunter," in *Renaissance Drama,* n.s. 14 (1983), p. 132, observes this pattern in Marston's *Satyra Nova.* Kerins, p. 136,

suggests that Jonson's choral figures "serve at every turn to counter-point the histrionics of this continually indignant satirist" Asper, but Kerins does not believe that Jonson is criticizing Asper's satirical efforts merely by exposing their histrionic tendencies. Instead, according to Kerins, Asper's weaknesses "illustrate the deficiencies of this ideal once it is realized in a sophisticated social environment." My suggestion is that a sophisticated dramatic environment exposes the deficiencies in any satiric approach more direct than Jonson's own parodic strategy.

8. Anne Barton, *Ben Jonson, Dramatist* (New York: Cambridge University Press, 1984), p. 62, suggests that Jonson "tries to fictionalize and distance Asper from himself by way of the initial criticisms of Cordatus," perhaps as a defense against attacks on Jonson's self-righteousness by rivals such as Dekker.

9. Judd Arnold, *A Grace Peculiar: Ben Jonson's Cavalier Heroes,* Pennsylvania State University Studies, vol. 35 (University Park: Pennsylvania State University Press, 1972), p. 22, describes Macilente as enduring a helpless rage of envy toward the world's comfortable fools, then changing as he "watches fools achieve nothing more than self-exposure and humiliation. Rather than seek to change their natures he begins to exploit them." This strikes me as suggestively similar to the process by which Jonson developed his own parodic strategy. Macilente also shares a number of Jonson's thematic concerns. For example, compare Macilente's efforts to rescue Deliro from the clichés of Petrarchan love with the argument of Jonson's masque *Lovers Made Men.*

10. Baskervill, *English Elements,* p. 160, sees "thoroughly conventional" foundations to Macilente's character, going back at least as far as *Piers Plowman,* and repeated up through Elizabethan satirists such as Nashe's Pierce Penilesse, whose traits "suggest Macilente very strongly," Greene's self-portrait as a malcontent scholar in *Repentance,* and figures in Lyly's *Campaspe,* Chapman's *An Humorous Day's Mirth,* and several other works (p. 163). There may even be a deliberate echo of Shakespeare's twenty-ninth sonnet; see Baskervill, p. 164. In any case, there is something emphatically derivative about some of Macilente's satiric postures, and Jonson never allows such derivative elements to rest in his works or his characters uncriticized.

11. Trans. in Wilkes, Oxford edition, I, 346 n.

12. Kerins, "Crafty Enchaunter," p. 141, describes Buffone as an epigrammatist. Barton, *Dramatist,* p. 73, uses Buffone's apparent quotation of an unidentified Elizabethan tragedy to include him in a list of characters whose literary allusions help reveal their follies.

13. J. Dover Wilson, "Ben Jonson and *Julius Caesar,*" *Shakespeare Survey,* 2 (1949), 37.

14. Herford, Simpson, and Simpson, *Ben Jonson,* IX, 471–472.

15. Robert Witt, *Mirror within a Mirror,* Salzburg Studies in English Literature, Jacobean Drama Studies, 46 (Atlantic Highlands, N.J.: Humanities Press, 1975), p. 22.

16. Barton, "Shakespeare and Jonson," p. 161.

17. Helena Watts Baum, *The Satiric and the Didactic in Ben Jonson's Comedy* (Chapel Hill: University of North Carolina Press, 1947), p. 68n; see also Baskervill, *English Elements,* p. 206.

18. Baum, *Satiric and Didactic,* p. 68n; see also Alexander Leggatt, *Citizen Comedy in the Age of Shakespeare* (Toronto: University of Toronto Press, 1973), p. 26n.

19. Jonson may be playfully accusing the farmers of their own piece of generic misprision here, inasmuch as the *Acts and Monuments* focused on those who *refused* to be converted.

20. Barton, *Dramatist,* p. 67; Randolph Parker, "A Rite for Scholars: The Experience of Jonsonian Comedy" (Ph.D. diss., Cornell University, 1975), p. 41.

21. William Kittle, *Edward de Vere, 17th Earl of Oxford, and Shakespeare* (Baltimore: Monumental Printing Co., 1942), pp. 187–192; also George Hookham, "Corporal Nym and Ben Jonson," *Times Literary Supplement,* 26 Jan. 1922, p. 61; and Edwin D. Lawrence, "The Player in Ratsei's Ghost and Sogliardo," *Baconiana,* 10 (1912), 207–209.

22. Herford, Simpson, and Simpson, *Ben Jonson,* IX, 425–427.

23. Gail Garloch, "Role-Playing and the Idea of the Play in Ben Jonson's Comedies" (Ph.D. diss., University of Tennessee, 1975), p. 25.

24. This belief that names have a deterministic power, as if baptism were casting, appears in many of Jonson's characters. But like many other gulls— most notably her male English namesake in *Bartholomew Fair,* Littlewit—Saviolina seems oblivious to the potentially degrading implications of her name.

25. Baskervill, *English Elements,* p. 202.

26. Ibid., p. 201.

27. Baskervill, *English Elements,* p. 212, cites these parallel stories, but from his perspective the fact that there are literary antecedents for such self-delusion is "unimportant."

28. Jonson uses Puntarvolo's play-ful marital fore-play to establish a systematic regression of plays within plays: Sordido and Fungoso are spectators at Puntarvolo's ritual, but are watched in turn by a critical chorus consisting of Brisk, Buffone, and Sogliardo, who are all characters in a play watched and criticized by Mitis and Cordatus, whom we in turn have been watching and criticizing. The situation warns us again that it is easy to criticize others for merely playing dramatic roles, but much harder to be sure one isn't doing so oneself. For other commentary on this regression, see Jackson I. Cope, *The Theater and the Dream* (Baltimore: Johns Hopkins University Press, 1973), pp. 226–228; Lawrence Danson, "Jonsonian Comedy and the Discovery of the Social Self," *PMLA,* 99 (1984), 184; and Garloch, "Role-Playing," p. 198–199.

29. Barton, "Shakespeare and Jonson," p. 161, asserts this connection to *Two Gentlemen of Verona.* Puntarvolo may also have taken inspiration from Thomas Heywood's plays in which "gentlemen travelled to the far ends of the world on ships which always moved through blue water, under a smart breeze, with a pirate or a Spaniard lurking menacingly to leeward"; see Esther Dunn, *Ben Jonson's Art* (1925; rpt. New York: Russell and Russell, 1963), pp. 132–133. It should be noted, however, that this characterization better suits the plays Heywood wrote after 1599 (the date of *Every Man Out of His Humor*) than the ones he wrote earlier.

30. Baskervill, *English Elements,* p. 199.

31. Barton, *Dramatist,* p. 73; Herford, Simpson, and Simpson, *Ben Jonson,* IX, 400, 403–404, 461.

32. Of course, as Macilente notes bitterly at 3.9.7–20, the entire world is so infected with Fungoso's and Brisk's way of thinking that good clothes can indeed be more valuable than any authentic personal virtue; this observation is Jonson's way of challenging his audience to move beyond the theatrical in evaluating each other, to become more sophisticated satiric spectators in the ongoing drama of society.

33. Herford, Simpson, and Simpson, *Ben Jonson,* IX, 450; Barton, *Dramatist,* p. 61.

34. Danson, "Jonsonian Comedy," p. 186, describes the "oddly cannibalistic" way this play aims at "the nullification of the characters that give it life."

35. Ian Donaldson, "Language, Noise, and Nonsense," in *"Every Man in His Humour" and "The Alchemist": A Casebook,* ed. R. V. Holdsworth (London: Macmillan, 1978), p. 208, observes: "A silent wife turns out to be no wife, a legacy turns out to be no legacy, an elixir fails to materialize, a project comes to nothing, a bride deserts her husband on their wedding day. The comic action is insistently negative." Virtually every critic who does not find the ending of *Volpone* immorally harsh finds the ending of *The Alchemist* immorally lenient. On the critical dissatisfaction with the ending of *The Alchemist,* see R. V. Holdsworth, Introduction to the volume cited above, p. 28.

36. Alastair Fowler, *Kinds of Literature* (Cambridge, Mass.: Harvard University Press, 1982), p. 47, observes that Patrizi marked the opening of new possibilities for Renaissance dramatists when "he not only denied that plot is the basis of unity, but even that it is a necessary element." Brian Gibbons, *Jacobean City Comedy,* 2nd ed. (London: Methuen, 1980), p. 61, describes the dual activity of this new dramatic form: "In the history of city comedy the special significance of Comical Satyre is two-fold; as propaganda, it gives assertive prominence to the need for self-conscious critical awareness in the audience and to the primacy of critically impelled general ideas as informing dramatic experience, while as theatre, it provides through its loose form in which self-sufficient scenes are suspended (by montage, not linear narrative) a new flexible mode for the expression of ideas and attitudes to which inherited Elizabethan genres of comedy were either formally inhospitable or ideologically hostile."

37. John Dryden, *Works* (Berkeley: University of California Press, 1971), XVII, 23.

38. This concern resembles the problem in Jonson's poetry explored by Stanley Fish, "Authors-Readers: Jonson's Community of the Same," *Representations,* 7 (1984), 28–56. Fish argues that many of Jonson's poems constitute less a positive statement than an occasion for "the recognition of one noble nature by another" (p. 50); a blank page can still function as a litmus paper (p. 42). This peculiarity in the poems, according to Fish, is Jonson's answer to the question, "how can a poet operating in a world of patronage maintain a claim of independence?" (p. 56). Perhaps the parodic strategy is an answer to an analogous question, no less important to Jonson's pride: how can a dramatist be in the popular theater but not of it?

### 3. *Volpone*

1. David R. Riggs, in his forthcoming biography of Jonson, convincingly documents this attitude. Joseph Loewenstein, "The Script and the Marketplace," *Representations,* 12 (1985), 106–107, discusses *Cynthia's Revels* as Jonson's attempt to exchange the loathed role of playwright for that of "patronized poet, a legislator of aestheticized morals." See also Joseph Loewenstein, *Responsive Readings,* Yale Studies in English, 192 (New Haven: Yale University Press, 1984), p. 77, on the ambivalence toward the theater in *Cynthia's Revels.*

2. Anne Barton, *Ben Jonson, Dramatist* (New York: Cambridge University Press, 1984), p. 247. Brian Gibbons, *Jacobean City Comedy,* 2nd ed. (London: Methuen, 1980), pp. 10–11, and Barton, *Dramatist,* pp. 243–247, describe *Eastward Ho* as a tongue-in-cheek parody of the city comedies so popular on the Jacobean stage. See, similarly, Richard Levin, *The Multiple Plot in English Renaissance Drama* (Chicago: University of Chicago Press, 1971), p. 89, and Alexander Leggatt, *Citizen Comedy in the Age of Shakespeare* (Toronto: University of Toronto Press, 1973), pp. 47–53. This strikes me as far more convincing than the assumption of earlier critics that the heavy-handed moralism is intended with all seriousness; see for example Robert E. Knoll, *Ben Jonson's Plays* (Lincoln: University of Nebraska Press, 1964), pp. 65–67, and Charlotte Spivack, *George Chapman* (New York: Twayne, 1967), p. 99.

3. John G. Sweeney III, *Jonson and the Psychology of Public Theater* (Princeton, N.J.: Princeton University Press, 1985), p. 75, tentatively suggests "an analogy between Jonson and his spectators and Volpone and his gulls," each using theater "to manipulate foolish and ignorant spectators, 'playing with their hopes . . . content to coyne 'hem into profit.' " But the joke is finally on Volpone, as it is on the form of Jonsonian comedy that indulges its clever rogues.

4. Edward Partridge, *The Broken Compass* (New York: Columbia University Press, 1958), p. 70. S. L. Goldberg, "Folly into Crime," *Modern Language Quarterly,* 20 (1959), 239, notes the ambivalence of the ending, to which "our judgment may assent, but our feelings are still lagging." To me, the same ambivalence reflects the discord between our rational moral faculties and our reflexive generic expectations.

5. Northrop Frye, *Anatomy of Criticism* (Princeton, N.J.: Princeton University Press, 1971), p. 165.

6. C. G. Thayer, *Ben Jonson* (Norman: University of Oklahoma Press, 1963), p. 50; see, similarly, Ralph Nash, "The Comic Intent of *Volpone,*" *Studies in Philology,* 44 (1947), 26–40; and William Empson, *"Volpone,"* *Hudson Review,* 21 (1968), 651–666.

7. Barton, *Dramatist,* pp. 118–119.

8. It is certainly not clear why the exploiters in the humors comedies and in *The Alchemist* escape unscathed, whereas those in *Volpone,* only a few years later, are severely punished. No great moral leap separates Mosca and Volpone from Brainworm and Clement before them, or Face and Lovewit after. The justification commonly offered for the fact that Brainworm and Face escape penalty—that they profit essentially by allowing the wickedness of their victims to punish itself—applies also to most of Mosca and Volpone's predations. In

*Volpone,* as in *Every Man In His Humor* and *The Alchemist,* the story line consists essentially of a struggle for control of the plot; Madeleine Doran, *Endeavors of Art* (Madison: University of Wisconsin Press, 1954), p. 329, vividly narrates this succession of superseding plots. The legacy hunters are scheming to take Volpone's possessions, while Volpone subsumes their plot into his own satiric stagecraft, unaware that Mosca himself might decide to put his own final self-serving twist on that plot. The usual moment when the master manipulators bring all the incompatible fantasies into an amusing and profitable collison occurs here when Volpone is reported finally dead (5.3). The mob scene at Volpone's house is much like the mob scenes at Cob's and Lovewit's houses: each legacy hunter confidently awaits the vindication of his glorious fantasy over the others, only to discover that Mosca has actually outwitted them all, led them all to gull themselves. Richard Dutton, "*Volpone* and *The Alchemist:* A Comparison in Satiric Techniques," *Renaissance and Modern Studies,* 18 (1974), 36–62, compares these plays extensively and informatively.

9. Thayer, *Ben Jonson,* pp. 62–63, sees in Volpone's sentencing "the rejection of the comic poet by a society unwilling to accept the implications of his art," with its dangerous Dionysian qualities.

10. Alexander Leggatt, "The Suicide of Volpone," *University of Toronto Quarterly,* 39 (1969–70), 19–32.

11. Leggatt, "Suicide," p. 25.

12. Ibid., p. 29.

13. R. B. Parker, "*Volpone* and *Reynard the Fox,*" *Renaissance Drama,* n.s. 7 (1976), 41.

14. For the classical allusions, see Herford, Simpson, and Simpson, *Ben Jonson,* IX, 689.

15. William Sylvester, "Jonson's 'Come My Celia' and Catullus' 'Carmen V,' " *Explicator,* 22 (1964), item 35, remarks on the ominous nature of this literary precedent.

16. L. A. Beaurline, *Jonson and Elizabethan Comedy* (San Marino, Calif.: Huntington Library, 1978), p. 185.

17. Barton, *Dramatist,* p. 117.

18. The disguised Volpone's exchange with Voltore at 5.7.20–21 turns on his "mistaking words, as the fashion is in the stage-practice" for constables (*Bartholomew Fair,* Induction, 39); Leggatt, "Suicide," p. 25, notes this connection.

19. Alexander Leggatt, *Ben Jonson: His Vision and His Art* (London: Methuen, 1981), p. 28. Sweeney, *Public Theater,* p. 75, similarly comments that life, for Volpone, becomes "a matter of one's either writing his own script or being forced to enact someone else's."

20. Beaurline, *Elizabethan Comedy,* p. 175.

21. Leggatt, "Suicide," p. 27.

22. Leggatt, *Ben Jonson,* p. 28.

23. Sweeney, *Public Theater,* p. 98, suggests that these characters belong in a "romance melodrama such as *A Woman Killed with Kindness.*"

24. Quoted in Partridge, *Broken Compass,* p. 71. This is not an anachronistic response. Leggatt, *Citizen Comedy,* p. 78, discusses the way "the conventional

sympathies of comedy are activated" in Renaissance drama toward the young people against forces such as age, money, and family, which conspire to keep them apart.

25. See, for example, Barton, *Dramatist,* p. 118, who observes that "despite this legal separation from Corvino, there is no suggestion that Bonario—or any other young man—will figure in her future. Jonson has avoided throughout doing what would have seemed only natural to most other dramatists of the period: establishing any emotional bond between these two which, in time, might ripen into love. Celia and Bonario are the only characters at the end of the comedy (apart from Peregrine, who is not present in the final scene) whose lives remain open and, to a large extent, undetermined. Yet Jonson turns away from them without interest," in order to focus on Volpone's fate. This is a classic instance of what I have been calling Jonson's strategic decentering.

26. Dutton, "Satiric Techniques," p. 41, observes that "throughout the last act, Jonson is playing upon that potential sentimentality of the audience, which is duped by tradition and convention into believing that 'justice' will prevail."

27. Thayer, *Ben Jonson,* pp. 52–53.

28. Daniel Boughner, *The Devil's Disciple* (New York: Philosophical Library, 1968), p. 122 and passim; Leggatt, *Ben Jonson,* p. 138, rightly observes that "Jonson does not dismiss [Celia] as a ninny . . . But she is placed in dramatic situations in which her virtue cannot operate effectively."

29. Dutton, "Satiric Techniques," p. 40, points out the "strained alliteration" of this speech, which marks the rescue as "melodrama, a ludicrous and meaningless make-believe in the grimmer reality of Volpone's Venice."

30. Alan Dessen, *Jonson's Moral Comedy* (Evanston, Ill.: Northwestern University Press, 1971), pp. 87–88. Leggatt, *Ben Jonson,* p. 139, effectively answers Dessen's objections, again emphasizing the generic dislocation: "Bonario . . . is vulnerable, not through any weakness in himself . . . but through the dramatic situations he is placed in." For another hagiographic view of these characters, based again on too straightforward a reading of the hinted allusions, see Gerard H. Cox III, "Celia, Bonario, and Jonson's Indebtedness to the Medieval Cycles," *Études Anglaises,* 25 (1972), 506–511.

31. Jonas Barish, "The Double Plot in *Volpone,*" *Modern Philology,* 51 (1953), 83–92, focuses especially on the devotion to mimicry, and the unwitting participation in a beast fable, of Sir Pol and his Lady. Many directors have actually excised these scenes from productions of *Volpone* as superfluous.

32. Knoll, *Jonson's Plays,* p. 100.

33. Dutton, "Satiric Techniques," p. 45, claims that Peregrine is "the only clear-sighted, uncorrupt character in the play, and as such has a special understanding of the other characters, with their blindnesses, which is equal to that of the audience." If that is true, it is only because the audience, like Peregrine, is blinded by literary convention from perceiving the true course of events in the final act.

34. J. A. Bryant, *The Compassionate Satirist* (Athens, Ga.: University of Georgia Press, 1972), pp. 83–84.

35. Barton, *Dramatist,* p. 186.

36. Sweeney, *Public Theater,* p. 88, argues perceptively that "in *Volpone*

identity is a function of theatricality, the repeated enactment of manipulative drama. Those who see themselves as centered individuals in this play are finally ridiculed. To succeed here, to actually define oneself, one must compel others to play roles in a drama of one's own making, without their knowing it." But it is hard for a character, no matter how clever, to maintain such control when his suddenly moralistic creator simply chooses to decenter him from the frame of the play the audience will see. Jonson can assert his sovereignty over his audience as well as his characters, through the strategically unconventional course of his play, precisely because they think they *do* know what sort of a play they are involved in.

Alvin Kernan's Introduction to the Yale edition of the play, pp. 1–26, thoroughly and skillfully documents a pattern of disastrous role-playing in *Volpone*. Authenticity and stability of identity are rare commodities indeed. The play-within-the-play staged by Volpone's dwarf, eunuch, and androgyne consists of "pleasing imitations / Of greater men's action, in a ridiculous fashion" (3.3.13–14); I believe that the play proper consists largely of less explicit versions of that same sort of parodic metadrama, as the attempts by various characters to play great roles entrap them in humiliating satire. Ironically, acting *can* control reality in this play, but (as in a fairy tale) not quite the way the wisher had hoped. Volpone becomes truly sick and immobile, the legacy hunters reveal themselves as essentially the animals after which they are named, and Sir Pol does indeed become a conspiratorial victim of his own grandiose politicking. Realistic twists thus spoil the conventional scenarios of good characters, of bad characters, and even of the audience. *Volpone* develops Jonson's parodic strategy not only in the specific peculiarities of its action, characterization, and genre, but also in its thematic concern with some new and dangerous ways in which theatricality attempts to insinuate itself into reality.

## 4. *Epicoene*

1. Ian Donaldson, "A Martyr's Resolution," in *Ben Jonson's Plays and Masques*, ed. Robert M. Adams (New York: Norton, 1979), pp. 428–429, comments on "the profusion of 'plots' (a word constantly used, and having obvious dramatic connotations)," all drawn together by "the masterplot of Jonson himself."

2. Edward Partridge, *The Broken Compass* (New York: Columbia University Press, 1958), pp. 168–169, and Leo G. Salingar, "Farce and Fashion in *The Silent Woman*," *Essays and Studies* (London), 20 (1967), 33, discuss this convention.

3. Jonas Barish, "Ovid, Juvenal, and *The Silent Woman*," *PMLA*, 71 (1956), 213–224; Edmund Wilson, "Morose Ben Jonson," in *The Triple Thinkers* (New York: Oxford University Press, 1948), pp. 213–232.

4. Donaldson, "Martyr's Resolution," argues that Truewit's abusive farces are the essence of the play. Judd Arnold, *A Grace Peculiar: Ben Jonson's Cavalier Heroes*, Penn State University Studies, 35 (University Park: Pennsylvania State University Press, 1972), p. 47, discusses the various critical advocacies of Truewit, Clerimont, and Dauphine as the play's true hero. See also Peter Hyland, *Disguise and Role-Playing in Ben Jonson's Drama*, Salzburg Studies in English Literature,

Jacobean Drama Studies, 69 (Atlantic Highlands, N.J.: Humanities Press, 1977), p. 103, who answers Barish's praise of Truewit with the observation that, though "Truewit is not an imbecile . . . he is finally immoral because he is inauthentic, a play-actor with too many roles."

5. Barish, *"The Silent Woman,"* passim.

6. John Ferns, "Ovid, Juvenal, and *The Silent Woman:* A Reconsideration," *Modern Language Review,* 65 (1970), 248–253.

7. Barish, *"The Silent Woman,"* expands on the treatment of this allusion in Herford, Simpson, and Simpson, *Ben Jonson,* X, 14–18. Intriguingly, Truewit warns that a wife might manifest an undesirable inclination to "censure poets and authors and styles, and compare 'em, Daniel with Spenser, Jonson with t'other youth, and so forth" (2.2.97–99).

8. E. K. Chambers, *The Medieval Stage* (Oxford: Clarendon Press, 1903), I, 152–154, cited in Donaldson, "Martyr's Resolution," p. 436.

9. Quoted in Donaldson, "Martyr's Resolution," p. 436. L. A. Beaurline, *Jonson and Elizabethan Comedy* (San Marino, Calif.: Huntington Library, 1978), p. 212, seems largely to share Truewit's supposition that this jest is the essence of the play.

10. O. J. Campbell, "The Relation of *Epicoene* to Aretino's *Il Marescalco,"* *PMLA,* 46 (1931), 752–762; also Daniel Boughner, "Clizia and *Epicoene,"* *Philological Quarterly,* 19 (1940), 89–91.

11. Anne Barton, *Ben Jonson, Dramatist* (New York: Cambridge University Press, 1984), p. 209.

12. J. A. Bryant, Jr., *The Compassionate Satirist* (Athens, Ga.: University of Georgia Press, 1972), p. 97, observes that "Truewit, whose lynx-eyed perception of the society's follies would have made him an admirable machinator in the simple world of *Every Man in His Humor,* only dimly perceives that the advanced decay of the people in his world has involved him too and reduced his role from that of prime machinator to one of garrulous supernumerary." I would only add that this seems to me the result of Jonson's deliberate shifting of his generic ground, whether or not it also reflects some general moral decay in society.

13. C. G. Thayer, *Ben Jonson* (Norman: University of Oklahoma Press, 1963), p. 79, makes this comparison.

14. Bryant, *Compassionate Satirist,* p. 97.

15. Jonson is here exploiting the paradoxical nature of dramatic characters, who are in one sense merely verbal artifacts with no existence outside of the play (as L. C. Knights has maintained in his famous essay "How Many Children Had Lady Macbeth?"), yet whose function within the play depends on our projecting onto them a more complete historical and psychological existence.

16. Barton, *Dramatist,* p. 125.

17. Arnold, *Grace Peculiar,* p. 49.

18. See Partridge's note in the Yale edition of the play, p. 179.

19. Jonas Barish, *Ben Jonson and the Language of Prose Comedy* (Cambridge, Mass.: Harvard University Press, 1960), pp. 148, 184. Michael Shapiro, "Audience vs. Dramatist," *English Literary Renaissance,* 3 (1973), 411, describes Morose as "the ascetic critic" of *Epicoene,* but notes that he is "neither a harmless

anti-social crank like Libanius' Morosus in Jonson's chief source nor an impassioned if self-destructive idealist like Molière's Alceste . . . no Crites, a humanist-scholar eager to restore court life to its pristine radiance." I think the fact that critics such as Shapiro feel compelled to raise and then reject such comparisons suggests how effectively Jonson has elicited, and then undermined, a sense that Morose derives from some literary model of the satirist.

20. Alvin Kernan, *The Cankered Muse: Satire of the English Renaissance*, Yale Studies in English, 142 (New Haven: Yale University Press, 1959), pp. 141–191, discusses the struggles of Jonson and his contemporaries to recast satire as a dramatic form.

21. Partridge, *Broken Compass*, pp. 10–11.

22. Barish, *Ben Jonson*, p. 161.

23. Barton, *Dramatist*, p. 123, even while maintaining that "Truewit is the master-wit of *Epicoene*," observes that his "words recoil ironically on to himself" in this exchange. Partridge, in the Yale edition, p. 18, points out Truewit's fantasy that the play is a legal proceeding in which he arrests and (with his fellow gallants) judges those guilty of foolishness.

24. Arnold, *Grace Peculiar*, p. 52.

## 5. The Alchemist

1. Herford, Simpson, and Simpson, *Ben Jonson*, II, 87–88, list several points of correspondence.

2. The correspondence between the evanescence of the gulls' empty hopes and the evanescence of a theatrical production is suggested similarly in *Every Man In His Humor*, 4.6.55, and in *Volpone*, 1.4.159; cf. Shakespeare's *The Tempest*, 4.1.148–158.

3. Anne Barton, *Ben Jonson, Dramatist* (New York: Cambridge University Press, 1984), p. 152, discusses this sad transformation.

4. Alexander Leggatt, *Citizen Comedy in the Age of Shakespeare* (Toronto: University of Toronto Press, 1973), p. 74.

5. Norman Rabkin, *Drama of the English Renaissance* (New York: Macmillan, 1976), II, 143.

6. Muriel C. Bradbrook, *The Growth and Structure of Elizabethan Comedy* (1955; rpt. London: Chatto & Windus, 1973), p. 78; on the same incident, see Herford, Simpson, and Simpson, *Ben Jonson*, X, 47–48; Herford, Simpson, and Simpson, X, 98, cite also the story of John and Alice West, who swindled other dreamy innocents by posing as "the King and Queene of Fayries."

7. Bradbrook, *Growth and Structure*, pp. 45, 154, and 251 n. 19, discusses this motif in the works of Marston and Middleton. Anne Barton, "Falstaff and the Comic Community," in *Shakespeare's "Rough Magic*,*"* ed. Peter Erickson and Coppélia Kahn (Newark: University of Delaware Press, 1985), p. 136, notes the way former prodigals thrive in Haughton's *Englishmen for My Money*, Middleton's *A Trick to Catch the Old One*, Rowley's *A New Wonder*, *A Woman Never Vexed*, and Cooke's *The City Gallant*. Shakespeare's contribution to this motif is Bassanio in *The Merchant of Venice*. Among the characters similarly redeemed in Fletcher's

plays are Valentine in *Wit without Money* and Young Loveless in *The Scornful Lady;* see Leggatt, *Citizen Comedy,* p. 47.

8. W. Gifford, ed. *Works of Ben Jonson* (London, 1816), IV, 114 n. 1; Charles Baskervill, *English Elements in Jonson's Early Comedy* (1911; rpt. New York: Johnson Reprint Corp., 1972), p. 12 n. 2.

9. F. H. Mares, "The Structure and Verse of *The Alchemist,*" in *"Every Man in His Humour" and "The Alchemist": A Casebook,* ed. R. V. Holdsworth (London: Macmillan, 1978), p. 179, suggests that "Drugger, almost certainly, was played by Robert Armin." It is interesting to consider the great prominence that the role of Drugger gained—it was chosen by Garrick, among others—as the fantasy of success by diligent and honest merchandizing became increasingly essential to England's economic system; see, for example, the brief history of the role provided by Holdsworth in his Introduction, pp. 34–35.

10. Bradbrook, *Growth and Structure,* p. 202.

11. The proof of this is largely negative: for all his effusive poetic praise of patrons and others, and for all the popularity of the notion of humanity transforming the world in the Renaissance, Jonson rarely wrote praise in this mode except in satiric contexts. It is also worth noticing that (as Drummond reports in the *Conversations*) Jonson condemned Donne's "First Anniversarie" for attributing to any single mortal the power to alter the condition of humanity as a whole.

12. Alan Dessen, *Jonson's Moral Comedy* (Evanston, Ill.: Northwestern University Press, 1971), p. 113, calls Mammon's declaration "a parody of the *fiat lux,*" but it is important to note that the parodist is not Mammon but Jonson, who is using the altered phrase to reveal Mammon's thoughtless and graceless conversion to his own desires of the greatest roles he has encountered in his reading.

13. Brian Gibbons, *Jacobean City Comedy,* 2nd ed. (London: Methuen, 1980), p. 18, remarks that "Sir Epicure is partly a parody, partly a comic counterpart of Faustus."

14. Holdsworth, Introduction to *"Every Man" and "Alchemist,"* p. 32, comments briefly on the Faustus parallel.

15. Leggatt, *Citizen Comedy,* p. 76.

16. Myrddin Jones, "Sir Epicure Mammon: A Study in 'Spiritual Fornication,'" *Renaissance Quarterly,* 22 (1969), 233–242, suggests that Mammon attempts repeatedly to cast himself as King Solomon, and is so taken with the glamour of the role that he overlooks its negative implications. Mammon's reference to himself as an amorous Hercules again recalls the second poem of the "Celebration of Charis," in which Jonson mocks himself for standing enthralled with love like Cupid "In a Hercules's shape" (l. 32).

17. Edmund Wilson, "Morose Ben Jonson," in his *The Triple Thinkers* (New York: Oxford University Press, 1948), pp. 213–232. In the *Discoveries* Jonson argues that "Language most shewes a man"; see Herford, Simpson, and Simpson, *Ben Jonson,* VIII, 625, ll. 2031–35. Jonas Barish, *Ben Jonson and the Language of Prose Comedy* (Cambridge, Mass.: Harvard University Press, 1960), comments extensively and brilliantly on the correlation between speech pattern and personality in Jonson's characters.

18. See Kernan's note in the Yale edition of the play, p. 81.

19. Herford, Simpson, and Simpson, *Ben Jonson,* X, 103, mention part of this parallel to the *Poenulus.*

20. Holdsworth, Introduction to *"Every Man" and "Alchemist,"* p. 27, comments that if Jonson had followed straightforwardly the formula of New Comedy, "Surly would be the play's hero and agent of release." William Empson, *"The Alchemist* and the Critics," in Holdsworth, ed. *"Every Man" and "Alchemist,"* p. 199, takes a similar view of Surly's defeat: "The moral atmosphere being so firmly like Dickens, one expects this good deed to be rewarded with an ample competence." Peter Fleming, "Harlequinade: *The Alchemist* at the New Theatre," in Holdsworth, ed., p. 222, remarks that "almost any other dramatist would have . . . put down Surly as an Honest Fellow or a Plain Dealer" and given him the right to the play's final triumph.

21. Katharine E. Maus, *Ben Jonson and the Roman Frame of Mind* (Princeton, N.J.: Princeton University Press, 1984), p. 84, observes that "Surly makes his fatal error when he treats [Dame Pliant] like a romance heroine."

22. C. G. Thayer, *Ben Jonson* (Norman: University of Oklahoma Press, 1963), p. 93, argues that Surly "would be effective if he were moral . . . Surly is a character who cannot be a good poet because he is not a good man." My feeling is that Surly's failure arises more directly from his mismanagement of poetry than from his misconduct as a gambler.

23. Judd Arnold, "Lovewit's Triumph and Jonsonian Morality," *Criticism,* 11 (1969), 160, argues that Jonson is here representing "a conventional sentimental or moralistic solution being overridden in order to clear the way for a more cavalier solution."

24. Holdsworth, Introduction to *"Every Man" and "Alchemist,"* p. 31, speculates that "*The Alchemist* might be said to dramatise the collision between Jonson the pessimistic *censor morum* . . . and Jonson the delighter in contrivance, who once himself dressed up as an astrologer . . . in order to play a joke on a lady." See also J. B. Steane, "Crime and Punishment in *The Alchemist,*" in Holdsworth, ed., pp. 187–189, on the role of Surly in representing this conflict and on the inducements it offers to the audience.

25. "To the Reader," ll. 14–18; for the parallel passage in *Discoveries,* see Herford, Simpson, and Simpson, *Ben Jonson,* VIII, 583, ll. 634–639.

26. Herford, Simpson, and Simpson, *Ben Jonson,* X, 108.

27. Wayne A. Rebhorn, "Jonson's 'Jovy Boy': Lovewit and the Dupes in *The Alchemist,*" *Journal of English and Germanic Philology,* 79 (1980), 355–375, argues for the identification of Lovewit with the audience—"those urbane gentlemen who habitually attended performances" in Blackfriars (p. 373)—rather than with the playwright; my argument suggests that both identifications may be active as part of a strategy to compel the audience's sympathetic participation in the transformation of standard comedy into Jonsonian satire.

28. Herford, Simpson, and Simpson, *Ben Jonson,* X, 111. Subtle evidently does not penetrate Face's Plautine pose as Lovewit does: he mistakes this wily servant of an ancient wit for "the precious king of present wits" (5.4.13–14).

29. Nancy Leonard, "Shakespeare and Jonson Again: The Comic Forms," *Renaissance Drama,* n.s. 10 (1979), 68.

30. Arnold, "Lovewit's Triumph," p. 161, suggests that Lovewit triumphs

because "He has no dream to sell himself"; my point is quite similar, though I would say "script" rather than "dream." Thayer, *Ben Jonson,* p. 106, maintains that because Lovewit "has donned the Spanish cloak and married Dame Pliant, both acts by now clearly associated with folly," Lovewit too is exposed as a fool. What this conclusion overlooks is the greater degree of ironic self-awareness in Lovewit's role-playing, which allows him to succeed precisely where the others have failed.

31. Herford, Simpson, and Simpson, *Ben Jonson,* X, 113.

32. See, for example, William D. Wolf, *The Reform of the Fallen World,* Salzburg Studies in English Literature, Jacobean Drama Studies, 27 (Atlantic Highlands, N.J.: Humanities Press, 1973), pp. 103–107; and Richard Levin, " 'No Laughing Matter,' " in *Ben Jonson: Quadricentennial Essays,* ed. Mary Olive Thomas; special ed. of *Studies in the Literary Imagination,* 6 (1973), 88–90.

33. John G. Sweeney III, *Jonson and the Psychology of Public Theater* (Princeton, N.J.: Princeton University Press, 1985), p. 151, discusses Face's "fascination for . . . the perfection of his work for its own sake . . . Subtle is running a con, but he lovingly imagines Mammon enacting this fantastic role simply because *he* has made it for Mammon. This is the Jonsonian 'hero' in his great moment, relishing as a spectator the drama he has compelled another to enact." My point is that Face is finally disqualified as a Jonsonian hero precisely because he becomes too enamored a spectator of his own role as a controlling playwright-figure.

34. Aside from its diabolical overtones, this fishing metaphor was evidently a conventional signature for witty coney-catchers in Elizabethan drama; see for example the remarks of Shortyard and Quomodo in Middleton's 1606 comedy *Michaelmas Term,* 2.3.155–157, 223–225, in *The Works of Thomas Middleton,* ed. A. H. Bullen (Boston: Houghton, Mifflin, 1885), I, 252, 255.

35. *Magnyfycence,* ll. 410–446, in John Skelton, *Complete English Poems,* ed. John Scattergood (New Haven: Yale University Press, 1983), p. 152.

36. Lois Potter, "The Plays and the Playwrights," in *The Revels History of Drama in English,* ed. Norman Sanders et al. (London: Methuen, 1980), II, 151, 172.

37. Dessen, *Moral Comedy,* p. 129; but Dessen assumes that Jonson intends this reminiscence only as a straightforward guide for the audience's moral response, not as something subliminally affecting the characters' own responses.

38. John S. Mebane, "Renaissance Magic and the Return of the Golden Age," in *Renaissance Drama,* n.s. 10 (1979), 127. Richard Dutton, "*Volpone* and *The Alchemist:* A Comparison in Satiric Techniques," *Renaissance and Modern Studies,* 18 (1974), 50, perceives "a hint in Subtle's claim that he carries a disproportionate part of the venture (1.1.144–145), that—without actually believing what he says—he is sometimes carried away by his own eloquence, by the artificial dignity of his disguise, which is potentially as much a flaw as the blindness of his dupes."

39. Coburn Gum, *The Aristophanic Comedies of Ben Jonson* (The Hague: Mouton, 1969), p. 165 and n. 32. In fact, through much of the play, Subtle seems to imagine he can take a standard Aristophanic role as an evil educator who is never punished for his knavery; see Gum, pp. 39–43.

40. Thayer, *Ben Jonson,* p. 86, notes this pun.

## 6. *Bartholomew Fair*

1. For summaries and bibliographies of this critical consensus, see Peter Hyland, *Disguise and Role-Playing in Ben Jonson's Drama,* Salzburg Studies in English Literature, Jacobean Drama Studies, 69 (Atlantic Highlands, N.J.: Humanities Press, 1977), p. 125; J. A. Bryant, *The Compassionate Satirist* (Athens, Ga.: University of Georgia Press, 1972), p. 135; and Thomas Cartelli, "*Bartholomew Fair* as Urban Arcadia," *Renaissance Drama,* 14 n.s. (Evanston, Ill.: Northwestern University Press, 1983), p. 154. Thomas M. Greene, "Ben Jonson and the Centered Self," *Studies in English Literature,* 10 (1970), 347, remarks that in *Bartholomew Fair* Jonson becomes "less ambiguously tolerant of the histrionic personality." Edmund Wilson, "Morose Ben Jonson," in his *The Triple Thinkers* (New York: Oxford University Press, 1948), pp. 213–232, portrays Jonson's works as the products of an anal-retentive psyche. The argument is not wholly convincing, but some traces of that syndrome may be visible in Jonson's punitive early comedies, in which he seemingly felt obliged to punish himself for his desire to retain and play with the ordinary waste products of the dramatic tradition, by punishing the audience for enjoying them. The generosity in *Bartholomew Fair* toward objects in general, and the specific acceptance of human digestive processes, show a significant deviation from that miserly and punitive pattern.

2. George Hibbard, Introduction to *Bartholomew Fair,* New Mermaids edition (London: Ernest Benn, 1977), p. xix.

3. Jonas Barish, *The Antitheatrical Prejudice* (Berkeley: University of California Press, 1981). It should be noted, however, that Puritanism was far from monolithic in its antitheatricalism. See David Norbrook, "The Reformation of the Masque," in *The Court Masque,* ed. David Lindley (Manchester: Manchester University Press, 1984), pp. 94–111; and Margot Heinemann, *Puritanism and Theatre* (New York: Cambridge University Press, 1980).

4. Katharine E. Maus, *Ben Jonson and the Roman Frame of Mind* (Princeton, N.J.: Princeton University Press, 1984), pp. 154–155. Jonson is not retracting his accusation that other playwrights are flawed. As Maus suggests, the puppet Dionysius is not so much "intimating the essential innocence of the theater" as pointing out that its corruptions are generated and shared by the follies of society in general, and such proud posers as the Puritans in particular. The assertion of the innocence of theater is quoted from Jonas Barish, *Ben Jonson and the Language of Prose Comedy* (Cambridge, Mass.: Harvard University Press, 1960), p. 237. In any case Barish, pp. 238–239, sees Jonson closing ranks in *Bartholomew Fair* with his dramatic rivals against the Puritan threat to the theater as a whole; I see that shift reflected in Jonson's redirection of his parodic attack.

5. Michael O'Connell, "The Idolatrous Eye," *ELH,* 52 (1985), 279–310, argues that the attacks on the theater were directed against what the Puritans saw as the essentially idolatrous character of visual representations.

6. Leo Salingar, "Crowd and Public in *Bartholomew Fair,*" *Renaissance Drama,* 10 n.s. (Evanston, Ill.: Northwestern University Press, 1979), p. 146, comments on this compromise.

7. On the complex nature of Bartholomew Fair in Jonson's time, see Frances

Teague, *The Curious History of "Bartholomew Fair"* (London: Associated University Presses, 1985), pp. 16–27.

8. From Horace's *Epistles*, II.i, 194–200, trans. in Hibbard, New Mermaids edition, p. 2.

9. R. B. Parker, "The Themes and Staging of *Bartholomew Fair*," *University of Toronto Quarterly*, 39 (1969–70), 305, remarks on the way this error erodes the boundary between the stage and the audience.

10. Parker, "Themes and Staging," p. 303, is one of several critics who comment on the correspondences between the puppet show and the play as a whole.

11. Edward Partridge, Introduction to *Bartholomew Fair*, Regents Renaissance Drama edition (Lincoln: University of Nebraska Press, 1964), p, xvi; Herford, Simpson, and Simpson, *Ben Jonson*, X, 198, discuss a ballad published shortly before *Bartholomew Fair* was written concerning an actor who wore a bear suit to act out a bear-baiting, probably at the Fortune theater.

12. Parker, "Themes and Staging," p. 301.

13. In any case, Winwife's praise of Win sounds less like a spontaneous appreciation than like a hollow borrowing from hackneyed Renaissance love poetry: "A wife here with a strawberry-breath, cherry-lips, apricot cheeks, and a soft velvet head, like a melicotton" (1.2.13–18). The fact that these comestible compliments are emulated by Littlewit, who is always susceptible to the most conventional tricks of courtly wit, effectively and accurately condemns them.

14. Anne Barton, *Ben Jonson, Dramatist* (New York: Cambridge University Press, 1984), pp. 211–212.

15. Ibid., p. 208.

16. Umphrey Lee, "Jonson's *Bartholomew Fair* and the Popular Dramatic Tradition," *Louisburg College Journal of Arts and Sciences*, 1 (1967), 6–16, demonstrates some striking parallels between the two plays, and argues (p. 10) that "Eleanor Cobham resembles Jonson's Grace Welborn in that both are rich orphans in the power of old and opinionated guardians. Each has one undesirable lover favored by the guardian . . . and two more acceptable lovers. At this point Jonson brings in the device of choosing between arbitrarily chosen words, and similarities diminish." If Chettle and Day's comedy was as popular as Lee suggests (pp. 12–13), then this sudden diminishment of such strong similarities may have been another Jonsonian trick on the audience, a trick which exalts those such as Grace who neither mistake the play world for a conventional melodrama nor attempt to play out the role of heroine on such a simplistic basis.

17. L. A. Beaurline, *Jonson and Elizabethan Comedy* (San Marino, Calif.: Huntington Library, 1978), p. 253.

18. Alexander Leggatt, *Citizen Comedy in the Age of Shakespeare* (Toronto: University of Toronto Press, 1973), p. 34; on p. 45 he mentions Wasp as a failed version of that figure, but he attributes that failure to Jonson's mistrust of bloodless moralism, rather than (as I do) to Jonson's mistrust of conventional literary self-conceptions. Alan Dessen, *Jonson's Moral Comedy* (Evanston, Ill.: Northwestern University Press, 1971), p. 155, observes that "ideally Wasp's task would be, like the Good Counsel or Charity figure of the morality tradition, to rise above temporary setbacks and educate Cokes . . . But this particular protector

or good counselor can only postulate the role he would like to play." For analogues in the Estates Moralities to Wasp's envisioned role, see Dessen, pp. 166–
176.

19. Irena Janicka, *Popular Theatrical Tradition and Ben Jonson* (Lodz: Uni-
wersytet Lodzki, 1972), p. 190.

20. Eugene Waith, ed., *Bartholomew Fair* (New Haven: Yale University
Press, 1963), p. 100, cites the *Oxford English Dictionary* definition of "overparted"
as meaning "having too difficult a part . . . to play."

21. Barish, *Ben Jonson*, p. 213, and Teague, *Curious History*, p. 23, mention
this suggestive parallel.

22. Cf. Cartelli, "Urban Arcadia," pp. 171–172, who associates the chastising of Wasp, Busy, and Overdo, with Jonson's surrender of his own overly
censorious attitude toward humanity as a whole, toward drama in general, and
toward Shakespeare in particular. Bryant, *Compassionate Satirist*, pp. 155–156,
speaks of "the reduction of the angry critic . . . to a mere Waspe" as "possibly
a part of Jonson's triumph over himself."

23. Eugene Waith, Introduction to the Yale edition of the play, p. 10,
mentions the dual implications of "hypocrite." Barish, *Antitheatrical Prejudice*,
pp. 91–92, quotes Prynne's attack on actors as "hypocrites."

24. Barish, *Ben Jonson*, p. 204, observes that "Busy has worn his mask so
long that when he comes to remove it, there can be nothing beneath but a replica
of the mask, now the authentic face—or voice—itself." The role acquires its
own momentum and supersedes identity.

25. Two good versions of such serious allegorical reading are Alvin B.
Kernan, "The Great Fair of the World and the Ocean Island," in *The Revels
History of Drama in English*, ed. J. Leeds Barroll et al., vol. 3 (London: Methuen,
1975); and Jackson I. Cope, "*Bartholomew Fair* as Blasphemy," *Renaissance Drama*,
8 (1965), 127–152.

26. Herford, Simpson, and Simpson, *Ben Jonson*, VIII, 597, ll. 1093–99.

27. See, for example, Barish, *Ben Jonson*, pp. 198–204.

28. Beaurline, *Elizabethan Comedy*, p. 239; the most explicit example is
3.2.40–42.

29. See George Lukàcs, *The Theory of the Novel*, trans. A. Bostock (1920;
rpt. Cambridge Mass.: MIT Press, 1971), pp. 98–100; also Mikhail Bakhtin,
"The Language of the Marketplace," in his *Rabelais and His World*, trans. Helene
Iswolsky (Cambridge, Mass.: MIT Press, 1968), pp. 145–195.

30. Barish, *Ben Jonson*, p. 199, demonstrates the Biblical roots of Busy's
inflated style. John Scott Colley, "*Bartholomew Fair*: Ben Jonson's *A Midsummer
Night's Dream*," *Comparative Drama*, 11 (1977), 70, observes that "Busy speaks
of his task as a kind of harrowing of hell."

31. T. W. Craik, *The Tudor Interlude: Stage, Costume, and Acting* (Leicester:
University Press, 1958), pp. 93–94, quoted by Dessen, *Moral Comedy*, pp. 188–
189.

32. Guy Hamel, "Order and Judgment in *Bartholomew Fair*," *University of
Toronto Quarterly*, 43 (1973–74), 64, and Barish, *Ben Jonson*, pp. 237–238, comment on the conversion of Busy into another puppet.

33. Hibbard, Introduction to New Mermaids edition, p. xxii, describes

·Overdo as futilely "attempting to combine the roles of Cicero and Sherlock Holmes."

34. Barton, *Dramatist,* p. 203; David McPherson, "The Origins of Overdo," *Modern Language Quarterly,* 37 (1976), 229; and Robert E. Knoll, *Ben Jonson's Plays: An Introduction* (Lincoln: University of Nebraska Press, 1964), p. 158, variously cite these plays as offering at least partial parallels to Overdo's stratagem. See also Salingar, "Crowd and Public," p. 158.

35. Herford, Simpson, and Simpson, *Ben Jonson,* X, 177; McPherson, "Origins of Overdo," p. 224 and passim.

36. This mayor has usually been identified as Sir Thomas Hayes, but a more recent study suggests that it was actually a man named Thomas Middleton—no relation, apparently, to the playwright, but the coincidence is nonetheless suggestive, considering how often Jonson shows characters foolishly imitating roles from Thomas Middleton's drama. For the Hayes identification, see, for example, Waith, Yale edition, pp. 190, 192; for the Middleton alternative, see McPherson, "Origins of Overdo," p. 224 and passim.

37. Cope, "Blasphemy," p. 128n.

38. McPherson, "Origins of Overdo," p. 230. See also Lee, "Popular Dramatic Tradition," p. 12.

39. Brian Gibbons, *Jacobean City Comedy,* 2nd ed. (London: Methuen, 1980), pp. 151, and McPherson, "Origins of Overdo," p. 230, suggest parallels between Fitzgrave's emergence from disguise and the emergence of Overdo.

40. Lee, "Popular Dramatic Tradition," p. 7 and passim.

41. McPherson, "Origins of Overdo," pp. 225–228.

42. Barton, *Dramatist,* p. 204.

43. Alexander Leggatt, *Ben Jonson: His Vision and His Art* (London: Methuen, 1981), p. 183, senses the same sort of betrayal, though he applies a slightly different specific precedent: "Justice Overdo aspires to be the ideal Jonson judge [but] the result is not a repetition but a parody of the moment when Cynthia unveils and sees through the disguises of the others."

44. Gibbons, *City Comedy,* p. 145.

45. Barish, *Ben Jonson,* p. 208; he asserts further (p. 212) that "the example of Overdo offers sufficient evidence that mimicry of the Great Books can be as perilous as mimicry of high society."

46. Barton, *Dramatist,* p. 211.

47. Barish, *Ben Jonson,* pp. 208–209.

48. Leggatt, *Citizen Comedy,* p. 45.

49. Barish, *Ben Jonson,* p. 206, remarks on Overdo's devotion to "oratorical mannerisms both advised and practiced by Cicero." He sees (p. 213) Overdo as Jonson's brutal parody of the moral and oratorical fervor—both his own and Cicero's—in *Catiline;* but perhaps Jonson is not attacking either his play or its hero, so much as he is demonstrating how preposterous such attitudes can appear in the degrading context of a realistically portrayed Jacobean London.

50. Barton, *Dramatist,* pp. 210–211.

51. John M. Potter, "Old Comedy in *Bartholomew Fair,*" *Criticism,* 10 (1968), 296.

52. Hyland, *Disguise,* p. 139, comments that Overdo's Stoicism is exposed as "no more than a pose."

53. Herford, Simpson, and Simpson, *Ben Jonson*, X, 207, note Overdo's debt to the language of Stoicism here, particularly the language of Epictetus.

54. Cope, "Blasphemy," pp. 129–130. On the whole, Cope's view grants Jonson less ironic distance from this blasphemy than mine. The general danger Cope stresses, of excessive literalness in interpreting the law, corresponds to the dangerous literariness I perceive in the way the characters construct their authority.

55. Robert N. Watson, "Overdo and Prospero," unpublished paper presented at the Shakespeare Association of America annual convention, Seattle, Washington, 1987, points out the possible connections between *Bartholomew Fair* and the All Saints' Day service. To be precise, *Bartholomew Fair* was first performed the previous day at the Hope theater, but that seems to have been essentially a public rehearsal for the court performance, which would presumably have been Jonson's main concern.

56. John B. Bender, "The Day of *The Tempest*," *ELH*, 47 (1980), 239. I am indebted to Bender's work on *The Tempest* for my approach to the liturgical context of *Bartholomew Fair*.

57. Watson, "Overdo," discusses the ways *Bartholomew Fair* functions as a parody of *The Tempest*.

58. Salingar, "Crowd and Public," p. 141, and Hamel, "Order and Judgment," p. 48, argue that in *Bartholomew Fair* Jonson deprives us of his usual plot, in which a master intriguer controls the single dominant story line. Barry Targan, "The Moral Structure of *Bartholomew Fair*," *Discourse*, 8 (1965), 277, argues similarly that the play lacks a center, largely because Quarlous is inadequate as a controlling spokesman for Jonson. I think the proliferation of incompatible plots these critics describe in *Bartholomew Fair* is very much in the tradition of the earlier plays; again, the dominant figure is the one who knows how to capitalize on the collision of those various plots. Salingar, p. 142, objects that Quarlous "only emerges as an active intriguer in the second half of the play," but that is considerably earlier than figures such as Clement and Lovewit emerge in the earlier plays. Hamel, p. 58, concedes that "only Quarlous, because he sees through the sham of the Fair and yet takes pleasure in its pretenses, might be said to share the perspective of the audience." A similar attitude toward the theater is what gives Quarlous his power and what Jonson sought to encourage his audience to imitate. Hyland, *Disguise*, pp. 140–142, summarizes a range of responses to Quarlous, with emphasis on the reservations about his morality and consistency.

59. J. W. Lever, "*The Wasp:* A Trial Flight," in *The Elizabethan Theatre*, vol. 4, ed. G. R. Hibbard (Toronto: Macmillan, 1973), p. 65, finds versions of this motif not only in the anonymous *The Wasp*, but also in Marston's *The Malcontent*, Chapman's *The Widow's Tears*, Middleton's *Michaelmas Term*, Beaumont's *The Faithful Friends*, and Rowley's *A Match at Midnight*; see also Haughton's *Grim the Collier of Croydon*.

60. Charles Baskervill, "Some Parallels to *Bartholomew Fair*," *Modern Philology*, 6 (1908–9), 109–127.

61. Barish, *Ben Jonson*, p. 212; Targan, "Moral Structure," p. 278, perceives Jonson reproving himself through Overdo's failures. See similarly Gibbons, *City Comedy*, pp. 151–152.

## 7. The Devil Is an Ass

1. Brian Gibbons, *Jacobean City Comedy*, 2nd ed. (London: Methuen, 1980), p. 156.

2. C. G. Thayer, *Ben Jonson: Studies in the Plays* (Norman: University of Oklahoma Press, 1963), p. 162, describes Pug as an "Everydevil."

3. Although sentimental comedy per se does not begin before Cibber's *Love's Last Shift* (1696), aspects of it are quite visible in the works of Shadwell and even Massinger.

4. Stephen Greenblatt, "Loudon and London," *Critical Inquiry*, 12 (1986), 326–346.

5. Herford, Simpson, and Simpson, *Ben Jonson*, X, 219.

6. Ibid., X, 217.

7. Thayer, *Ben Jonson*, p. 161.

8. See for example Marston's *The Malcontent*, Chapman's *The Widow's Tears*, Middleton's *Michaelmas Term*, Beaumont's *The Faithful Friends*, Rowley's *A Match at Midnight*, and the anonymous *The Wasp*. Jonson alludes to this convention, I have suggested, in *Bartholomew Fair*.

9. Gibbons, *City Comedy*, p. 156.

10. The Vice in *Mundus et Infans* (1520) wins employment with Manhood by a similar name change and offer of free service; see Herford, Simpson, and Simpson, *Ben Jonson*, X, 228.

11. It is interesting to compare Pug's dilemma with that of his kinsman, Robin Goodfellow, who finally gains admission to Jonson's 1612 masque *Love Restored* only by playing himself.

12. Peter Hyland, *Disguise and Role-Playing in Ben Jonson's Drama*, Salzburg Studies in English Literature, Jacobean Drama Studies, 69 (Atlantic Highlands, N.J.: Humanities Press, 1977), p. 148, discusses Fitzdotterel as a spectator who mistakes himself for an actor. Anne Barton, *Ben Jonson, Dramatist* (New York: Cambridge University Press, 1984), p. 227, sees Fitzdotterel's faults as a spectator as Jonson's warning that "we complacently mock the very vices and follies which we ought with shame to acknowledge as our own." While accepting that Fitzdotterel serves that standard satiric purpose, I would add that the parodic elements of his character remind us of the opposite, that we complacently claim as our own the grandiose conduct we witness at the theater, which we ought instead to dismiss as folly and even vice.

13. See, for example, Fitzdotterel's complaint at 4.7.78 and his simulation of diabolical possession at 5.8.27. He proudly if unwittingly proclaims himself such an ass when he thanks Engine for saying that no one should "doubt his ears" for such projects as Merecraft offers (2.1.30–32). He later confirms the identification by the way he declares himself "not altogether an ass" at 3.3.116, and by his dangling response to Wittipol at 2.7.13–14. In the first Intermean of *The Staple of News*, shortly after a specific allusion to *The Devil Is an Ass*, Gossip Tattle mentions her husband's conflation of cuckold's horns with those of a devil.

14. Herford, Simpson, and Simpson, *Ben Jonson*, X, 234, demonstrate that this list is itself derived from Plautus' *Aulularia*.

15. Herford, Simpson, and Simpson, *Ben Jonson*, X, 255.

16. Alan Dessen, *Jonson's Moral Comedy* (Evanston, Ill.: Northwestern University Press, 1971), p. 233, discusses the dual meaning of "possession" in these two comparable scenes. See also Greenblatt, "Loudon and London," passim.

17. Barton, *Dramatist*, p. 228, builds on an editorial suggestion in Gifford's 1816 edition of Jonson's works.

18. Dessen, *Moral Comedy*, p. 231, and Barton, *Dramatist*, p. 230, suggest this comparison.

19. Barton, *Dramatist*, p. 230, remarks on Merecraft "blinding Plutarchus with visions of himself as a future captain."

20. Gibbons, *City Comedy*, pp. 156–157, has observed that "Jonson seems to be . . . gesturing toward clichés of Middletonian plot such as the cycle of rich tradesman cozening landed gentry, going to live in the country, seeing his children grow up as gentry, the young prodigals coming to the city . . . and being cozened of their inheritance by city sharks, Coney-Catchers and tradesmen in their turn." Plutarchus seems oddly conscious of the usual arc of these plots, as if he assumes life will necessarily imitate art. He complains that he does not want to become a gentleman, because—despite the fact that he is even more cautious and miserly than his father (3.1.14–43)—he fears that the family will soon necessarily become prodigals "fit to be cozened."

21. Hyland, *Disguise*, p. 152, notes the theatrical overtones of this project in cosmetics.

22. John J. Enck, *Jonson and the Comic Truth* (Madison: University of Wisconsin Press, 1957), pp. 213–214, complains about this stilted quality.

23. In terms of chronology, biography, and what we know of immediate reception, it makes more sense to group *The Devil Is an Ass* with the great comedies of Jonson's middle period, as indeed Swinburne did; but the voices (and, more damningly, the silences) of modern criticism usually place it among the "dotages." See Larry Champion, *Ben Jonson's "Dotages"* (Lexington: University of Kentucky Press, 1967), pp. 3, and 24.

24. Herford, Simpson, and Simpson, *Ben Jonson*, X, 216 and 238; since we do not know the composition date of the "Celebration of Charis," it is impossible to be sure whether Jonson adapted the poem into this play, or scavenged the play for the poem.

25. Barton, *Dramatist*, p. 221, is one of a number of critics who cite this parallel to the fifth tale of the third day in the *Decameron*. Wittipol may conceivably be intended to embody the spirit of a new age in poetry, as well as in drama. His method of using conventional motifs of verse courtship, while still implicitly announcing his ironic distance from them, resembles a common practice among seventeenth-century love poets. Even the projection of Mrs. Fitzdotterel's response is a characteristic device of Metaphysical seduction poems.

26. Barton, *Dramatist*, p. 226.

27. Marvin Herrick, *Italian Comedy in the Renaissance* (Urbana: University of Illinois Press, 1960), p. 80.

28. Daniel Boughner, *The Devil's Disciple* (New York: Philosophical Library, 1968), pp. 222–223; see similarly Enck, *Comic Truth*, pp. 212–213.

29. Barton, *Dramatist*, p. 224. Celia in *Volpone* and Grace Wellborn in *Bartholomew Fair* certainly have their virtues, but those virtues do not finally place

them at the center of the action. See also the final pages of my chapter on *Every Man Out of His Humor.*

## 8. The New Inn

1. L. A. Beaurline, *Jonson and Elizabethan Comedy* (San Marino, Calif.: Huntington Library, 1978), p. 260.

2. That this is less a class distinction than a distinction between types of drama is clear from the banishment of the *miles gloriosus,* Sir Glorious Tipto, to the cellar, and the promotion up the stairs of the virtuous servant Pru. C. G. Thayer, *Ben Jonson* (Norman: University of Oklahoma Press, 1963), pp. 210–223, argues that the below-stairs world represents satiric Old Comedy, while the upstairs world is occupied with the business of New Comedy. Anne Barton, *Ben Jonson, Dramatist* (New York: Cambridge University Press, 1984), p. 272, argues that the "underworld of characters below stairs . . . exists primarily to express the chaos of society when it does not admit the ordering influences of true valour or true love." I would only add that one could say precisely the same thing about the world of Jonson's satiric city-comedy.

3. See for example Douglas Duncan, "A Guide to *The New Inn,*" *Essays in Criticism,* 20 (1970), p. 318.

4. There are suggestive parallels between these two plays, each emphasizing not only its own fictionality, but also the power of such fictions to reveal true identities and fulfill dreams of reunion. Barton, *Dramatist,* p. 281, remarks on the Shakespearean quality of the ending of *The New Inn,* "a palpable but highly charged fiction that gains strength from the very honesty of its admission that this is how we should all like the world to be, but know it is not."

5. Herford, Simpson, and Simpson, *Ben Jonson,* II, 194, reflect the early twentieth-century consensus that *The New Inn* is Jonson's ungainly but sincere attempt to write romance. More recently, some critics have perceived quality as well as sincerity: see Beaurline, *Elizabethan Comedy,* pp. 257–274; Duncan, "Guide," 311–326; and Barton, *Dramatist,* pp. 258–284. Richard Levin, "The New *New Inn* and the Proliferation of Good Bad Drama," *Essays in Criticism,* 22 (1972), 41–47, argues that the play is simply bad romance, and that efforts to rescue it by viewing it as ironic are misguided. Several critics, however, assert quite forcefully that Jonson is writing at least passable burlesque rather than execrably bad romance: see Larry Champion, *Ben Jonson's "Dotages"* (Lexington: University of Kentucky Press, 1967), pp. 76–103; Edward Partridge, *The Broken Compass* (New York: Columbia University Press, 1958), pp. 189–205; and Robert Knoll, *Ben Jonson's Plays* (Lincoln: University of Nebraska Press, 1964), pp. 181–190. Alexander Leggatt, *Ben Jonson* (London: Methuen, 1981), pp. 43–44, comes closest to my own position in arguing for "some sort of balance between a delight in the creative fantasy and a satire on its absurdity."

6. I would not go as far as Thayer in describing *The New Inn* as Jonson's elaborate allegorical commentary on his career as a playwright, but Jonson does arrange his story so that it summons for reexamination many of the critical attitudes that shaped his earlier comedies. It is interesting how closely this surrender of his parodic strategy corresponds to the supposed decline in Jonson's

literary genius and popular success. Naturally, I am tempted to adduce this correspondence as evidence that the parodic strategy was an essential aspect of Jonson's comedic power.

7. This harsh rejection of his indulgent fantasy may help to explain why Jonson returns to a more straightforward—though somewhat hollow—version of the parodic strategy in his next play, *The Magnetic Lady* (1632). Its Induction is an elaborate warning to Damplay—Jonson's quintessential bad spectator—that "a good play is like a skein of silk: which . . . if you light on the wrong end, you will pull all into a knot" (116–121), a metaphor renewed several times later in the play. In the Chorus at the end of the fourth act, Damplay wonders why the playwright has not "spared us the vexation of a fifth act yet to come, which everyone here knows the issue of already, or may in part conjecture." Jonson characteristically uses a fourth-act *catastasis* to mortify precisely such conjectures; as the Boy replies, the conventional outcome "was never in the poet's purpose perhaps."

Compass has hold of "the right thread" (5.10.81), and he uses it to make himself the husband of the best girl, the holder of the biggest legacy, and the hero of the plot that outlasts and outflanks the others. His name suggests both his ability (shared with Jonson) to show us the true way to the Magnetic Lady, and his ability (similarly shared) to encompass all the lesser plots of those around him. He promises to prove his "wit is magisterial" and to provide his audience with "infinite delight" by bringing the "several humours" into conjunction for a few hours (1.1.5–14). Compass describes himself as

> a scholar,
> And part a soldier; I have been employed
> By some the greatest statesmen o' the kingdom,
> These many years: and in my time conversed
> With sundry humours . . .                                      (1.1.19–23)

As if these biographical hints were not clear enough, Compass extensively and acknowledgedly plagiarizes Jonson in the scene that follows.

The noble Ironside also echoes Jonson, but his dramatic quotations are neither conscious and exploitative, like those of Compass, nor unwitting and exploited, like those of the lesser characters. Ironside's comments on valor cause Diaphanous Silkworm to remark,

> Oh, you ha' read the play there, "The New Inn,"
> Of Jonson's, that decries all other valour
> But what is for the public.
> *Ironside*                               I do that too,
> But did not learn it there.                                      (3.6.92–95)

As in *The New Inn,* it is possible to act like the hero of a play because you truly are heroic in that way, and not merely because you were enthralled with how it looked on stage. Silkworm, in contrast, understands his own valor only in terms of the prescribed roles "which the town calls valor," as Compass' reply emphasizes: "Yes, he has read the town, Towntop's his author!" (3.6.111–113). Silkworm goes on to categorize his own undertakings with those "which in the brave historified Greeks / And Romans you shall read of" (3.6.157–158). Because he always thinks by the book, Silkworm fails when he tries to spin out his own plot, his own version of the skein of silk.

Item attempts to stage the same type of counterplot attempted in *Volpone* and *The Devil Is an Ass,* assigning Needle to feign possession, which Jonson again presents as a highly theatrical phenomenon. Claiming to be possessed by the ghost of a secretly rich woman, Needle seems able only to play the somnambulistic Lady Macbeth, and the men's reactions to his performance unwittingly parody the reactions of Lady Macbeth's doctor and waiting-women (5.5.1–46). Needle's soliloquy, furthermore, fits so neatly with a fantasy native to Sir Moth's covetous imagination that the old miser scrambles farcically off in pursuit of treasure supposedly buried in a well, into which he plummets. Even the slow-witted Doctor Rut can draw the moral: "With what appetite / Our own desires delude us!" (5.7.23–26).

What weakens the parodic strategy in *The Magnetic Lady* is the fact that the self-dramatizing postures, though still ridiculous, do not consistently lead to the posers' downfall by any clear pattern of poetic justice or theatrical logic. For example, Compass plays up to Bias' image of himself as a brilliant Jacobean Machiavel (see Champion, *Dotages,* p. 125), but never takes tactical advantage of that delusion. Mistress Polish constructs a plot directly out of romantic comedy, by switching her low-born infant with the heiress Placentia (see Champion, *Dotages,* p. 117); but it fails only because her daughter goes into labor prematurely, not because Polish is deluded into complacency by literary precedents; nor is the audience given enough information to join in any such delusion. (By contrast, her ally, the midwife Mistress Chair, makes a more formidable counterplotter precisely because she is aware of her theatricality; see 4.7.40–46.)

In the Chorus at the end of the first act, the Boy mocks Damplay's suggestions for revising *The Magnetic Lady* by equating them with various moldy antique plays (such as the lost *Guy of Warwick* and *Huon of Bordeaux,* and with some suggestion of Shakespeare's *Pericles* as well) that Jonson openly scorned:

> So, if a child could be born, in a play, and grow up to a man i' the first
> scene, before he went off the stage: and then after to come forth a
> squire, and be made a knight: and that knight to travel between the acts,
> and do wonders i' the Holy Land, or elsewhere; kill paynims, wild
> boars, dun cows, and other monsters; beget him a reputation, and
> marry an emperor's daughter for his mistress; convert her father's country; and at last come home, lame, and all-to-beladen with miracles.
>
> *Damplay*   These miracles would please, I assure you: and take the people!
> For there be of the people that will expect miracles, and more than miracles from this pen.                                                        (14–25)

As in the similar discussion in the Prologue to *Every Man In,* the miracles of popular dramas are, to Jonson, monstrous. At home and lame at the end of his adventurous life, Jonson would like to be thought of as a miracle-worker, but not of this sort; his quest was to convert a country of base posers into upstanding citizens, and of complacent audiences into alert critics. His flirtation with romantic scenarios and popular favor in *The New Inn* had ended in a quick and bitter divorce; that failure, rather than debility or death, may explain why he never completed *The Sad Shepherd,* which appears to be another nostalgic indulgence of popular literature.

8. Herford, Simpson, and Simpson, *Ben Jonson,* X, 301.

9. Thayer, *Ben Jonson,* p. 230. David R. Riggs, in his forthcoming biography of Jonson, further elucidates this point.

10. Barton, *Dramatist,* p. 270, observes that Pru, by acting "the part of a great lady, mistress of the day's entertainment, as Gonzaga's Duchess had been at Urbino, in Castiglione, comes into triumphant possession of aspects of her real self formerly stifled and hidden by her inferior social position." Pru thus fulfills what had been a hollow literary fantasy for characters like Fallace in *Every Man Out* and Gertrude in *Eastward Ho.*

11. Partridge, *Broken Compass,* p. 205, concludes his analysis of the play by claiming that the role of clothing in shaping the reality of characters in *The New Inn* "is characteristic of Jonson's method . . . The folly detested by Jonson becomes the virtue cherished by the characters he creates [who] are turned loose in a world of their own making and create their own hell, usually unaware of the hell of it." It is hard to see why characters joyously united in long-sought marriages and joyously reunited with long-sought kinspeople should deduce that they are being punished in hell. Knoll, *Jonson's Plays,* p. 188, sees evidence in the play that Jonson "is too old to think us able to attain our aspirations." Although it is true that Lovel cannot perfectly embody the principles of love and valor he advocates, the play as a whole culminates in the miraculous attainment of aspirations considerably greater than any the younger Jonson was willing to endorse.

12. Harriett Hawkins, "The Idea of a Theatre in Jonson's *The New Inn,*" *Renaissance Drama,* 9 (1966), 214n.

13. This began as early as Owen Feltham's "Ode against Ben Jonson" and has been reaffirmed by Coleridge and many other critics. Barton, *Dramatist,* pp. 273–276, comments insightfully on the peculiarities of naming in this play, and on the contrast in the ways names are used below and above stairs.

14. Barton, *Dramatist,* p. 270.

15. Thayer, *Ben Jonson,* p. 230, comments briefly on this contrast.

16. Duncan, "Guide," p. 326, on a rather different basis, reaches a similar conclusion: "the play fails because it is too personal, too much determined by subjective interests, too much a game on the author's own terms. But for the same reason it is a clear index of his thinking about his life's work."

17. Barton, *Dramatist,* p. 269, points out the autobiographical overtones of this list. It should be noted, however, that it is not clear at what point in the preparation of *The New Inn* Jonson suffered his stroke, nor whether Jonson was really as badly impoverished as one might infer from the grant of five pounds "to Mr Beniamin Ihonson in his sicknes & want" on the same day *The New Inn* was licensed; see Michael Hattaway, ed., *The New Inn,* The Revels Plays (Manchester: Manchester University Press, 1984), p. 1.

# INDEX